The
Day-to-Day Life
of the
Desert Fathers
in
Fourth-Century Egypt

LUCIEN REGNAULT

TRANSLATED BY
Étienne Poirier, Jr.

ST. BEDE'S PUBLICATIONS
PETERSHAM, MASSACHUSETTS

Originally published in France under the title *La Vie Quotidienne des Pères du Désert en Egypte au IVᵉ Siècle* © 1990 by Hachette. All questions concerning the rights of translation, reproduction, adaptation, in any language or in any manner other than what appears in this volume must be addressed to the editor of the original French edition.

Map on p. iv and cover: Competitive Edge Graphic Design

LIBRARY OF CONGRESS CATALOGING-IN-PUBLICATION DATA

Regnault, Lucien.
    [Vie quotidienne des Pères du désert en Egypte au IVe siècle. English]
    The day-to-day life of the Desert Fathers in fourth-century Egypt/ Lucien Regnault : translated by Etienne Poirier, Jr.
        p.   cm.
    Includes bibliographical references and index.
    ISBN 1-879007-34-7
    1. Desert Fathers.   I. Title.
BR190.R6413   1998
271'.02062 — dc21   98-45678
                                                                      CIP

Published by: St. Bede's Publications
            P.O. Box 545
            Petersham, Massachusetts 01366-0545

Contents

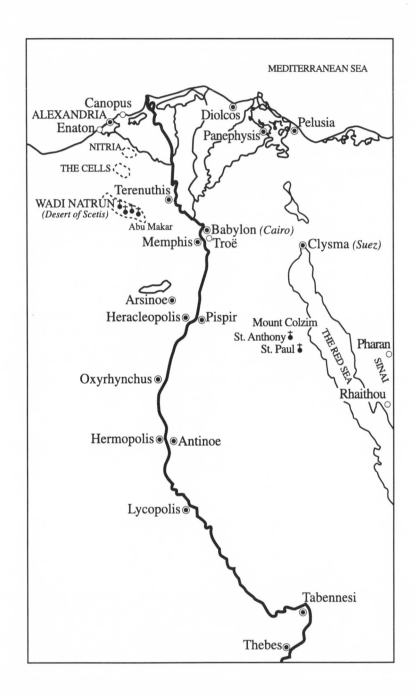

MEDITERRANEAN SEA

Canopus
ALEXANDRIA
Enaton
NITRIA
THE CELLS
Terenuthis
WADI NATRUN
(Desert of Scetis)
Abu Makar
Memphis
Diolcos
Panephysis
Pelusia
Babylon (Cairo)
Troë
Clysma (Suez)
Arsinoe
Heracleopolis
Pispir
Mount Colzim
St. Anthony
St. Paul
THE RED SEA
Pharan
SINAI
Oxyrhynchus
Rhaithou
Hermopolis
Antinoe
Lycopolis
Tabennesi
Thebes

MONASTIC EGYPT

Abbreviations

For the most part, the footnotes in the text refer to the apothegms of the Fathers. In order to simplify the references, the author always refers to the French translation edited by Solesmes under the title *Les Sentences des Pères du désert* (SP). We give these references as they appear in the French text and supply the English sources where available.

A　　　　SP, Alphabetical Collection, Solesmes, 1981. Most of these apothegms can be found in Benedicta Ward (trans.), *The Sayings of the Desert Fathers: The Alphabetical Collection*, Kalamazoo, 1975.

Am　　　Apothegms translated from the Coptic in SP, 3rd collection, Solesmes, 1976, pp. 139-194.

Arm　　Apothegms translated from the Armenian, in SP, new collection, 1970, pp. 253-274.

Bu　　　Apothegms translated from the Syriac, in SP, new collection, pp. 219-251. These can be found in E.A.W. Budge, *The Wit and Wisdom of the Christian Fathers of Egypt*, London, 1934.

Ch　　　Apothegms translated from the Coptic, in SP, new collection, pp. 277-285.

CSP　　Apothegms translated from the Latin, in SP, 3rd collection, pp. 129-137.

Eth　　　Apothegms translated from the Ethiopian, in SP, new collection, pp. 287-331.

Evelyn White　H.G. Evelyn White, *The Monasteries of Nitria and Scetis*, New York, 1932.

Guillaumont　A. Guillaumont, *Aux origines du monachisme chrétien*, Spiritualité oriental, no. 30, Bellefontaine, 1979.

HL　　　Palladius, *The Lausiac History*.

HM　　　*The Lives of the Desert Fathers, The History of the Monks in Egypt*, trans. by Norman Russell, London and Kalamazoo, 1981.

HM Latin　*History of the Monks in Egypt*, according to the Latin translation of Rufinus, (Migne, PL 21).

Isaiah　*Recueil ascétique*, Spiritualité orientale, no. 7 bis, Bellefontaine, 1985.

N　　　　SP, Série des anonymes, Solesmes-Bellefontaine, 1985. (The Anonymous Series. Some of these apothegms can be found in English in Benedicta Ward [trans.], *The Wisdom of the Desert Fathers*, Oxford, 1986.)

v

PA   Apothegms translated from the Latin, in SP, 3rd collection,
    pp. 125-128.
Regnault   L. Regnault, *Les Pères du désert à travers leurs Apophtegmes,*
    Solesmes, 1987.
SC   Sources chrétiennes, Paris.
Sy   Apothegms from the Greek systematic collection, in SP, 3rd
    collection, pp. 65-121.
VA   *Life of Saint Antony.*
Veilleux   *Life of Saint Pachomius,* trans. by Armand Veilleux,
    Pachomian Koinonia, vol. 1, Kalamazoo, 1980.

Introduction

A governor of Egypt journeyed one day to the desert of Scetis to see Abba Moses, a former bandit who became a famous hermit. Approaching the site with his retinue, he came across an old man on the road and asked him to show him where to find the great Anchorite's cell. "What do you want of him?" the old man asked. "He's a fool and a heretic." The governor traveled on, regardless, and came to a church where he was told that the old man was none other than Moses himself.[1]

As this shows, it isn't easy to identify the Desert Fathers and establish relations with them. More than forty-five years ago, full of the enthusiasm—and the rashness—of my monastic youth, I set out to discover all I could about these strange and mysterious figures. I had the good fortune to find an excellent guide in the person of Father Irénée Hausherr. On the advice of this eminent historian of Eastern spirituality, I decided to search everywhere for the words of the Fathers and collect them, as one collects rare stamps or other precious objects. Why? Because these pearls from Egypt are dispersed in multitudinous collections of manuscripts or printed in Greek, Coptic, Latin, Syriac, Arabic, Armenian, Georgian and even Slavic. Like a jigsaw puzzle revealing its image, this mass of some 3,000 items, patiently collected and translated into French, finally showed me the world of the Fathers in all its unity and infinite variety, becoming very concrete and familiar. A sojourn of two years in Egypt and contacts with contemporary Coptic monks gave me a better understanding of the elements and aspects of the life of their fourth-century spiritual ancestors. This is the picture I have tried to recreate and present here.

The reader who only knows the Desert Fathers through the works of Gustave Flaubert, Anatole France and other modern

---

[1] A 502 (Ward, p. 140) according to the authentic lesson of PA 33, 13.

vii

novelists may be surprised to see them in a new light. There is really no unique "type" of Desert Father. Each has his own personality — and had to, in order to have enough courage to live in the heart of the desert. But quickly enough, living conditions in solitude imposed habits and customs which helped regulate such an original existence. I will try to present these consistencies, while respecting the individual traits of each personality.

In order to narrow the scope of the picture, I must point out that I use the term "Desert Fathers" not in the larger sense usually given it, but in the narrow one of the original.[2] At the end of the fourth century, it referred to the most famous Egyptian anchorites who had left the fertile and inhabited regions of the Nile valley or delta to plunge into the desert. Very quickly some distinguished themselves for their holiness and drew to their neighborhood many imitators and disciples who looked upon them as their fathers. Until this time, only bishops had been recognized as Fathers by Christians, including ascetics and monks. "The bishops are our fathers who teach us according to the Scriptures," said Pachomius. But little by little, in the eremitic groups far from the communities of the faithful, a new spiritual paternity would appear, linked not to an official and hierarchical function within the Church, but to exceptional gifts of wisdom and speech. The newcomer to the desert gets his schooling from an elder he calls his "abba," meaning his father in God. And quite naturally, the Christian people begin to call all the elders directing the other anchorites "Fathers of the Desert." The title appears in writings from the beginning of the fifth century. In the following century, among the monks in the Judean desert, it would also apply to the elders in eremitic circles of Lower Egypt, well-known in Palestine through collections of apothegms. In Upper Egypt, Pachomius, founder of cenobitism, and his successors would also be called Fathers, though not "Desert Fathers," since their communities were not set up in the heart of the desert but near market towns in the Nile valley.

The main source to be drawn upon, of course, will be the words of the Fathers or, more specifically, their maxims or

---

[2]Regnault, pp. 19-20.

"apothegms." In fact, this term is the only one that expresses the very character of these texts. They are not idle words, written aphorisms or beautiful stories, but words that were spoken first of all in distinct circumstances, always with the aim of edification, connected to the lifestyles of the desert anchorites. They are fragments, slices of life, or something like flashes from the lives of these anchorites. This explains why the collections of these words were often entitled "Lives of the Fathers,"[3] and why they are so valuable in helping us get to know the concrete and daily reality of the first desert monks.

Other documents of the era complement, in a useful way, this fundamental source. First of all are three biographies, of which the most ancient is the *Life of Antony*, usually attributed to the Bishop of Alexandria, Athanasius, and written soon after the Saint's death in 356 A.D. The *Life of Paul of Thebes* and the *Life of Hilarion*, written by St Jerome, have less historical value.

A second category of documents includes some types of investigative reports carried out by foreign monks who came to visit the Egyptian anchorites or spend a few years with them. The *Lausiac History*, so named because it is dedicated to Lausus, chamberlain to the Emperor, is written by Palladius, deacon of Constantinople and friend of St John Chrysostom. The *History of the Monks* is the account of a trip to Egypt in the winter of 394-395 by a group of Palestinian monks. Written in Greek by one of them, this account was then adapted into Latin by Rufinus of Aquilea, who had visited monastic Egypt himself before founding a monastery on the Mount of Olives in Jerusalem. We can link these two "histories" to the works of John Cassian. After embracing the monastic life in Bethlehem, Cassian spent fifteen years among the monks of Lower Egypt (385-400), and recorded their customs and teachings in his *Institutes* and *Conferences* for the monks of Provence.

Finally, I draw some information from the writings of Evagrius and Isaiah. Originally from Asia Minor, Evagrius was a great intellectual who came to live in Nitria and the Cells until his death in 399. Isaiah, who received his monastic training in

---

[3]Regnault, pp. 57-63.

Scetis, then spent most of the rest of his life in Gaza, where he became a renowned spiritual master.

From these different sources I endeavored to gather everything that could help me recreate as faithfully as possible the life of the ancient Egyptian anchorites. It would be vain to try to unravel this documentation and choose between historical reality and legend. Even so, one can see there is no reason to quibble with secondary details, when there are no edifying motives involved, and which are nevertheless most worthwhile for placing the Fathers in their environment. The role of the supernatural is important and one cannot exclude it without distorting the picture. It is enough to not take everything as factual and to take into account the imagination of disciples and admirers from whom these accounts were handed down to us. It was certainly not very often that a hermit met the Devil in person or a visible angel, a debonair lion or a pleasant crocodile but, whenever this happened, it seems that no one—neither beast nor man—was surprised by it and found it normal in the desert.

"The true Christian epic begins with the lives of the Desert Fathers." Quoting these words of Gaston Paris, Jean Brémond asked himself if "this epic character doesn't rob our heroes of their reality...

> ...their acts take place in a pleasant light of legend, the combat between Antony and the demons, the discovery of Paul as the first hermit, the desert wildcats tamed, the crocodiles serving as ferries...the eccentricities of one Dorotheus, they seem like the exploits of Roland and Isengrin.[4]

It is certain that during their lives these heroes of asceticism and virtue were surrounded by a halo of the supernatural which led, for instance, to Macarius being called a "god on earth," after the fashion of the pharaoh who held this title in ancient Egypt.[5]

---

[4]H. and J. Brémond, *Le Charme d'Athènes*, Paris, 1925, p. 160.

[5]A 485 (Ward, p. 134). Cf. H. Grapow, *Die bildlichen Ausdrucke des Aegyptischen*, Leipzig, 1924, p. 178. The title is also given the Bishop in *Constitutions apostoliques*, XI, 26. Cf. P. Brown, *The Making of Late Antiquity*, Cambridge, MA, 1978, pp. 98ff.

But if we put them back in their historical and geographical context, see them living in solitude in their cells or relating to others, we find men who are closer to their peers—those of yesterday and today—than we can imagine. Otherwise, we won't grasp the fascination they had—and continue to have—even among unbelievers. Flaubert, who thought himself free of prejudice and any belief, was literally obsessed for more than thirty years by the personality of Antony, and one can say that the work he dedicated to him consumed his entire life.[6] Closer to our times, in his work *Les Hommes ivres de Dieu*, Jacques Lacarrière categorically declares, "I feel myself to be a total atheist and I wrote the history of these saints without ever sharing either their choice or their faith," and yet, gazing at them on frescoes in a monastery on Mount Athos, he admits to having understood "that they were not just painted to depict an irreplaceable experience, to anchor us in a bygone era, but to erupt at any moment into the present life of men."[7]

*   *   *

I wish to thank all the friends who agreed to read the manuscript of this work and suggest useful corrections. I am especially grateful to Antoine Guillaumont, honorary professor at the Collège de France, whose encouragement and advice as well as writings have always been invaluable to me.

---

[6]Gustave Flaubert, *The Temptation of Saint Antony*, English translation by Kitty Mrosovsky, Ithaca, NY, 1980/81, Intro., pp. 12ff.

[7]J. Lacarrière, *Les Hommes ivres de Dieu*, 3rd edition, Le Seuil (Points Sagesse 33), 1983, pp. 10-11. (Eng. trans. *The God-Possessed*, London, 1963.)

The Day-to-Day Life
of the Desert Fathers
in Fourth-Century Egypt

ONE

꒦✝꒦

In the Heart of the Desert

The Desert in Egypt

Every tourist visiting Egypt notices the omnipresence of the desert. One who goes to Cairo by jet today notices the pyramids alongside the desert, and the airport where travelers land is in the full barren zone. If he or she flies over the Valley of the Nile to reach Luxor, Aswan and Abu Simbel, the desert is constantly in view, hemming in on both sides a narrow, cultivated and inhabited strip by the river. In no other country is the desert so close to the populated world. To every Egyptian it imposes its continual presence. It is at his door, at the end of his field, of his glance, of his life. And in no other place is the contrast between cultivated land and the desert, between the black soil irrigated and fertilized by the Nile and the sterile sand here and there throughout the valley, so startling. Ever since Pharaonic Antiquity, the valley is "the domain of the god of life, Osiris, and his son Horus, opposed by Seth, the god of the hostile and wicked desert."[1] The valley is the domain of death, not only because it is a place of sterile soil and tombs, but because death often comes from bands of looters or wandering ferocious animals. The Egyptian had every reason, faced with the desert, to feel a sacred terror and an instinctive revulsion. Before he would ever agree to venture there, he really needed an urgent motive.

So it was that some Christians, during the persecution of Decius in the mid-third century, sought refuge in the desert to

---

[1]Guillaumont, p. 77. Cf. P. Brown, *Society and the Holy in Late Antiquity*, Berkeley, U. of Calif. Press, 1982, pp. 110ff.

escape torture and death. According to St Jerome, this was the case with Paul the Hermit, who of necessity fled to the desert to save his life, then remained there for reasons of virtue.[2] But most of the refugees were able to return to their villages after the persecution ended.

During this era, the Egyptians converted *en masse* to Christianity and, for Christians nourished by the Bible, the desert could appear less fearsome and even, to a certain extent, attractive. It was to the desert that God took his people, after freeing them from Egyptian captivity, to lead them to the Promised Land. John the Baptist had grown up in the desert and Jesus himself had gone there to confront the Devil. Many fervent Christians decided to remain celibate for the Lord and lead an ascetic life, first of all among their families, then somewhat cut off from the confines of the villages, that is, on the borders of the desert. Thus, at the end of the third century, there were, all along the Nile Valley and the branches of the Delta, monks who lived either in grottos on the slopes of the cliffs above the river, or in huts built nearby. Among them the most famous was Antony, who lived in Pispir, a few miles northeast of the modern city of Beni Suef.

Antony's Exodus

Apart from Paul the Hermit who had fled towards the Red Sea (but whose story poses many problems for historians), all these monks lived in the desert close to the Nile and populated areas. Yet it is understandable that they would develop a taste for the desert and some would one day feel like disappearing there in order to benefit from its solitude and silence. After living for ten years or so in a tomb not far from his village on the left bank of the Nile, Antony crossed the river to withdraw to a small abandoned fort a few miles from today's El-Maimoun. He remained hidden there for twenty years, after which many disciples came to join him. Then, guided by celestial inspiration, he began to tackle the "inner desert." Joining a caravan of Bedouins,

---

[2]*Life of Paul* 5.

he traveled some ninety miles to the foot of a mountain with a spring and a few palm trees, the spot where the monastery that bears his name was later built.[3] A modern highway now follows approximately the route Antony took from the Valley of the Nile. It connects with the low-lying area of Wadi el-Araba which, since Antiquity, had been one of the roads traveled by caravans from the Nile to the Red Sea.

The desert east of the Nile, the Arabian Desert, rocky and stony, is made up mainly of mountainous chains with an altitude in some spots of 6,560 feet. To the west of the river, the Libyan Desert has a limestone plateau about 656 feet high, with occasional outcrops among the sand dunes. It was to the northern part of this desert, the closest to the Delta, that Amoun and Macarius withdrew.

Just about everywhere alongside the Nile, emulators of Antony left the valley and its immediate surroundings to withdraw "to the deepest part of the desert." But none appear to have founded any notable group of hermitages. Those of Upper Egypt depicted in the *History of the Monks*, Or, Apollo and Patermuthius, did live for several years in total solitude, but returned later to the "near desert," where they attracted numerous disciples.[4] As for Amoun and Macarius, they left to settle in the great desert and this is where they attracted innumerable monks, founding there the eremitic centers of Nitria, along with an affiliated brotherhood of kindred spirits in the Cells and Scetis.

Nitria, The Cells and Scetis

At the same time as Antony was wending his way to his mountain, sometime around the year 313, a rich young man—an orphan living somewhere in the Delta—was forced by his uncle to get married. On the evening of their nuptials, he suggested to his bride that they both dedicate their chastity to the Lord. This they both did and lived together under the same roof for eighteen years, during which time they had no sexual relations whatsoever and maintained a perfect state of chastity. Urged by

---

[3]VA 1-2, 8, 11, 49-50.
[4]HM, 2, 3; 8, 3-7; 10, 8.

5

his wife, Amoun left for the desert, where he built himself a cell near the village known today as El-Barnougi, about twelve miles southwest of Damanhûr.[5] And this is how the desert of Nitria became so famous—the desert where Amoun attracted numerous monks—so much so that the area soon became over-populated. For those in search of more solitude, Amoun, on the advice of Antony, set up new cells ten or twelve miles from Nitria.[6] And so the desert of the Cells (or Cellia) came to life and is today well known due to excavations by French and Swiss archeologists in the last thirty-two years. In this region, the desert rises no more than a few miles above sea level. Altitude increases towards the south where it reaches thirty miles or so.

Some thirty miles from Cellia, we find a large basin about eighteen miles long and three to four miles wide, whose floor is above sea level, with lakes that gave their name to Wadi Natrun because of the niter gathered there from the days of Antiquity. This is the area of the desert of Scetis where Macarius settled around 330 A.D. He knew the places well because, as a camel driver, he used to go there looking for niter. After becoming an ascetic and a cleric near his village, he fled to the desert to escape from human glory.[7] It didn't take long for Scetis to become the most flourishing center of anchoritic life, and the most renowned Fathers lived there.

A Decisive Step

In the three vocations of Antony, Amoun and Macarius, we find the same progressive retreat from the world which culminates in the creation of fervent centers of monastic life in the heart of the desert. The decisive step involves leaving the "near desert" or "exterior desert," what one might call the fringe of the desert, to reach the "great desert," which ancient texts call the "faraway desert," the "interior desert," the "deeper desert" or again, the "full desert." This was the major event which occurred in Egypt at the beginning of the fourth century in monastic cir-

---

[5]HL 8.
[6]A 34 (Ward, p. 8). Cf. Guillaumont, pp. 151-152.
[7]A 454, A 484 (Ward, pp. 124, 134).

cles. It isn't a simple phenomenon, a news item, but the beginning of what can be called a true epic, due to its heroic character and immense impact. When we take into account the revulsion felt by Egyptians for the desert, already noted, we can sense how it must have taken truly powerful motives to drag them into these arid and desolate spots. And they weren't just taking off for a limited time, but had the firm intention of spending their entire lives there. In Antony's case, his biographer says he was advised by "a voice from on high" to go "into the interior desert." But heavenly inspiration came only after Antony had decided to move, because he "could not live in solitude as he wanted, and was afraid of boasting about what the Lord was doing for him."[8] For the same kind of motive, Macarius also went to live in Scetis.

Evangelical Renunciation Pushed to the Limit

Historians have put forth all kinds of reasons to explain this withdrawal to the desert: economic, political, sociological…and while it is possible that, in the long run, these reasons did influence the vocations of certain men, in the case of the three great pioneers we're talking about, nothing leads us to suppose that such motives prompted them to completely and definitively leave the world. The reasons for such a radical making up of one's mind could only have been religious, like those which led them to renounce marriage. It is remarkable that Amoun and Macarius, like Antony, were already living in chastity and asceticism before deciding to depart for the desert. They left the world in order to carry out, in a better way, the renunciation they've embraced. As has been shown by Professor Antoine Guillaumont, the evolution of the meaning of the word "monk" well conveys the ongoing discovery of all the requirements of monastic renunciation.[9] After giving the word "alone" the meaning of "single," it also expressed the desire to unify one's heart and life by getting rid of everything that distracts and divides, that is to say, all earthly goods and human concerns. And it is, finally, this

---

[8]VA 49.
[9]Guillaumont, pp. 218-222.

7

desire to remove oneself completely from the world's grasp so as to fully belong to God that led the monk to the solitude of the faraway desert. So long as he lived near his village, the anchorite took the risk of again allowing himself to be distracted by various preoccupations—family or other matters—by the attractions of pleasures here below and the trap of vainglory. By staking out a greater distance between himself and the world, he achieved a radical break, a veritable and voluntary death inspired, as Athanasius put it, "by the remembrance of the love God showed us, he who didn't spare his own Son, but delivered him up for us."[10] If the call to live in the desert isn't found explicitly in the Gospels, it nevertheless appears as a privileged way of achieving totally the teaching and imitation of Christ: "If someone doesn't renounce all that he owns, he cannot be my disciple...whosoever leaves his house, brothers, sisters, father, mother, children or fields, because of my Name, will receive much more and inherit eternal life."

The Anchorite's Truly Authentic Christian Character

There had certainly been precedents in pagan and Jewish Antiquity. Greek philosophers, notably the Stoics, had advocated a certain ideal of solitude and withdrawal in order to achieve wisdom more easily. Some Jewish ascetics, contemporaries of Christ, the Essenes, had come together on the banks of the Dead Sea, living chaste and austere lives, all taken up with praising God and praying. During the same era, Philo tells us about a community of "Therapeutae," meaning "servants of God," who lived in the suburbs of Alexandria, away from the noise and bustle of business, so as to devote themselves to contemplation of the divinity.[11] Yet nowhere else but among the Christian anchorites does one see such a complete break with the cultured and inhabited world. And what is also completely new and unique to Christian monasticism is that the exodus to the desert isn't undertaken for an abstract and distant god but for God incarnated in Christ, the intention being to better respond to the

---

[10]VA 14.
[11]Guillaumont, pp. 13-37.

immense love that God showed us by sending his Son, who became human like us, suffered and died to save us. Without the Incarnation of Christ, the departure of the monks to the desert makes no sense at all, and never could only a few individuals ever have drawn thousands of Christians to follow in their wake. This unusual step, this separation from the ecclesial community, could have been seen as a desertion, an exaggeration, even an aberration, and yet in no time at all it became admired, praised, exalted as the summit of virtue and saintliness. St Athanasius himself, the great bishop of Alexandria, who was the ardent defender of Christ's divinity against the Arians, turned out to be a fervent apologist of the monastic life. By composing and publishing the *Life of Antony*, this eminent theologian in a way authenticates via the seal of his authority this singular innovation. In his hero he gives us not only a role model for monks but a beautiful example for all Christians and even an eyewitness account that would touch the pagans. And soon, from all sides, people turned towards the deserts of Egypt, going there on pilgrimages with the same fervor as to the Holy Places in Palestine, spreading a thousand anecdotes about the Desert Fathers, spreading their words with almost as much zeal as that devoted to the Gospels. For Christian people, this amounts not only to a canonization of these saintly personages, but to an implicit approval of their lifestyle, of what was most original about it, this withdrawal to the desert which they had initiated.

An Uninhabitable Land

To retreat to the desert was first of all, for Antony and the early hermits, to "flee from people," flee from the inhabited regions, the towns and villages. But the desert is not only an inhabited place, but also an uninhabitable land because it is sterile and unsuited for supplying men with the barest essentials of livelihood. True, nomads can travel from oasis to oasis there, making plundering forays into populated regions to get what they need. But sedentary people can only lead a miserable and uncomfortable life there. This is precisely what the Desert Fathers wanted. As Abba Isidore asked one day, "Isn't it to work

9

hard that we've come to this place?"[12] In quitting the outskirts of the cultivated country, they knew very well what they were doing. One day Abba Abraham told Cassian,

> We could have set our cells on the banks of the Nile and had water at our doors. We would have saved ourselves the trouble of having to go four miles to fetch it.... Nor are we ignorant that there are even in our country some pleasant places where...fertile ground would furnish the food we need.... But we despised all these things and scorn them together with all the pleasures of this world, we delight only in this squalor, and prefer to all luxuries this dreadful and vast desert and cannot compare any riches of a fertile soil to these barren sands ....[13]

How far this is from the idyllic portraits painted by Philo of the lives of the Therapeutae in suburban Alexandria, where the air is pure and velvety, the gardens green and flourishing and where one enjoys peace and quiet, far from the razzle-dazzle and pollution of the towns![14] It's undeniable that these Jewish ascetics had religious preoccupations, but they just wanted to live in the most favorable conditions for contemplation of God, while the Christian anchorites sought first of all to imitate a crucified God. It wasn't for nothing that they painted crosses all over the walls of their hermitages, as can be seen today in the ruins of the Cells.

Even in Our Own Day

The first monks to live in the desert did not enjoy for long the total solitude they had journeyed there to seek. According to Palladius, at the end of the fourth century, Nitria had 5,000 monks and the Cells, 600.[15] We have no figures for Scetis but soon after the death of Antony in 356, Sisoes was already grumbling about there being too many monks, and this is why he then

---

[12]A 618 (Ward, p. 173).
[13]Cassian, Conf. 24, 2.
[14]Guillaumont, pp. 29-30.
[15]HL 7, 2.

went to live by himself on Mount Colzim.[16] Other anchorites, insatiable for solitude, took off for deeper parts of the desert, such as Paphnutius, spoken of by Cassian, who had earned the nickname "Bubalis," the Wild Roamer.[17] Soon Poemen was deploring the fact that "there's scarcely any desert left."[18] At any rate, at the time of the Desert Fathers and afterwards, an anchorite seldom spent his entire life in total solitude. But the decisive step taken by those who became the first to reach the deep desert never lost any of its importance or impact. They are truly the "Fathers of the Desert" because it was through their work that the monastic desert came into being, not only as a spirituality, but as a place separated from the world, where certain Christians wish to live the Gospel more completely.

"In the Heart of the Desert" — this is the title given by Saint-Exupéry to the chapter in *Terre des Hommes* where he tells about his plane crash in the Lybian Desert. The aviator already knew the fringes of the desert, having visited Cape Juby on the Moroccan coast. But, he wrote, "It was given to me one day to reach it by the heart." He almost died of thirst during the long walk he had to undertake before being rescued by a Bedouin near Wadi Natrun on January 2, 1936. At a particular moment, he thought he saw a cross in the distance.[19] The monastery shown on maps would have been one of four still in existence today in Scetis, the most easterly one being El-Baramus. Saint-Exupéry certainly fraternized with the spiritual descendants of the Desert Fathers who have lived in these arid lands for fifteen centuries. In his works, did he not often mention and praise the desert where, he says, "we were entrusted to the discretion of God."[20]

---

[16]A 831 (Ward, 218).

[17]Cassian, Conf. 3, 1.

[18]Eth 14, 66.

[19]A. de Saint-Exupéry, *Terre des hommes*, Paris, 1958, pp. 209, 228. (Eng. trans., *Wind, Sand and Stars*, New York, 1967.)

[20]*Ibid*, p. 214.

TWO

ﯫ✝ﯫ

The Men

Why Egypt

For several decades now, many works on the origins of monasticism have brought to light the existence—from the end of the third century—of many monks just about everywhere in the different regions where Christianity took root. Before that, there were already ascetics and virgins living in celibacy for God right within Christian communities. More and more they isolated themselves from society, living apart and reducing relations with their neighborhoods to a minimum. It was a universal phenomenon which was not, however, restricted to Christianity. But why was it in Egypt of the fourth century that the new event we have just mentioned, the exodus to the desert, took place—and that this occurrence very soon caused an extraordinary stir throughout the Christian world? From all quarters people turned to Egypt as the favored land of monasticism and the homeland of the monks. And soon the apothegms of the Desert Fathers, recounting their words and acts, would be translated into all languages and spread everywhere, while in monastic circles, in all places and all eras, venerable elders would say and also accomplish marvelous things. At the beginning of this movement, we find only a few Copts of modest background and little education. How do we explain the immense influence of these men who withdrew to the heart of the desert in order to hide out there and vanish completely from the eyes of their fellow creatures?

Already in the fourth century, Antony's biographer asked himself this question and wondered, "How could the renown of this man, hidden on his mountain, have reached Spain, Gaul, Rome, Africa, without the will of God who makes known everywhere those who belong to him...? These men act in secret and wish to remain hidden, but the Lord shows them to everyone as torches."[1] Obviously God wanted it, but the All-Powerful does not intervene in the course of human history without preparing the ground first. Egypt's geographical configuration is not without merit, as we have seen, in the great anchoritic movement. The founder of the Community of the Lion of Judah and the Sacrificial Lamb, Ephraim, writes, "To those who think that geography has nothing to do with religion, I would say that it is intimately connected to the plan of God."[2] The Creator had placed the desert within reach of the Egyptians, but did he not also prepare men to be drawn there, to live there and, for many, to die there? It was in Egypt that the God of Israel began training his people before leading them to the desert. It seems that he also gave the Egyptians some predispositions to depart for the desert.

A Profoundly Religious People

Herodotus remarked that Egyptians are the most religious of all peoples.[3] As Amélineau put it,

> It does seem that in ancient Egypt, in the highest classes of society as well, perhaps, as in the lowest, all life had religion as its main and sufficient reason, since present life is but a preparation for the much more important one to come.... Religion and the gods were implicated in all of life's activities. The same was true for the Christians on the banks of the Nile.[4]

A very ancient tradition dates the commencement of Christian preaching in Alexandria back to the evangelist St Mark in the mid-first century. However, the progress of Christianity was apparently somewhat slow during the first two centuries. At the

---

[1]VA 93.
[2]Ephraim, *Déjà les blés sont blancs*, Paris, 1987, p. 40.
[3]Herodotus, *History* II, 37.
[4]E. Amélineau, *Contes et romans de l'Egypte chrétienne*, Paris, 1888, p. XXIX.

beginning of the third, according to Origen, the Christians were still "no doubt few in numbers but truly faithful." There still exists in Alexandria a famous school of biblical exegesis and theology, of which Origen was the prestigious master. At the same time, we find there a strong current of asceticism preparing the dawn of monasticism. But it is especially the persecutions of the second century which reveal the existence of large Christian groups all through the Nile Valley. To quote the historian Eusebius, the persecutions by Diocletian and Maximian in Upper Egypt produced thousands of victims. "I'm persuaded," writes Amélineau, "that Egypt is the country that supplied most of the martyrs for the Christian religion during this persecution."[5] What is remarkable is that Coptic chronology numbers the years beginning with the 284 A.D. accession to power of Diocletian, who launched the most violent persecution. From these fervent Christians, it is not surprising that many ascetics, keen on renunciation and the anchorites, became the very first to go live in the deep desert. Prepared to shed their blood for Christ, they were ready to give up the world in order to belong totally to him. When Maximinus Daia's persecution came to an end, Constantinian peace would allow a prodigious expansion of Christianity throughout Egypt and also the rapid development of monastic life in the desert.

Human Qualities and Virtues

It is hard to detect with certainty, in the temperament and character of the Egyptians, any predispositions favorable to anchoritic life. Nevertheless, could we perhaps put forward a few inborn qualities and virtues which predisposed them to a rough and austere life in the body, but also an equally spiritual and deep one in the soul? In race and language, the Desert Fathers were almost all Coptic, coming usually from peasant stock, used to a tough and hardworking life, a frugal lifestyle and the lack of all comfort. These "fellahs" had strong constitutions and could put up with anything.[6] Bossuet had this to say about them: "The

---

[5]*Ibid.*, p. L.
[6]H. Ayrout, *The Egyptian Peasant*, Boston, 1963, p. 53.

never-changing temperature of Egypt gave them solid and constant minds."[7] Herodotus had already noted that "the Egyptians are, after the Libyans, the healthiest people in the world,"[8] which must be understood as applying as much to psychic stability as to physical health.

Egyptian anchorites are often depicted as primitive and savage, crude and uncouth. Could all Egyptians have been looked upon like this by the Greeks? The reality is that they had generally preserved from their ancient civilization an accumulation of nobleness, a nobility of soul, of pride and of urbanity which we still find today among the humble villagers of Upper Egypt. Most had little culture but had intellectual strength plus a remarkable subtlety of mind, wisdom and shrewdness. All these qualities are found again in the Desert Fathers, brought into service to develop in them and the souls of their disciples the spiritual life, by adhering to a uniquely demanding discipline. Gifted also with extraordinary memories, the Egyptians could amass and carefully preserve all their knowledge and experience. This ability to collect, preserve and transmit to their descendants traditions received from their ancestors was especially prevalent among them, as Herodotus pointed out,[9] and it is mostly because of this that we have the apothegms of the Fathers.

We could certainly point out other aspects of the Coptic temperament which might have furthered the flowering of Egyptian monasticism, but there were also some which could have caused it to wilt and wither. Even the attachment to tradition, mentioned above, could have diverted the first anchorites from a step which had no precedent, the initiative of cutting themselves off completely from the world so as to live in the desert. "As observers of ancestral customs," wrote Herodotus, "the Egyptians add not a single new one."[10] And yet, what a dimension of novelty there was to Antony's decision!

---

[7] J.-B. Bossuet, *Discourse on Universal History* III, 3.
[8] Herodotus, *History* II, 77.
[9] *Ibid.*
[10] *Ibid.*, 79.

Antony suggests to his "elder" that they depart together but the latter declines, citing his advanced age and the unusual character of the mission.[11] Never had anything like this been done! So the youthful Antony must have had either a first-rate audacity or a serious thrust from God — or rather both — for him to conceive and realize his project.

Attachment to One's Land and Family

One must also imagine what it represented for an Egyptian to leave his land, his neighborhood, his family and his friends. The fellah especially is sedentary and a homebody. "He stays riveted to his native village, which represents for him the security of the present and the past."[12] When Antony set off for the desert, he was an orphan, had left his sister and rid himself of all his possessions. But he still had many relatives and acquaintances in the village. And he was giving up not only the relatives he had left but also the family he might have started. In no other country of the world were family ties as strong as in Egypt, and this undoubtedly still holds true today.

Many ancient paintings and sculptures still evoke in a marvelous way the joys of family life in Pharaonic Egypt. We know that the Devil often used the remembrance of family to tempt an anchorite. He did this to Antony and many others, especially, those who had been married and missed the wives they left behind. The first anchorites would have required an uncommon detachment to make up their minds to abandon the family circle. Only the words of Jesus could have moved them to such a radical and definitive separation.

Cheerfulness and Sociability of the Egyptians

One doesn't have to spend much time in Egypt before noticing the sociability of its inhabitants, their need for contacts and exchanges with others. They are certainly not inclined by nature to isolation and solitude. This is another trait underlined

---

[11]VA 11.
[12]Ayrout, *op. cit.*, p. 16.

by Amélineau: "The Egyptian race was one of the most playful on the face of the globe. From remotest Antiquity to our times, Egyptians have been grown-up children, lovers of pleasure and joy, sociable to the utmost degree."[13] Happy to be alive, they are joyful, optimistic and carefree. How do we explain that these men—generally so cheerful, playful, so fond of jokes, laughter and irony—should have embraced in such large numbers an ideal of gravity and seriousness that excluded all entertainment? Again on this point, it must be recognized that the Desert Fathers were not as strict as they've been made out to be. Antoine Guillaumont thought he could soften the somewhat categorical judgments of K. Heussi and Irénée Hausherr by showing that the Egyptian anchorites didn't lack good humor and could occasionally show it,[14] in the spirit of their ancestors who didn't mind painting amusing caricatures on the walls of their tombs. We're too inclined to imagine them with sad and severe looks, constantly busy weeping over their sins. For every Pambo who, we are told, never laughed,[15] there must have been many others who at least cracked a smile and showed a happy face. This was the sign by which Antony was recognized and the subject of one of his favorite recommendations for visitors.[16] "Be joyful at all times," was the order given by Benjamin to his disciples.[17] Joyful John of Lycopolis greeted the travelers in the *History of the Monks* with a smile.[18] These describe with enthusiasm the elation of Apollo and his disciples: "We could see them exulting in the desert to such an extent that nowhere on earth could one find such jubilation, such physical contentment."[19]

---

[13]Amélineau, *op. cit.*, p. VI.
[14]A. Guillaumont, "Le rire, les larmes et l'humour chez les moines d'Egypte," in *Hommages à François Daumas*, Montpellier, 1986, pp. 373-380.
[15]A 774 (Ward, p. 197).
[16]VA 67 & 92; VA 42.
[17]A 171 (Ward, p. 44).
[18]HM 1, 18.
[19]HM 8, 52-53.

Past Lives of the Anchorites

We would like to learn more about the Desert Fathers' past histories: their social backgrounds, their younger years, the education they received and the trades at which they worked before becoming monks. The stories of Coptic lives of the seventh and eighth centuries are full of details but instead of this legendary proliferation, it is best to rely on more ancient sources, especially the apothegms, where the information about the past lives of the Fathers is much more invaluable because it is rarer and has no hagiographic motive. As was said, most came from the peasant class. If this isn't often set forth explicitly in the texts, it is precisely because this was true for most of them. But there were variations in the lot of the fellahs. Antony had inherited 300 acres of excellent land[20] and wouldn't have had to work the land himself. His disciple, Paul the Simple, was returning from the fields when he caught his wife committing adultery, which caused him to leave for the desert.[21] Amoun was a manufacturer of balm,[22] while Macarius used his camels for transporting—and perhaps dealing in—natron.[23] In other words, they worked for the funeral parlors of the day, since balm and natron were used to mummify cadavers.

According to Palladius, Macarius of Alexandria, in his youth, used to sell "sweets,"[24] no doubt candies, dried fruit and all kinds of pastries still sold today in the streets of Cairo and Alexandria. Not much of a job but one that can be very profitable. The two brothers, Paësius and Isaias, were sons of a rich merchant of Spanish origin.[25] John of Lycopolis had learned the carpenter's trade in his youth while his brother worked as a dyer.[26] Apollonius was a former merchant and Apelles worked

---

[20]VA 2.
[21]HL 22, 1.
[22]HL, 8, 3.
[23]A 484 (Ward, p. 134).
[24]HL 17, 1.
[25]HL 14, 1.
[26]HL 35, 1.

as a blacksmith.[27] Some anchorites had also been slaves.[28] One
followed his master to the desert and became his disciple.[29]

Before becoming a monk, Dioscorus had been a scribe,[30]
Mark and others had been calligraphers,[31] which means they had
some education. Antony himself couldn't have been as illiterate
as his biographer makes him out to be since he could read and
write letters.[32] Poemen knew no Greek but this was not the case
with all the Coptic monks.[33] Cassian mentions an Abba Joseph
who was well-versed in the language.[34]

Recruits from Paganism

The Pachomian communities of the Thebaid territory
included a number of recruits from paganism who were baptized at the monastery. Did this also take place in the anchoritic
circles of Lower Egypt? We know that Macarius, traveling one
day from Scetis to Nitria, converted a pagan priest impressed
with his kindness: "We made him a monk and many pagans
became Christians because of him."[35] Another pagan priest decided to embrace the monastic life after hearing about the gentleness and patience of a monk.[36] A young Theban, son of another
pagan priest, became a monk after witnessing, at a gathering of
demons, one of them receiving a palm branch for having finally
enticed into lust a monk he had been after for more than forty
years.[37]

Because Christianity had undergone a tremendous expansion in Egypt in the second half of the third century, one can
assume that most of the monks were already Christians before

[27]HL 13, 1; HM 13, 1.
[28]N 53.
[29]N 540.
[30]Ch 252, Ch 256.
[31]A 526 (Ward, p. 145); N 375, N 517, N 520.
[32]VA 1.
[33]A 757 (Ward, p. 192).
[34]Cassian, Conf. 16, 1.
[35]A 492 (Ward, p. 137).
[36]N 77.
[37]N 191.

departing for the desert. This was true for Antony, born in a Christian family and brought up as a Christian.[38] Of the monks from Cellia, Palladius says they had also been "obedient to God from infancy and born to Christian parents."[39] However, Macarius of Alexandria was only baptized at the age of forty.[40] His monastic vocation must have coincided with his conversion and baptism in 333 A.D.

Former Bandits

A few well-known bandits became monks who were just as famous. We know the story of Patermuthius, leader of a gang and looter of tombs who, through his crimes, developed quite a reputation. One night he attacked the hermitage of a virgin consecrated to God. He climbed up to the roof, fell asleep and in a dream saw "a kind of king who suggested he abandon vice for virtue" and join his service. Upon awakening, he saw the virgin near him, asking what he was doing there. She showed him the road to the church where the priests taught him a few verses of a psalm, after which he left for the desert. Three years later he returned there to be baptized and then went back into solitude and soon had many disciples.[41]

Even more famous at Scetis was Moses, the Ethiopian, who spent some time working for an official but was banished for his immorality and robberies. As a gang leader, he became known for his perversity and cruelty. After recounting one of his feats, Palladius tells us he was led to repentance one night following a "problem." Cassian explains that Moses was pursued by the forces of justice for murder.[42] He became a monk and they say that one day four thieves, unaware who they were dealing with, came to attack him in his cell. He tied them up, stacked them on his back and carried them to the church where he let the

---

[38]VA 1.
[39]Palladius, *Dialogue on the Life of John Chrysostom* 17, SC 341, p. 331.
[40]HL 18, 28.
[41]HM 10, 3-8.
[42]HL 19, 1-4; Cassian, Conf. 3, 5.

priests decide what to do with them. When they learned they had attacked the great Moses, they too converted.[43]

We also know of another murderer who became a monk at Scetis—a shepherd called Apollo. He had ripped open a pregnant woman's stomach just to see "how the baby is situated in the womb." Stricken with remorse, he came to confess his crime to the elders at Scetis. He was forty and had never prayed. He decided to do nothing but pray for the rest of his life.[44]

From these beautiful examples of penitence, one should not assume that most of the Desert Fathers had guilt-ridden pasts to expiate. The *History of the Monks* mentions another Apollo who retreated to the desert at the age of fifteen and a Helle who also persevered in asceticism from childhood days.[45] We have every reason to believe that Poemen and his six brothers had led blameless lives before coming to Scetis, as did Macarius who, in the desert, still blamed himself for a peccadillo of youth: while taking some calves to pasture with other boys, he had picked up and eaten a fig stolen by his companions.[46] The apothegms even mention an elder who left the world "still a virgin and totally ignorant of fornication" as well as another who, while still young, arrived in Scetis with his father and didn't even know women existed until the Devil showed him one in a dream.[47]

Foreign Monks

Next to the Egyptians of the Delta and the Thebans of the Nile Valley, there were in the deserts of Lower Egypt some strangers whose number is difficult to estimate but who appear to have never been more than a small minority. We're not talking about the numerous visitors who came to be instructed and uplifted for a time near the Fathers of the Desert but of those who established themselves for good in Nitria, Cellia and Scetis. The most famous are Evagrius and Arsenius but there were

---

[43]HL 19, 4.
[44]A 150 (Ward, p. 36).
[45]HM 8, 3; HM 12, 1.
[46]A 490 (Ward, p. 136).
[47]N 426; N 171.

others less well-known: for instance, the two little foreigners received at Scetis by Macarius who were involved in the beginnings of the El-Baramus Monastery.[48] A legend makes them Maximus and Domecius, sons of the Emperor Valentinian,[49] but it is best to respect the mystery concealed in the apothegms of the luminous figures of these two young anchorites predestined to die prematurely after only three years in the desert.

A native of Asia Minor, Evagrius had fled Constantinople to evade the attentions of an official's wife. Withdrawing to Palestine on the advice of a saintly moniale,[50] Melania, he passed through Egypt and settled first in Nitria, then in Cellia, where he died in 399 A.D. He lived there among a circle of learned and cultivated monks, fervent admirers of Origen, but also attended the Desert Fathers' school, notably that of the two Macarii. Evagrius had arrived in Nitria around 383.[51] A few years later, a high dignitary of the imperial court, named Arsenius, also left Constantinople for Egypt. He became a monk in Scetis alongside John Colobos.[52] He certainly had dealings with Evagrius. The latter asked him one day, "Why is it that we, with all our culture and wisdom, have nothing, while these uneducated Egyptians have acquired so many virtues?" To which Arsenius replied, "We gain nothing from our worldly culture, but these uneducated Egyptians work hard to acquire the virtues."[53]

According to another apothegm, "seven senators, imitating Arsenius, renounced all their goods, began working with reeds, and used worthless pottery."[54] One can easily imagine what such a harsh and modest existence in the midst of aging fellahs must have meant for these well-to-do and cultured Greeks and Romans. Several apothegms mention it. While the majority of

---

[48]A 486 (Ward, pp. 134ff.).

[49]Evelyn White, pp. 102-103.

[50][Ed. note]: The word *moniale* is the feminine form of *monk*, though in the 4th-5th centuries, that term would have been unknown. The Desert Fathers generally referred to women in the desert as virgins or mothers, "ammas."

[51]Guillaumont, pp. 186-187.

[52]Regnault, pp. 42-43.

[53]A 43 (Ward, p. 10).

[54]N 14.

Egyptian peasants did not find material conditions in the desert much different from those in their villages, for these lofty personages from well-heeled backgrounds, it was a complete change which made their renunciation all the more heroic.[55]

Regardless of their past lives, backgrounds, social conditions and spirituality, these men came to the desert with the same firm decision to live only for and with God. In the rugged school of anchoritic life, they lost no time in adopting a common spirit and many similar traits; yet each would retain his unique personality. We have met some of them. We will meet them again along with many others. Many remarkable personalities emerge among hundreds of desert dwellers whom we know by name or physiognomy. They all do credit to humanity.

---

[55]A 74; A 233; A 799 (Ward, pp. 17, 64, 297).

THREE

✠

Women and Children

Women in the Desert?

When Abba Sisoes had become old and infirm, his disciple suggested they move closer to inhabited regions. To which the old man replied. "Let's go where there are no women!" "But," the disciple went on, "what place has no women if it isn't the desert?"[1]

People sometimes speak of the "Desert Mothers." Palladius himself, in the prologue to his *Lausiac History*, announces that he will report the feats of "our holy fathers, the desert monks, as well as those of the venerable mothers who, with a virile force, led the battle for asceticism in a perfect way right to the end."[2] Of all the saintly women introduced in his work, none lived in "the great desert." When one considers the insecurity that reigned there, we can see that a woman, be she ever so valiant, could never live by herself without taking tremendous risks, as much for her honor as for her very life. Furthermore, as notes Jacques Lacarrière, "In the view of the anchorites of Egypt, the desert was not the place for women,"[3] for the simple reason that one among them would pose a permanent temptation. The

---

[1]A 806 (Ward, p. 213).

[2]HL Pr 1.

[3]*The God-Possessed*, p. 144. The same author unfortunately invented a Mary of Egypt (*Marie d'Egypte*, Paris, 1983) whom he claims lived and died in the desert in a manner which honors neither women nor the Fathers of the Desert. [Ed. note: Contrary to the author's statement here, Lacarrière did not "invent" Mary of Egypt. Her story has been told in monastic circles in the East since the sixth century. See Benedicta Ward, *Harlots of the Desert*, p. 26.]

"Ammas" who appear in the collection of apothegms did not live in the heart of the desert. Amma Sara, the most famous one, "lived sixty years near the river," meaning the Nile.[4] Theodora,[5] like Syncletica,[6] probably lived in the suburbs of Alexandria.

One must nevertheless take into account the moniales who, dressed as monks, lived incognito in the desert. Hagiography records many such cases whose historicity is hard to evaluate.

In the deserts of Lower Egypt, the most famous are Apollinaris, Hilary and Anastasia. Apollinaris was the daughter of Emperor Anthemius. She fled to the Scetis desert to escape from a marriage her father wanted to arrange. After being disfigured by mosquitoes in the Scetis swamps, she lived in the vicinity under the name of Dorotheus. One of her sisters was possessed by the Devil, and Anthemius sent her to the Fathers in Scetis for healing. She was referred to the so-called monk, Dorotheus, who sent her back to her father, healed. But shortly afterwards, "the Devil made her appear pregnant." Furious, the Emperor ordered Dorotheus to be brought before him and only then did he recognize her as his daughter Apollinaris, which didn't prevent her from returning to Scetis, still incognito, where she lived again for a time. Only after she died, at the moment of the funeral ablutions, was her real identity revealed.[7]

This life of Apollinaris, which would make a good film script, is, from beginning to end, a tissue of improbabilities. The same goes for Hilary, so-called daughter of Emperor Zeno, who did exactly the same as Apollinaris by living in Scetis under the name of Hilarion, the eunuch. She also cured her sister, possessed by the Devil, but was never recognized or seen again. Zeno, knowing his daughter to be in the desert and rightly afraid for her safety, is said to have erected in each of the monasteries a fortified tower where the monks could find refuge when in danger.[8] When today's visitors reach the monastery at Wadi Natrun, the guide never fails to recall—gravely or with a smile—

---

[4] A 886 (Ward, p. 230).
[5] A 309-315 (Ward, pp. 82ff.).
[6] A 892-909 (Ward, pp. 230ff.).
[7] Evelyn White, pp. 117-118.
[8] *Ibid.*, pp. 224-227.

this legend to explain the origins of the dungeons which still survive in the four monasteries.

In one of the sixth-century narratives by Daniel of Scetis, we find another version of the legend. A noble patrician, Anastasia, wanting to hide from Emperor Justinian's advances, went to see Daniel who gave her monastic clothing and an out-of-the-way cell. She lived there for twenty-eight years and only after her death did Daniel reveal her identity.[9]

The following also would have occurred in the sixth century. In the more ancient tradition of the apothegms, we find only two histories of holy women living in a desert grotto. One, told by Doulas, a disciple of Bessarion, concerns a moniale first thought to be a man and found to be a woman after her death.[10] The other comes from two great old ones who, walking in the Scetis desert, heard "the weakened sound of a voice coming from the ground," and found in a cave a little old lady, sick and lying down, who had been there for thirty-eight years and, she tells them, "serving Christ without lacking for anything and without seeing anyone. God sent you to bury my body."[11] This story, the most sparing in details, is the most plausible one, without its authenticity being for that matter a sure thing. Stories such as these obviously have an edifying purpose. They were intended to remind the anchorites that they shouldn't boast about their withdrawal to the desert since women were doing the same. "See," Bessarion told his disciple, "how even women triumph over Satan!"[12]

Diabolical Illusions

In the end, it is Satan who is defeated in these cases since, ordinarily, women encountered in the desert are either real beings sent there at his instigation or, more often, phantoms created by him to seduce an anchorite. For example one woman, taking advantage of a caravan, came to rejoin her cousin "in the

---

[9]N 596/2. Cf. Evelyn White, pp. 244-246.
[10]A 159 (Ward, p. 41).
[11]N 132C.
[12]A 159 (Ward, p. 41).

faraway desert, egged on by the Devil," and did lead him into sin.[13] Pachon, in Scetis, and more than fifty years of age, was attacked without mercy day and night for twelve years by the demon of fornication. Finally, the demon came to him in the guise of a young Ethiopian he had spotted during his youth gathering grain in a field. She plunked herself on his knees and got him so excited, he thought they had copulated. Furious, he slapped her face and she disappeared. But for two years, his hand gave off an intolerable stench.[14]

Sometimes a tempted monk didn't stop at a slap. One shameless hussy boasted among her young friends that she would be able to corrupt an illustrious anchorite. She turned up one evening at his cell door, pretending to be lost. He let her in but, sensing that the Devil was starting to tempt him with this woman, lit a lamp and put all his fingers, one by one, into the flame, to the point where he had only one left in the morning. Stricken, the woman dropped dead. The young people then came to the anchorite to see if the temptress had succeeded.

"Didn't a woman come here last evening?" they asked.

"Yes," he replied, "she's in there — asleep."

They went in and found her dead.

The elder, showing his missing fingers, told them, "This is what this daughter of the Devil did to me, but," he added, "it is written, 'You will not render evil for evil.' " He then prayed and revived the woman; she left and lived a chaste life from then on.[15]

Sometimes the demons would join forces. Four of them, metamorphosed into gorgeous women, harassed a brother for forty days. But he put up a courageous fight and, after this harrowing ordeal, God never again allowed him to suffer any carnal temptation.[16] One day in Cellia, a priest, standing near a brother's cell, saw a multitude of demons disguised as women, saying and doing indecent things.[17]

---

[13]N 176.
[14]HL 23, 3-5.
[15]N 189.
[16]N 188.
[17]N 166.

Shunning Women

In general, a clairvoyant monk knew how to spot the presence of the Devil in disguise, but this was not always the case. This explains why the anchorites had to shun women as a matter of principle or, as some said, "like wine or bishops."[18] To interpret the meaning of this phrase, one must understand that it was, rather, a case of giving up wine as well as women, since drunkenness easily ends in debauchery; and fleeing from the bishops, as well as women, since they can tear the monk from his monastic life by conferring upon him the priesthood.

In this mistrust of women, though, we see that some Desert Fathers went to extremes: for example, the one who spotted a woman's footprint in the road and made it disappear,[19] or one who, while traveling with his elderly mother, covered his hands before carrying her from one bank of a river to the other.[20]

One day a woman disembarked at Diolcos and remained seated nearby. A brother who came to fetch water saw her and ran to warn his elders, shouting: "Help, brothers, thieves!"[21] Another, upon meeting some moniales on his way, left the road, and one of them shouted to him: "If you were a perfect monk, you would not have noticed that we were women!"[22]

Cassian the sage, on this subject, tells the delightful story of one Abba Paul who "had made such progress in purity of heart, in the stillness and silence of the desert, that he did not suffer... even the clothes of [a woman] to appear in his sight." One day while going to an elder's cell, Paul accidentally met a woman on the way. He fled immediately, "running faster than one would at the sight of a lion or a terrible dragon...." This went beyond the bounds of observance and of proper austerity. He was punished for this by being paralyzed to such an extent that he had to be carried to a virgins' monastery and consigned to the care of feminine hands who, for four years, nourished him and "looked

---

[18]N 592/55; Cassian, Inst. 11, 18.
[19]N 480.
[20]N 159.
[21]N 459.
[22]N 154.

after all the necessities of nature."[23] Cassian is also credited with an apothegm about an elder who, served by a moniale, was criticized and damned by some. After his death, a miracle proved that he had always maintained perfect chastity.[24]

Some measures of prudence were indeed required of these men who had dedicated their celibacy to God and, after a long sojourn in solitude, could be more sensitive and impressionable in their very rare meetings with the other sex. We easily understand the interdictions of the elders: "Allow no woman into your cell"; "sleep not where there is a woman"[25]; "never eat where there is a woman."[26]

Normally, as we said, there were no women living in the desert and certain anchorites, such as John of Lycopolis, had not seen a woman for forty or more years.[27] But many were sometimes obliged to return to the inhabited regions in order to sell their baskets there, to get fresh supplies, or for other reasons. They then had many opportunities to meet women, to desire them and eventually to sin with them.[28] They couldn't help seeing them but were supposed to avoid staring at them. Of one elder it is said that, during his sixty years of monastic life, he had not looked at a woman.[29] One must therefore assume this was exceptional.

On the other hand, the sight of certain women could be a subject of edification. Poemen and Anoub spotted a woman in a cemetery, crying abundantly, and this reminded them that they must cry over their own sins with as much ardor.[30] Likewise Pambo, noticing a prostitute in an Alexandrian street, broke into tears and later explained to his companions: "Two things struck

---

[23]Cassian, Conf. 7, 26.
[24]A 428 (Ward, p. 113).
[25]A 870, A 284 (Ward, pp. 225, 76).
[26]A 184 (Ward, p. 51); Evagrius, *Praktikos* 96.
[27]HM 1, 4.
[28]N 49, N 50, N 52, N 179.
[29]N 418.
[30]A 646 (Ward, p. 177).

me: First, this woman's perdition, then, that I don't have as much zeal in pleasing God as she has for pleasing sinful men."[31]

No Contempt of Women Among the Desert Fathers

Anatole France had his Thaïs say: "I know the saints of the desert detest women who, like me, are made to give pleasure."[32] One can assert that, in all the documents about the Desert Fathers, there is not a single fact or a single word justifying this statement. Arsenius could greet very warmly a grand Roman lady come to Egypt just to see him[33] or rebuff in no uncertain terms a young Ethiopian girl who, on the banks of the Nile, came to touch his coat. Yet he took as a lesson the girl's retort: "If you're a monk, go to the mountain!"[34] Even towards prostitutes, he shows no contempt. Several apothegms tell of an anchorite going to one of them either to convert her or rescue a brother and take him back to the desert.[35]

In trying to console the matron dismissed by Arsenius, Archbishop Theophilus told her: "Don't you realize that you are a woman and that, through women, the Enemy fights the saints?"[36] In fact, we see in the maxims several women seducing or trying to seduce monks,[37] but we also see others resisting monks who want to lead them into wrongdoing and who try to keep them faithful to their monastic profession,[38] which contradicts in advance the much-too-pessimistic quote from John Moschus (seventh century): "Salt comes from water and if it approaches water, it dissolves and disappears. Similarly, the monk comes from woman and, if he approaches a woman, he dissolves."[39] Evagrius fled Constantinople to elude a woman he

---

[31] A 765 (Ward, p. 196).
[32] *Thaïs*, Paris, p. 123.
[33] A 66 (Ward, pp. 13-14).
[34] A 70 (Ward, p. 15).
[35] A 355, A 875, A 917 (Ward, pp. 93-94, 226-227, 237); N 43, N 44, N 179.
[36] A 66 (Ward, pp. 13-14).
[37] N 176, N 189; Bu II 420.
[38] N 49, N 52.
[39] J. Moschus, *Pratum Spirituale*, 217.

loved,[40] but it was another woman, Melania, who put him back on the right path in Palestine.[41]

Proof that the Desert Fathers did not detest women is that they voluntarily performed miracles to help them. John of Lycopolis brought sight to the blind wife of a very important man.[42] Longinus cured the gangrenous hand of a woman who presented herself at the window of his cell.[43] During his life, Antony healed several girls, though most often from a distance,[44] while, to bring healing to a woman stricken with breast cancer, Longinus did not hesitate to touch the affected organ with his hand.[45] In the same manner, Macarius cured a possessed woman by rubbing her with holy oil for twenty days.[46]

But there is even better proof: the goodness with which the Desert Fathers treated women who misbehaved with a monk. One day some brethren came to Ammonas to denounce a monk who had a woman in his cell. The brother was hiding the woman in a large earthenware jar. When Ammonas entered the cell with the accusers, he discerned the stratagem and sat on the jar. The others searched the cell in vain. After they left, feeling sheepish, Ammonas simply took the brother by the hand and told him: "Look after yourself, brother."[47] Another monk lived with a woman. Upon hearing that she was in labor, Poemen sent his disciple with a jug of wine to celebrate the birth.[48] And what do we say of an elder who took into his cell for one night a monk and a moniale? Lying down between the pair, he knew they came together to do wrong, but he said nothing and let them leave the next morning. He had, however, prayed for them and the two culprits returned to ask his pardon.[49] Even if such stories were only edifying anecdotes fabricated from

---

[40]HL 38, 3.
[41]HL 38, 8-9.
[42]HM 1, 12.
[43]Sy 19, 7.
[44]VA 48, 58, 61, 71.
[45]A 451 (Ward, p. 123).
[46]HL 18, 11.
[47]A 122 (Ward, p. 28).
[48]Sy 9, 20.
[49]N 13.

various sources, they would still attest to the fact that the anchorites did not detest women.

Sexuality in the Desert

Some often attribute to the Christianity of the first centuries—and more so to monasticism—a phobia and an obsessive fear of women. At least for the Desert Fathers, this opinion is contradicted, it seems, by the simplicity and ingenuousness with which some of them illustrate their metaphors borrowed from the female sex. Arsenius, like Macarius, compared the anchorite in his cell to the virgin confined to her bedroom before her wedding.[50] In his parables, John Colobos wasn't afraid to mention two naked women or a prostitute who had many lovers.[51] Another elder used the image of a woman who rubs her breasts with a sour plant in order to wean her infant. This sour plant is the thought of death which the monk must use to chase away impure fantasies![52] Longinus even went so far as to compare the soul, which has conceived the Holy Spirit and is purified of the passions, to the woman for whom the blood stops flowing once she has conceived.[53] Harassed by the demon of lust which tried to force him to leave the desert to get married, Olympius took clay and sculpted a woman and a girl, telling himself: "There, you have a wife and a daughter, you have to work hard to feed them!" By his dedication to work, he obtained, by the grace of God, an end to his temptations.[54]

One might find a few sexually-obsessed monks in the desert, as anywhere else, but they were extremely rare and we find only two references among three thousand known apothegms. There was a brother who, during the harvest, thought he saw another lying with a woman in a field. As he approached the couple to put an end to the scandal, he saw they were nothing but two sheaves of wheat, lying one against the

---

[50]A 82, A 474 (Ward, pp. 19, 132).
[51]A 330-331 (Ward, p. 88).
[52]N 182.
[53]A 453 (Ward, p. 123).
[54]A 572 (Ward, pp. 160-161).

other.[55] Another monk went to an elder to accuse two brothers of "being together and committing evil." When night came, the elder summoned the two brothers and had them sleep on the same mat, under the same cover. Then he told his disciple: "Put this brother in a separate cell because he is the one who is tempted."[56]

The rich literature we have on the Desert Fathers shows that there was no stench of Manichaeism which would have made them detest the body, sex or women, but only a solid realism faced with the fleshly condition. The anchorites remained normal men with their instincts and lusts. None among them went as far as Origen, mutilating themselves in order to better observe continence, but they understood the full impact of renunciation in the words of Jesus about those "who become eunuchs for the kingdom of heaven." They are not astonished by the sometimes fierce desires they might feel. Didn't one of them go so far as to say that ten women would not be enough to satisfy his desire?[57] An elder used to say: "It is written of Solomon that he loved women. Assuredly all that is masculine loves what is feminine, but we tackle our thoughts and constrain nature, so as to bring it to purity and prevent it from succumbing to sensual delight."[58] Perhaps Evagrius and his disciples dreamt of an impassivity allowing them to feel no emotion whatsoever at the sight of a nude woman in their arms,[59] but the more reasonable among the Fathers were more realistic, like Abba Abraham who went to teach a lesson to an elder who claimed to be totally freed of fleshly lusts: "If you were to find a woman lying on your mat when you entered your cell, would you think it is not a woman?" "No," replied the other, "but I would resist the thought of touching her." "Thus the passions are still alive," concluded Abraham, "they are merely restrained by the saints."[60]

[55] A 688 (Ward, pp. 183-184).
[56] N 181.
[57] A 789 (Ward, p. 203).
[58] N 593.
[59] Cassian, Conf. 15, 10; cf. 12, 7.
[60] A 140 (Ward, p. 34).

If we collected all the stories about physical temptations to which some monks succumbed, this could make an impression on us,[61] but there are also many more temptations which they conquered. On the other hand, almost all who fell then pulled themselves up and resumed their monastic life with even more fervor and humility. In our modern society, where sex and sexuality have become so overwhelming, it's hard to think of a chastity lived serenely without any fleshly satisfaction. This is reason enough to avoid judging severely the ancient monks in this regard.

The Desert Fathers and Children

Whether they are houses of detention, barracks or monasteries, all environments where women are excluded always present dangers of homosexuality. We know that pederasty was widespread in ancient times. If Egypt in general seems to have known less of this depravity, the regions imbued with Hellenism—such as Alexandria—couldn't avoid it. When Athanasius, through the words of Antony in his philosophical discourse, denounces homosexual perversions, he is speaking to Greeks and not Egyptians.[62] Some weaknesses must have shown up among the thousands of anchorites but one would be wrong to assume they were common.

The Desert Fathers had no a priori mistrust of children. Unlike Pachomian communities, anchoritic areas were unable to attract and welcome children. The tough and solitary life was not for them. Most of the children who appear in the apothegms are not monks, nor are they destined to be. The boy Macarius met in the desert was leading cattle to pasture.[63] Throughout Egypt we see children leading cattle or donkeys. They are often mis-

---

[61]Especially if one unduly raises the significance of the texts, as is sometimes done by Aline Rouselle in her work, *Porneia, On Desire and the Body in Antiquity*, Oxford, 1988, when she writes, for example, about sexual relations between anchorites and women haphazardly encountered on their trips: "This was such a common occurrence that pregnant girls who did not want to betray their real lovers falsely accused the anchorites," (p. 145).

[62]VA 74.

[63]N 490A.

chievous, loud and boisterous.[64] However, some young boys
might come to the desert with their father or older brother.
Carion, for example, brought with him his son Zacharias, predestined to become prematurely an "elder"[65]; and among the
seven brothers which included Poemen and Anoub, there was
young Paësius who was not always sensible, so much so that the
others thought of abandoning him.[66] We also know that a child
from the Cells had an amazing knowledge of Holy Writ.[67]

In our times, Ephraim devoted a chapter of one of his books
to the "apothegms of the desert children."[68] The point is that his
community includes single persons, dedicated or not, along with
married couples and their children. There's nothing like this in
the desert of the Fathers. The best we can do is cite the wise
replies to Macarius by a young herdsman:

> [Macarius:] "What must I do, son, because I'm hungry?"
> He said: "Well, then, eat!"
> "I've eaten and I'm still hungry."
> He then told me: "Maybe you're a donkey, Father,
> because you always want to chomp."
> And I left, uplifted by this reply.[69]

To Be on Guard Against the Snares of the Devil

Frequently the apothegms give dire warnings against the
danger presented by children in the desert. The elders used to
say: "More than women, children are a snare of the Devil for
monks. Where there is wine and children, Satan is not needed."[70] The Fathers said that "it isn't God, but Satan, who leads
children into the desert."[71] The monk must never stare at anyone,
least of all a child. He must not "eat with a woman nor have any

---

[64]A 490 (Ward, p. 136), A 729 (Ward, p. 189); N 338.
[65]A 243-247, A 441 (Ward, pp. 67ff., 117ff.).
[66]A 747, A 754 (Ward, pp. 191, 192); N 448.
[67]Arm 10, 149; SP, New Collection, p. 263 (II 148).
[68]Ephraim, *Déjà les blés sont blancs*, Paris, 1987, pp. 103-121.
[69]N 490A.
[70]N 544-545.
[71]N 458.

familiarity with a child, and neither must he sleep in the cell of a brother who has a bad reputation."[72] Poemen said: "If a man cohabits with a child who arouses in him any of the passions of the old man, and he continues to keep him with him, he is like the owner of a field devoured by worms."[73] As far as he was concerned, John Colobos said, "He who eats without self-control and chats with a child has already fornicated with him in thought."[74]

Such insistence leads to the conclusion that it was not just an imaginary peril. And yet we find, in all of our sources, only one account of a sin committed by a monk with a child, and this concerns a brother "come from a monastery in Egypt," and not of an anchorite.[75] There are also two accounts of homosexual temptations admitted by an elder.[76] So we know the apothegms in no way hide the faults and temptations of the monks. Some good historians think that pederasty was practically unknown in the desert throughout the whole period when fervor reigned in the Cells and Scetis but that the situation must have changed with the decline in discipline at the end of the fourth century and the beginning of the fifth.

Macarius the Egyptian (390 A.D.) proclaimed the first devastation of Scetis, which probably occurred in 407, thus: "When you see a cell built near the marsh, know that its devastation is near; when you see trees, know that it is at the door; and when you see children, take your coats and leave."[77] So there were no children at Scetis during Macarius' time. Later Isaac of the Cells, a priest, would tell the brothers: "Don't bring children here,

---

[72]N 533; A 523 (Ward, p. 145), A 482 (Ward, p. 133); N 125, N 412; Sy 5, 53.

[73]A 750 (Ward, p. 191).

[74]A 319 (Ward, p. 86).

[75]A 416 (Ward, p. 107). Here again, A. Rousselle makes affirmations which go way beyond the significance of the texts; "The monks make it clear that these children did represent a temptation and that sexual acts did take place.... Macarius had doubtless seen so many sexual relationships develop with children that he strongly advised monks not to take them in..." (*Porneia*, p. 148).

[76]A 129 (Ward, p. 30); Cassian, Inst. 12, 20.

[77]A 458 (Ward, p. 128).

because four churches in Scetis have become deserted due to children."[78]

According to Cassian, there were, at the end of the fourth century, four monastic groups in Scetis, each with its own church.[79] It was therefore all of Scetis which was deserted in 407 following a Bedouin raid. The elders attributed this disaster to the monks' slackening of discipline. Moses had predicted it: "If we keep the commandments of our Fathers, I assure you the barbarians will not come here, but if we do not keep them, the area will be devastated."[80] The fact that children were involved in the affair, according to Isaac, doesn't necessarily mean that pederasty had become a scourge in Scetis. Children could be the source of temptations, it's true, but they were first of all a cause of noise and distractions. The brothers of Abba Poemen complained about it: "Now the grousing of children prevents us from meditating." Poemen, always indulgent and kind, asked them: "Is it because of angels' voices that you want to leave here?"[81]

Angels or Demons?

A demon could appear to an anchorite in the guise of a child. One day, old Nathaniel in his cell heard himself being called by a young boy, not far from there, pushing a donkey with a basket of bread. The donkey had apparently fallen down and the boy cried: "Abba Nathaniel, have pity on me, come and help me!" The old man half-opened the door and guessed it was a demon disguised as a child; he refused to go out or allow the boy in.[82] But a child can also hide an angel. Lost one night in the Scetis desert, Zeno saw before him a small boy with bread and a jar of water. Thinking it a mirage—or a ruse of the Devil—Zeno tried three times to pray. Each time the boy told him: "Well

[78]A 376 (Ward, p. 100).
[79]Cassian, Conf. 10, 2.
[80]A 503 (Ward, p. 140).
[81]A 729 (Ward, p. 189).
[82]HL 16, 4-5.

done!" Then the boy invited him to eat, led him to his cell and disappeared.[83]

The desert anchorites did not despise children anymore than they did women. If they appeared prudent and reserved towards young boys, it was evidently because they knew of the danger these represented, like women, for single men who want to safeguard their purity of heart and body.

When he went to see Paphnutius to become a monk in Scetis, young Eudemon was ushered out because he had "the face of a girl."[84] Zacharias came as a young child, as already noted, with his father Carion. When he had grown, there were rumors about him among the brothers. So he jumped into the lake which was full of niter "up to his nostrils," stayed there as long as he could, and emerged so deformed and disfigured that his father had trouble recognizing him. The holy priest Isidore received a revelation from God about what had happened. The following Sunday, when he saw him coming up for communion, the priest said with admiration: "The young Zacharias communed last Sunday as a man but now he has become like an angel."[85] So long as Zacharias was as physically attractive as an angel, he could be a demon tempter. But as soon as he proved, by his heroic act, the authenticity of his virtue, he appeared as an angel of purity and holiness. The young anchorite would die prematurely, beatified again by Isidore: "Rejoice, Zacharias, my child, because the doors of the kingdom of heaven have opened for you."[86]

---

[83] A 239 (Ward, p. 66), A 926 (Ward, p. 241).
[84] A 234 (Ward p. 64).
[85] A 441 (Ward, p. 118).
[86] A 247 (Ward, p. 68).

FOUR

❧✝❧

Habitat

Need for Shelter in the Desert

We can easily imagine the Desert Fathers, as they are portrayed in age-old descriptions, at the entrance to a humble hut
with a small garden and two or three palm trees. The monks of
the Cells, says Palladius, lived "in huts just good enough to protect them from sunburn and heaven's dew."[1] In Upper Egypt we
find some of these huts at the end of fields where the fellahs took
their siestas and eventually spent the night when the field they
were working was far from their homes. In the deserts of Lower
Egypt, these huts could only be temporary shelters because one
had to be protected not only from the heat and dew but from the
nocturnal cold and especially the violent winds and rain which
fell from time to time. Excavations in the Cells over the past
twenty-five years reveal solid and well-cared-for hermitages of
which certain parts could date back to the fifth century.[2]

The desert might have had a few monks who spent more or
less of their time in the open air: vagabonds like Bessarion, or
a John spoken of in the *History of the Monks*,[3] or sedentary ones,
like the two naked men discovered by Macarius on an islet way
out in the desert.[4] But these could only be very rare cases or
temporary exploits. Serapion (nicknamed Sindonites), Palladius

---

[1]Palladius, *Dialogue on the Life of Jean Chrysostom* 17, SC 341, p. 331.

[2]S. Favre, "L'architecture des ermitages," in *Dossiers Histoire et Archéologie*,
No. 133, December 1988, pp. 20-29.

[3]A 167 (Ward, p. 42); HM 13, 3.

[4]A 455 (Ward, p. 125).

tells us, couldn't live under a roof.[5] Palladius also mentions one
Macarius the Younger who lived three years in the open air to
atone for an involuntary murder, but who later built himself a
cell.[6] Another Macarius, the famous Alexandrian, considered it a
feat to have remained twenty days in the open air "on the one
hand, burnt by the sun and on the other, frozen to the marrow at
night by the cold. Had I spent any more time before seeking
shelter, my brain would have dried out and made me lose my
mind."[7] As for Evagrius, who spent forty days under the stars
and sun, his body had become "like those of animals' crawling
with ticks."[8]

Even had he not had to put up with bad weather, the hermit
would have needed a shelter to assure him the solitude for
which he had come to the desert. As long as the first arrivals had
unlimited space, they could spread themselves out and avoid all
enclosures. But as soon as they became more numerous, usually
rallying around a well-known elder, the anchorites had to find
a spot to build a rudimentary house to protect their bodies and
especially to allow each to escape from the demands of others
and hide his asceticism from inquisitive eyes.

Grottoes and Caverns

Like the men of prehistory, the first anchorites just naturally
found refuge in the caves — almost everywhere among the rocky
slopes bordering one or other of the banks of the Nile valley.
Here lived most of the saintly figures mentioned in the *History of
the Monks*: Elias, Apollo, Helle, John, Pityrion and his disciples,[9]
along with other monks near Antinoë.[10] In the desert close by
some inhabited spots, the anchorites could set themselves up in
a tomb or some building in ruins, as did Antony at the beginning of his monastic life.[11] Poemen and his brothers, driven from

[5]HL 37, 1.
[6]HL 15, 1-2.
[7]HL 18, 3.
[8]HL 38, 11.
[9]HM 7, 1; 8, 5 and 38; 12, 4; 13, 3.
[10]HL 57, 1.
[11]VA 8 and 12-13.

Scetis by the barbarians, took refuge in an old temple.[12] After reaching Mount Colzim, Antony established himself in a cave on the mountainside. This cave is not mentioned in the *Life* written by St Athanasius nor in the *Lausiac History*, but we learn of its existence from the explicit testimonials of Macarius, Ammonas and the *History of the Monks*.[13] Sisoes, who occupied it after Antony's death, said, "In the cave of a lion lives a fox."[14] This cave, still visited and revered today, is about 165 miles above the actual monastery of St Antony. It provides a magnificent view of the desert and the Red Sea.

Some thirteen miles from there, Paul of Thebes moved into a larger cave with a vestibule in the open.[15] Above this cave has been constructed a church enclosing it, much like the *Sacro Speco* of St Benedict at Subiaco. The apothegms often speak of anchorites living in caves but all cannot be located. Several were in the deserts of Nitria and Scetis — Chaeremon and Elpidius, for example.[16] In fact, there are numerous caves in Wadi Natrun among the limestone projections in the sand. Some might have been dug by the first anchorites.

An ancient Coptic *Life* of Macarius speaks of two caverns dug by him in rocky crags.[17] Palladius mentions only an underground passage Macarius made, beginning from his cell and ending up in a small grotto where the Saint would hide in order to avoid the pleas of visitors.[18] The monks of the monastery of St Macarius show a grotto situated less than a mile south of the monastery, inside which a subterranean passage ends. This could be the grotto mentioned by Palladius. Other grottoes are found in these parts, where one or other of the monks of the monastery of St Macarius (Deir Macarius, *Deir* is Coptic for "monastery") still withdraw today for a more or less extended term. Before coming to restore this monastery in 1970, Father

---

[12]A 138 (Ward, p. 32).
[13]A 119, 457 (Ward, pp. 27, 127); HM 24, 2.
[14]Bu II 103.
[15]*Life of Paul*, 5.
[16]A 932; N 627A.
[17]*Annales du musée Guimet*, Vol. XXV, p. 76.
[18]HL 17, 10.

Matta-el-Meskin had lived a dozen years with his disciples in the Wadi Rayan grottoes, right in the open desert, some forty miles west of Beni-Suef.[19] Many are still nostalgic for this primitive life, recreating faithfully that of the Desert Fathers. The other three Wadi Natrun monasteries also have hermits living in grottoes a few miles to the south.

In Nitria and the Cells, where the whole desert is flat, there appears to have been no cave to serve as shelter for the anchorites. Palladius says that when Amoun reached the Nitria desert, he immediately built himself a cell.[20] Pambo died in the cell he built for himself when he arrived there.[21] New excavations in Cellia reveal that some cells had been dug out of the earth, like the hermitages rediscovered and explored in the Esna Desert of Upper Egypt by S. Sauneron. Sometimes the grottoes where the anchorites lived were joined together in the front by small areas made of bricks. This is the case with certain hermitages occupied today by monks of Deir Macarius in the Wadi Natrun.

Choosing the Right Spot

The anchorites who had no grotto at their disposal were forced to build cells. Yet they couldn't just stake out a place anywhere at all. They at least needed water and this explains the development of Cellia and Scetis. Water is found near the surface and wells are easy to dig. Even today, in the lower parts of the Wadi Natrun, as soon as one digs five feet deep, water, though salty, is found, which the fourth-century monks no doubt found acceptable. Most of the cells were built in this part of the Wadi; however, monks seeking more solitude built their cells out-of-the-way and at some distance from the wells. Cassian tells how Paphnutius, the Scetis priest, spent ninety years in the desert, always living in the cell in which he had first established himself upon his arrival, five miles from the church. Each Sunday when returning from the liturgy, he would collect and carry on his

---

[19]O. Meinrardus, *Christian Egypt*, 2nd ed., Cairo, 1977, pp. 468-482.
[20]HL 8, 5.
[21]A 769 (Ward, p. 197).

shoulders the water he needed for the week.[22] One old father, it seems, lived a dozen miles from water, some eighteen kilometers. One day while struggling to carry his water, he told himself it would be better to live closer to the wells. But turning around, he saw an angel counting his footsteps to determine his reward. He was fortified on the spot and moved five miles further out.[23] Chaeremon, at Nitria, had built his grotto forty miles from the church and ten from the marsh and water.[24] To water his dead wood, John the Dwarf used to spend all night carrying water.[25] Arsenius' cell was thirty-two miles from the church.[26] Macarius had predicted: "When you see a cell built near the marsh, know that the devastation of Scetis is approaching."[27] It was a sign of relapse for the monks to want water at their doors and not feel too isolated.

We know that in Cellia they were careful not to build cells too close to each other, "so that none could be recognized from afar by another nor be seen at first glance, nor hear the sound of a voice."[28] According to Philo, it was the same with the houses of the Therapeutae: neither too close, to avoid promiscuity, nor too far apart, so as to rally the community and give help.[29] The first arrivals could freely choose sites that suited them, but after the rapid increase in the number of monks, it probably became more difficult to find the ideal spot, not too close to one another, nor too far from the church and water.

Building the Cells

Usually the monk, upon reaching the desert, would build his own cell, as Amoun and Pambo had done at Nitria. In Scetis, the two young strangers greeted by Macarius built themselves a cell on the spot indicated by the elder and according to his

---

[22]Cassian, Conf. 3, 1.
[23]N 199.
[24]A 932 (Ward, p. 244).
[25]A 316 (Ward, p. 85).
[26]A 59 (Ward, p. 12).
[27]A 458 (Ward, p. 128).
[28]HM Latin 22 (PL 21, 444); cf. 20, 7.
[29]Philo, *On the Contemplative Life*, 24. Cf. Guillaumont, p. 25.

instructions.[30] Sometimes an elder would give his own cell to a newcomer and go build himself another further away. At Diolcos, Archebius gave his cell to Cassian along with the furnishings and built himself another elsewhere; some time later he did the same for other newcomers.[31] In Cellia, a monk with a second cell as a "secondary home" lent it for a time to a brother who had none.[32] Another old man was visited by a brother looking for a cell. He told him: "Sit down. I'll go fetch it." He didn't return for three years, but found the brother still waiting.[33]

In some places, when a newcomer arrived, the elder started building him a cell right away, with the help of his disciples, and the job was done in a day. This is what Abba Or used to do.[34] An apothegm describes Abba Agathon devoting a very long time to building a cell with his disciples.[35] Dorotheus the Theban, who lived in a grotto a few miles from Alexandria, spent his days collecting stones to build cells. He built one a year.[36] In Scetis, an elder would always lend a hand to brothers building cells.[37]

The work would take more or less time depending on the importance of the construction, materials used, as well as the number, strength and ability of the builders. In the beginning, the structure would have been very modest and simple, like many of the Egyptian country houses today. Upon reaching the desert, Or put up "a small cabin."[38] Yet in Nitria, Amoun built himself "two rooms with vaulted ceilings."[39] A cell was usually square but could also be circular, in the shape of a tower.[40] We see houses built like this in the villages of Upper Egypt, no doubt to facilitate building the cupola on top. Walls were of stone or brick or even clay or cob. One of the apothegms tells of Or and

---

[30]A 486 (Ward, p. 134).
[31]Cassian, Inst. 5, 37.
[32]N 451.
[33]Ch 272.
[34]HM 2, 11.
[35]A 88 (Ward, p. 21).
[36]HL 2, 2.
[37]N 361.
[38]HM 2, 5.
[39]HL 8, 5.
[40]Arm 5, 127; SP, New Collection, p. 169 (I 27, 3).

Theodore preparing clay to build a cell.[41] In Scetis, the cells
of Macarius' young disciples were made of stone dug out on
the site.[42] Cassian tells the story of one monk who spent his
time restoring and rebuilding useless lodgings. A demon held
the hammer with him and urged him to waste his time on the
hardest rocks.[43]

Most often a brick or stone cupola served as a roof, due
to the scarcity of wood needed for the joists of a cob ceiling. John
of Lycopolis was cloistered in a cell made up of three vaulted
rooms, "one for the needs of the flesh, another where he worked
and ate and the third for prayers."[44] However, for the cells
of Macarius' young disciples, there is mention of "wood for the
roof."[45] Whether vaulted or flat, the cell roof could also have a
terrace[46] which wasn't always very solid and could crumble
easily, as happened one day in Cellia.[47] At first, the monks didn't
worry too much about laying foundations, but the use of them
spread little by little[48] — for example, in the Cells — which made it
possible for very ancient remnants of construction to be exca-
vated. Certain elders criticized this method of "putting down
roots" and settling somewhere. Zeno said, "Never put down
foundations when you build a cell."[49]

Multiple Cells

At the end of the fourth century, Abbot Isaac lamented to
Cassian that certain monks were not content to build one or two
cells but were putting up four or five, all spacious and richly
furnished.[50] Until then, no doubt, most cells had only one room
where the anchorite prayed, ate, worked and slept. The young

---

[41]A 934 (Ward, p. 247).
[42]A 486(Ward, p. 134).
[43]Cassian, Conf. 9, 6.
[44]HL 35, 1.
[45]A 486 (Ward, p. 134).
[46]A 495 (Ward, p. 138).
[47]N 148.
[48]N 361.
[49]A 235 (Ward, p. 65).
[50]Cassian, Conf. 9, 5.

strangers received by Macarius in Scetis had this type of cell.[51] The unknown or little known anchorite, alone in his corner of the desert, could be content with this unique cell, or "single cell" as the texts put it.[52] But as soon as he became the slightest bit known, his fame attracted admirers and often irksome suppli-cants. It was then useful to have at least two rooms to safeguard his solitude and the needs of charity. Amoun had built himself a double cell in Nitria.[53] There also, it is said that Ammonius "had choice cells, a yard, a well..." but this is to emphasize his detach-ment which he proved by abandoning everything to a newcomer and moving to a small cell further away.[54] Macarius of Alex-andria had several cells but they were dispersed: one in Nitria, another in Cellia and a third in Scetis. He spent Lent in one that had no windows, the second was so tiny that he couldn't stretch his legs and the third, more spacious, doubled as a reception room and parlor.[55] Macarius the Egyptian had his two grottoes and an underground passage.[56]

In the apothegms, there are several accounts of a "back cell" or "inside cell."[57] This was the second room of a double cell. In the front room, opening to the outside, the anchorite worked, ate and greeted visitors; in the second, he prayed and slept. We know from Philo that the Therapeutae also had a special room for praying, separate from those where they ate and worked.[58] Sometimes an elder, Achilles in this case, would put up a brother for a night in the front room, while he himself slept as usual in the second.[59] But occasionally an elder would also hide a brother there who had sinned and wanted to do serious penance under his guidance.[60] In the recent restoration of the monastery of St

---

[51] A 486 (Ward, p. 134).

[52] G. Husson, "L'habitat..." IFAO 82, Cairo, 1979, p. 195; pp. 205-206.

[53] HL 8, 5.

[54] HM 20, 9.

[55] HL 18, 10.

[56] HL 17, 10.

[57] A 132 and 415 (Ward, pp. 30, 107); N 177, N 181, N 435, N 627; Eth. 13, 14 and 13, 55.

[58] Philo, *On the Contemplative Life*, 25.

[59] Eth. 13, 55.

[60] N 177; Eth. 13, 14.

Macarius, the old cells were demolished but a few were kept as evidence of the past. These cells have two rooms, one in front with door and window, and the other at the back, with no opening to the outside, which served as bedroom and chapel. In the new cells with several rooms, the bedroom is also the chapel and the monks must never take anyone there.

Doors and Windows

Like many of the village houses in Egypt, the cells of the anchorites had only rare and small openings, so as to keep out the sun and heat. The door was usually left open and provided enough light and ventilation. It is reported of certain elders, Macarius and Sisoes for instance, that they closed their cell doors,[61] thus the others must have had the habit of leaving theirs open. This door could have a bolt or lock. Traces of such locks were found in the Esna and Cellia hermitages. An apothegm tells how one monk made a skeleton key in order to enter another brother's cell and steal his earnings.[62]

Wood being scarce, doors were precious things in Egypt. If there was no door, one would hang a mat in the opening. This is what Dioscorus did after giving his door to a brother who needed one for his cell.[63] The Pachomian documents also tell of a small vent covered by a detachable mat.[64] But there were also glass windows, attested to by glass fragments found at Cellia near some openings. Moreover, vestiges of ancient glassworks have been discovered in Wadi Natrun. At any rate, with or without windows, with or without glass, some elders enjoyed a supernatural light which allowed them to work at night as well as during the day.[65] This light was sometimes produced by the Devil, as was the case with an elder spoken of by Moses in Cassian.[66]

---

[61]A 469 and 827 (Ward, pp. 131, 217).
[62]N 7.
[63]Ch 258.
[64]Veilleux, p. 136.
[65]N 425.
[66]Cassian, Conf. 2, 7.

As for the recluses, they blocked up their doors and sometimes walled the openings. They then needed a window to communicate with the outside, either to get supplies or give advice, or indeed to grant a healing or blessing to some obstinate beggar. John of Lycopolis thus spent thirty years "completely locked up and receiving needed items through a window from the one helping him."[67] On Saturdays and Sundays, he would sit at the window, ready to comfort those who came.[68] As for Theon, he was a recluse for twenty years. Every day a crowd of sick people came to him; he healed them by the laying on of his hands through the window.[69] These two recluses lived in the Nile Valley. A few miles from Alexandria, Longinus also performed healings through his window without leaving his cell.[70] Others remained locked up without ever seeing anyone.[71] A temporary reclusion might also be a penance imposed by the elders on brothers who had sinned grievously.[72]

Enclosures and Walls

The anchorite who found himself in the open desert didn't have to cloister himself to obtain solitude. But as more and more people came to Nitria, then to Cellia, it became customary to enclose the cell in a large yard, surrounded by a wall. Thus the hermit could "take the air" without leaving his cell and the enclosure often included a small garden with a well for water, where the anchorite cultivated a few vegetables.[73] Was it the same in Scetis?

At Wadi Natrun the monks had more space and there was less need to be fenced in. However, when a great elder had disciples, these wished to live near their master. Silvanus had twelve and each had a separate cell not far from his. The group also had its kitchen and garden surrounded by a fence that was easily

---

[67]HL 35, 2.
[68]HL 35, 4.
[69]HM 6, 1.
[70]Sy 19, 7.
[71]N 622.
[72]N 186.
[73]HM 20, 9.

moved.[74] When the famous Moses died, he had, said Palladius, seventy disciples,[75] but we don't know how they were housed.

Probably the rallying of disciples around an elder is the reason for the origin of the four separate communities in Scetis, each with its own church and priest, spoken of by Cassian.[76] Little by little, devastating raids by Bedouins led the monks to reorganize their cells near a fortified tower where everyone could seek refuge in case of danger. In the middle of the fifth century, forty-nine monks in Scetis were massacred by the barbarians, and the story of their martyrdom mentions a tower where some had found refuge.[77] It seems that the tower came before the setting up of a protective wall around the cells. Such a wall was already in place in the Thebaid in the Pachomian monasteries. It is impossible to determine the date when the monks of Scetis decided to surround their monasteries with a fortified enclosure. At the end of the sixth century, Scetis was again totally ravaged by the barbarians,[78] but the monasteries were rebuilt in the middle of the following century.[79] It was probably then that the walls were erected which still exist around the four Wadi Natrun monasteries, not any longer to maintain their security but to assure separation from the world.

Cellia underwent the same evolution as Scetis.[80] Cells were regrouped and isolated hermitages abandoned. There, too, one finds fortified towers and walled enclosures. But from the beginning of the ninth century, the site was abandoned, no doubt because, like Nitria, it was too close to populated regions and therefore more likely to be invaded by the world and the world's spirit. It is undeniable that the hermitages discovered by recent excavations, like those of Esna, reveal a marked contrast between the most ancient cells, undoubtedly quickly constructed by the monks themselves, and later buildings "made by teams of highly

---

[74]A 526, 528 and 863 (Ward, pp. 145, 146, 224).
[75]HL 19, 11.
[76]Cassian, Conf. 10, 2.
[77]Evelyn White, pp. 164-165.
[78]*Ibid.*, pp. 249-250.
[79]*Ibid.*, pp. 268-269.
[80]Guillaumont, pp. 164-167.

qualified workmen." The latter have "impeccably built hydraulic and sanitary facilities...."[81] In his cell with walls of smooth-downed coatings and with paintings, "the hermit was no longer at the mercy of the desert"; one hopes, however that he was still "at the mercy of God."

---

[81]P. Bridel, *Le site monastique des Kellia*, Research for years 1981-1983, Louvain, 1984, pp. 21-27; *Dossiers Histoire et Archéologie*, No. 133, pp. 44-59.

FIVE

Clothing

Nudity and Deprivation

The anchorite is in the desert because he has heard, like Antony, the Lord's call: "Go, sell all that you have...; then come and follow me." He has left everything to "follow, naked, the naked Christ," as St Jerome puts it, to imitate him "who had no place to lay his head"; because "the desert loves naked people."[1] If some Desert Fathers wanted to attain this stage of deprivation, it was simply to observe the Gospel to the letter and not to compete with Hindu gymnosophists. Our sources mention several completely naked anchorites in the desert. One, an old weaver in a monastery in the Thebaid, had lived for many years right among the buffalo. His clothes were in tatters and he had no hair.[2] Another was a bishop who, for forty-eight years, lived in the desert atoning for his apostasy during a persecution. Only his hair covered him.[3] A third, similarly garbed, ran off when a monk wanted to come near him and only allowed himself to be met when the other had also discarded "the things of this world," and dropped all his clothing.[4] For his part, Macarius had found in the heart of the desert two naked monks drinking water with animals in a pond.[5] And, again, we learn from Sulpicius

---

[1]St Jerome, *Letters* 14, 1 and 125, 20.
[2]N 132A.
[3]N 132B.
[4]N 132D.
[5]A 456 (Ward, p. 125).

Severus of another anchorite who had lived naked for fifty years in the Sinai.[6]

Did these desert nudists really exist? One is tempted to think that these stories were concocted only to remind the anchorites of the perfect ideal which they could never hope to attain. It is with this in mind that Macarius concludes his account: "Excuse me, brothers, I've not yet become a monk but I've seen monks."[7] In any case, if these men had really existed, they were but rare exceptions. The objective reporter for the Desert Fathers, Cassian, takes the figurative meaning of "the perfect nudity of Christ"[8] which he had adopted. A candidate for monastic life could well depart and arrive completely naked in the desert, but in such a case the Lord took care to warn an elder: "Get up and greet my athlete."[9]

One day, a great anchorite stripped himself completely so as to discount the honors they wanted to bestow upon him.[10] And for a monk stung by temptation, nudity could also be a way of humbling himself, of confessing his trial before his brothers.[11] It was also an eloquent way of showing the total deprivation, the lot of the monk. One day, Ammoes asked his disciple John to show his visitors how one becomes a monk. To everyone's astonishment, John took off his clothes and simply said: "If a man doesn't strip himself of this world's honor and praise, like this, he can absolutely not become a monk."[12]

The later tradition watered down this apothegm by showing the disciple removing only his hood and stamping on it, saying, "If a man is not trampled underfoot like this, he cannot become a monk."[13] Certainly the desert "athletes" were not inclined to show themselves off like the Greek ephebes in the

---

[6]Sulpicius Severus, *Dial.* I,17.
[7]A 456 (Ward, p. 125).
[8]Cassian, Inst. 10, 19.
[9]N 51.
[10]N 61.
[11]N 64.
[12]Eth 13, 61. Cf. Am 337.
[13]A 245 (Ward, p. 68).

stadium. The *Life of Antony* says "no one ever saw him naked"[14] and that one day, Amoun, blushing when he saw himself naked, was miraculously transported to the other bank of the Nile.[15] The Pachomian Rules for monks living in a community give precautions required to prevent others seeing one's nudity. But the anchorite who ordinarily lived alone had no witness who might be scandalized when he changed his tunic. Only while changing it? Perhaps to wash it too, in which case he would be naked at the river's edge doing his laundry.[16] This is what the fellahs in Upper Egypt still do, since they have no running water at home, while the women keep all their clothes on to do their ablutions, their dishes and their laundry in the Nile or nearby canals.

Clothing of the First Anchorites

The Desert Fathers generally didn't have a river near them so they couldn't worry about washing their clothes. St Jerome said that Hilarion "never washed the sackcloth he wore, declaring it useless to look for cleanliness in a hair shirt. And he only changed shirts when one fell in tatters."[17] Hilarion had inherited a skin cloak from Antony before his death.[18] As for Antony, after having buried Paul of Thebes in one of the two cloaks he received from Athanasius, he took Paul's as a relic, made of interlaced palm leaves, and wore it during the Easter season.[19] One sees how Jerome insists on associating his heroes with the prestigious Antony. Of his clothing, Athanasius says only that he wore on his body a garment made of hair on the inside, while the outside was an animal hide.[20] And Antony washed this hide at least once in his lifetime, when he went to Alexandria to render homage to the confessors of the faith.[21]

---

[14]VA 47.
[15]VA 60.
[16]N 61.
[17]*Life of Hilarion*, 10.
[18]*Ibid.*, 4.
[19]*Life of Paul*, 12 and 16
[20]VA 47.
[21]VA 46.

The clothes of the first anchorites were certainly always very plain, perhaps inspired by what the Bible says concerning Elijah and John the Baptist.[22] Elijah wore a skin loincloth, John a garment of camel hair and a skin belt. The wild animal hide normally worn as a cloak was in use among the Pachomian cenobites as well as the anchorites.[23] Most likely the clothing of the Desert Fathers was generally coarse and seedy-looking. The *History of the Monks* speaks of two monks named Macarius sitting atop a ferry crossing the river and "wearing old rags."[24] Helle also wore "a garment in tatters and full of patches."[25] Pambo said "a monk should wear the kind of garment he can leave outside for three days without anyone taking it."[26] Serapion the Sindonite had that nickname because he wore an old shroud around his body.[27] From an old basket an elder made himself a tunic.[28] A monk "who wore a mat" is also mentioned.[29] This must have been the plainest and coarsest garment possible, which the monk fashioned himself with braided palm leaves. And no doubt this bizarre garment was an invention of the desert monks who were the only ones to wear it.

A Special Monastic Costume

The accounts about the vocation of Paul the Simple and his coming to Antony don't tell us that the latter gave him monastic clothing. The same is true of the very detailed account of how Macarius the Egyptian greeted the two young strangers in Scetis. Yet he tells us that at night, before going to sleep on their straw mat, the two young monks removed their belts and scapulars, which they put back on after getting up to pray.[30] So it appears that at this period — the middle of the fourth century — there was

---

[22]Cassian, Inst. 1, 1.
[23]HM 3, 1.
[24]HM 23, 3.
[25]HM 12, 8.
[26]A 383 and 767 (Ward, pp. 101, 197).
[27]HL 37, 1; N 565.
[28]N 662.
[29]A 116 (Ward, p. 26).
[30]A 486 (Ward, pp. 134ff.).

already some special monastic garb. When Macarius the Egyptian went to the Thebaid to visit the monks at Tabennesis, he changed clothes so as not to be recognized and dressed as a workman.[31] Pinufius did likewise.[32] Around 375, Porphyry, future bishop of Gaza, went to "the desert of Scetis where, after a few days, he was given the venerable habit."[33] A few years later, around 382, Evagrius received the habit from the hands of Melania in Jerusalem. Actually, Palladius says that Melania gave Evagrius "a change of clothing."[34] She undoubtedly gave him a coarse garment to replace the elegant one he had worn until then. It was probably not yet the garb of the monks of Egypt as described later by Evagrius and Cassian.

This attire, which soon became classical and traditional with the anchorites as well as the cenobites, could have existed from the time of St Pachomius, around 320. Pachomius would have received his from his master Palamon following three months' probation: "After having seen his courage and firm intention, the elder took a monk's habit with the belt and placed it upon the altar, then they spent the night praying over it. He then clothed him with it at dawn."[35] This mention of the altar makes of this clothing in the habit a liturgical ceremony. It is surely an anachronism, Pachomius' biography having been inspired by the customs of his time among Pachomian communities.

According to Copres whose *History of the Monks* tells about it, it was Patermuthius who was the inventor or "creator" of the monastic habit. Receiving a young man who wanted to become his disciple, he clothed him in the short-sleeved tunic, the cuculla (a cowl covering the head), a pelt on the shoulders and finally the belt.[36] According to Cassian, the tunic was made of linen like the scapular. Not mentioned by Copres was a type of suspenders or girdle tying back the tunic, which allowed the monk to work

---

[31]HL 18, 12.
[32]Cassian, Inst. 4, 30.
[33]Mark, *Vie de Porphyre*, Paris, 1930, p. 4.
[34]HL 38, 9.
[35]Veilleux, p. 30.
[36]HM 10, 3.

more comfortably.[37] Evagrius had already mentioned in his *Praktikos* all these items of monastic dress in explaining their symbolism.[38] According to the sources at our disposal, it is certain that at the end of the fifth century, this costume had spread just about everywhere in Egypt and clearly set the monks apart from the secular clergy.

It also appears that during this era, the custom of receiving the habit from the hands of an elder had become widespread. To a brother who apparently knew nothing about monastic courtesy, the monks of Scetis demanded, "John, who gave you the habit? Who made you a monk?"[39] An apothegm denounces the imprudence of this young man who had "taken the cloth and immediately became a recluse, declaring, 'I am an anchorite.' "[40] An elder would give the habit to a new disciple and if he became unworthy, would take it away.[41] When important groups were organized in Nitria, Cells and Scetis, it was the priest who gave the habit to newcomers and took it away from any monks to be expelled from the desert.[42] From then on, taking the habit became a solemn rite. A great elder said he saw divine virtue descending upon the monk taking the habit, as upon the newly baptized.[43]

What color were these garments? Today black is *de rigueur* among the Coptic monks, but it seems that in the beginning, white predominated. At least it is in white that we see the monks of Or and Apollo in the *History of the Monks*.[44] Daniel says that the dying Abba Arsenius left him "his tunic made of hide, his white hair shirt and his sandals of palm leaves."[45] One can suppose that the anchorites generally left intact the natural tint of their garments.

---

[37]Cassian, Inst. 1, 4-5. Cf. Veilleux, p. 293 n.
[38]Evagrius, *Praktikos*, Pr.
[39]A 356 (Ward, p. 96).
[40]N 243.
[41]Bu I 613.
[42]A 585 (Ward, p. 168).
[43]N 365.
[44]HM 2, 12; 8, 19.
[45]A 80 (Ward, p. 19).

Quality and Number of Garments

Even after the habit of the anchorites became standardized, there were still many differences in quality. Certain Fathers always distinguished themselves by their miserable attire, among them Moses,[46] the former bandit, and Arsenius, the former courtier of whom it was said: "No one at the palace wore more splendid garments and none at the church wore cheaper ones."[47] But a monk had better not think of wearing an elegant outfit in public. At the church in the Cells, a brother wearing a fine hood was expelled by the priest Isaac.[48] Another time, the same Isaac loudly deplored the sartorial elegance of the monks of his day: "Our Fathers and Abba Pambo wore old garments woven from pieces of palm; now you are dressed in costly garments. Get out of here!"[49] It was generally advisable not to be noticed by wearing either sordid old cast-offs or clothing that was too neat. "Because," as Cassian put it, "when the Devil has not been able to arouse vanity by well-fitted and clean clothing, he then tries to do so by a dirty and totally-neglected garment."[50] Agathon was praised since his dress was neither too fine nor too cheap.[51]

Christ had told his apostles to have but one cloak. The first Desert Fathers took this commandment to heart. Cassian notes that, in areas where winter is harsher, a tunic like those worn by the Egyptians was not enough.[52] And yet early on, custom decreed that one should have a better tunic to wear to church on Saturday and Sunday. For example, this is what Isaiah, Theodore of Pherme and Dioscorus did. As soon as he returned to his cell on Sundays, Isaiah put away this tunic.[53] One day when thieves came to rob him, Theodore succeeded in retrieving from them

---

[46]A 502 (Ward, p. 140).
[47]A 42 (Ward, p. 9).
[48]A 379 (Ward, p. 100).
[49]A 378 (Ward, p. 100).
[50]Cassian, Inst. 1, 2.
[51]PA 19, 1.
[52]Cassian, Inst. 11, 4.
[53]Eth 13, 79.

"the tunic he wore before the congregation."[54] Likewise, Dioscorus had a second tunic for church, which was better than the one he normally wore. He gave it to a beggar. The priest asked, "Why didn't you give him the shoddy one and keep the one you wear at the liturgy?" He simply answered, "Would you give the shoddy one to Jesus?"[55] Charity comes before liturgical splendor.

Abbot Phocas, an emigré from Egypt in Palestine at the end of the fifty century, testified that "the Egyptian Fathers have the custom of preserving until death the cloak they received when they took the habit and the cowl. They have themselves buried with these garments. They wear them only on Sunday for Holy Communion and put them away right after that."[56]

Sandals

Like their secular compatriots, the Egyptian monks traveled most of the time barefoot without sandals. On this subject, Cassian mentions the injunction of Christ but adds that the Fathers "protect their feet with sandals when illness, the morning cold of winter or the heat of summer requires it."[57] Evagrius says nothing about it and sandals are mentioned in the apothegms only four times,[58] two of which deal with Arsenius' sandals. A monk, a former fellah, was shocked one day to see "the Roman," as they called him, with clean feet shod with sandals.

Like everyone who usually goes around barefoot, the soles of the monks' feet had to be like shoe leather and one can understand the full sense of Paphnutius' words: "Unless a man makes the skin of his face like the soles of his feet, he can in no way become a monk."[59]

---

[54] A 296 (Ward, p. 78).
[55] Ch 254 and 260.
[56] A 926 (Ward, pp. 240-241).
[57] Cassian, Inst. 1, 9.
[58] A 80, 315, 799 (Ward, pp. 19, 84, 209); N 592/15.
[59] Eth 13, 81.

Hair and Beards

We have mentioned anchorites whose beards and hair were their only garments. Others were clothed but never cut their hair. St Jerome described Paul of Thebes as having hair down to his ankles.[60] Apollo found fault with long-haired monks,[61] but they must have been rare. Only one shows up in the apothegms.[62] On the other hand, concerning the beard, the general custom was to let it grow like the old fellahs who did not shave. Some anchorites had impressive beards. One Abba John "looked like Abraham and had a beard like Aaron."[63] At eighty-four, Abba Or had "a snow-white beard that fell right down to his chest."[64] So did Arsenius.[65] But there were some glorious exceptions. John of Lycopolis "had such a tired-out body, a result of asceticism, that not even a whisker grew on his face."[66] At the end of his life, Macarius of Alexandria was still beardless also, "having no whiskers above the lips or on his chin because an excessive asceticism had prevented the hair on his cheeks from growing."[67] Happily, he had arrived in the desert at a time when there was no one yet to repel beardless postulants.

This Macarius was, it seems, very personable. The Desert Fathers have often been depicted as coarse men by those who like to stretch the truth, such as Patermuthius who was introduced by a contemporary author as having "a face half-hidden under a beard which he dirtied on purpose, allowing lice to make their way there."[68] Though some were undeniably not very clean, never was filth lauded by them as a mark of virtue, as will be seen in a later hagiography. Of course, it was impossible to take baths in the desert or frequent the public baths of the nearest town. As Athanasius said, Antony had never washed his

---

[60]*Life of Paul*, 1.
[61]HM 8, 59.
[62]N 418.
[63]HM 26.
[64]HM 2, 1.
[65]A 80 (Ward, p. 19).
[66]HM 1, 47.
[67]HL 18, 29.
[68]F. Weyergans, *Macaire le Copte*, Paris, 1981, p. 44.

feet.[69] But the account is given only to emphasize the old man's perfect health and it was certainly not a general rule since the apothegms show us Arsenius and Poemen pouring water on their feet.[70] To Isaac who took offense at this, Poemen gave this wise response: "We haven't learned to kill the body but to kill the passions."[71]

A brother on his way to Scetis was walking by the Nile. Tired from the trip and exhausted by the heat, he removed his garments and went for a swim. If he was punished by being devoured by a crocodile, it was less for having bathed than for having taken off his clothes. The crocodile couldn't have known he was dealing with a monk and thought he had eaten a secular person,[72] because at this time in Egypt, as everyone knows, the crocodiles respected the monks and served as makeshift ferries for them when needed.

---

[69]VA 93.
[70]A 799 (Ward, p. 209).
[71]A 758 (Ward, p. 193).
[72]Sy 18, 53.

SIX

❧✝❧

Diet

If there is one area in which the Desert Fathers have a well-established reputation, it's that of their diet, or rather restrictions on food. We'll see that this renown is justified, but that it is often misunderstood and misinterpreted. No doubt the fault lies with the early writers not having the documentation we now possess on this subject. Because if we collect and read all the texts well, they show that the ordinary practice and teachings of the Fathers refute the ideas and images customarily given about emaciated beings of skin and bones who no longer looked human because they deprived themselves of food and drink.

Lengthy Fasting

It is undeniable that there were in the desert, especially in the early years, astonishing feats of fasting and abstinence. But accounts about them are very rare. We know of a few monks who went for forty days without eating, but this was either during Lent or to conquer violent temptations. For example, James, tempted by the demon of impurity, retired to a grotto where he fasted for forty days. Finally, he was found to be half-dead.[1] Assailed by similar temptations, Moses stayed in the open desert for forty-two days without eating or drinking. Suddenly he was freed from his temptations for good.[2] Probably neither repeated this exploit. Sarmatas is the only one who is said to have fasted often for forty days at a time, but it was on the advice of Poemen,

---

[1] A 927 (Ward, p. 241).
[2] Eth 14, 26.

the best guarantee of wisdom and discretion.[3] Palladius also tells of Macarius of Alexandria's Lenten visit to the monks of Pachomias: for forty days, he took neither bread nor water, being satisfied to chew a few cabbage leaves on Sundays "just to give the impression he was eating."[4]

In the Old Testament, Moses and Elijah had already carried out this feat with the Lord's help. Their imitators in Egypt were able to benefit from a similar privilege. Abba Or even spent ten years without taking any earthly food.[5] God often decides to nourish miraculously the anchorites who wholly commit their subsistence to him. Like Martha Robin in our own century, some among them were sustained only by the Eucharist brought to them either by an angel or a priest. This is how it was for Anouph and John.[6] Heron also spent up to three months taking nothing but the Eucharist, but he then fell into drunkenness and almost ended badly.[7] Others received their earthly food in mysterious ways. John of Lycopolis, for instance, found a loaf of bread on his table every two or three days.[8] Patermuthius only received a loaf every Sunday but this was sufficient for him until the following Sunday.[9] After three weeks of fasting, Helle all of a sudden found a spring with vegetables erupting around him in the desert sand. Another day he discovered fresh bread, honey and various fruits.[10] But more often than not God didn't spoil his servants and sent them only that which was needed. However, Palladius' companion one time did receive wine with his bread.[11]

Normally a man cannot remain forty days without eating or drinking, even if he follows the progressive training suggested by Eulogius to his disciple: "Train yourself to shrink your stomach little by little through fasting. The same as a stretched

---

[3]A 872 (Ward, p. 226).
[4]HL 18, 14.
[5]HM 2, 9.
[6]HM 11, 5; 13, 4.
[7]HM 1, 47.
[8]*Ibid.*
[9]HM 10, 8.
[10]HM 12, 3-4.
[11]HL 71, 3.

water skin shrinks, so it is with a stomach that takes in a lot of food. If on the contrary, it takes in little, it shrinks and needs less and less."[12] The advice could prove useful to a beginner not yet accustomed to the rigors of desert life, but the Fathers knew very well that food is, along with clothing and sleep, something that cannot be completely cut out.[13] The monk might dream sometimes of a completely celestial life, totally removed from the concerns of the flesh but, as Chaeremon reminded him, "we have a body that is a poor beast of burden. You must think about it, considering the wonderful providence of our Savior, for fear of flinching on the road, because 'the spirit is willing but the flesh is weak.' "[14]

Lent was a privileged time for fasting, but most monks did not go forty days without eating. Some spent the whole year— and all their lives—fasting the way others did during Lent. One day in Scetis, as the beginning of Lent was being proclaimed, an elder, to whom a brother came to announce it, replied, "It has been fifty years now that I've ignored when the fasts about which you speak begin and when they end. My whole life is a fast."[15]

Frequency of Meals

If a total fast of forty days in the desert was exceptional, on the other hand a few days' fasting was frequent enough, without it necessarily being continuous in the life of a monk. One day Macarius the Egyptian imposed on his namesake from Alexandria the penance of eating but once a week for three weeks, but he had no doubt that this was, in fact, the habitual practice of the great elder.[16] This was also Abba Elias' diet in his youth.[17] Or and Apollo often went six days without eating but this was not a weekly affair. Apollo always ate with his brothers on Sunday.[18]

---

[12]Arm 4, 54; SP, New Collection, p. 256 (I 580).
[13]A 759 (Ward, p. 193).
[14]Cassian, Conf. 11, 15.
[15]Sy 4, 104.
[16]A 474 (Ward, p. 132).
[17]HM 7, 3.
[18]HM 2, 5; 8, 9.

Pityrion took his ration of gruel Thursday and Sunday.[19] We also know of an elder who fasted from Monday to Saturday.[20] Palladius says Antony ate only on Saturday and Sunday; this explains how he left Paul to shiver and fast for four days.[21] But according to the *Life*, he ate every two days, often every four days.[22] For any one anchorite, the diet could vary according to his age, his state of health or diverse circumstances. Cassian tells us of an elder who ate only during the week if a visitor arrived. On Saturday and Sunday, he arranged to bring a brother back to his place and ate with him.[23]

An apothegm thus summarizes the different practices in effect during the high point in the history of Scetis: "Among the monks of Scetis, one ate every two days, another every four days, another every seven days."[24] The most common practice was to abstain completely from food every second day. This was the habit with Sisoes, Megethius[25] and no doubt many others. In addition, it was often a penance imposed on a brother who had sinned grievously.[26] In any case, little by little, experience showed the Fathers that it was better to eat a bit each day than a lot every two days. This was the advice given by Agathon and Poemen.[27] In his youth, the latter would often pass two, three, four days or the whole week without eating, but later found it better to eat a little each day.[28] This he called "the royal path of the Fathers."

And Cassian, faithful witness of the Fathers, also remarked that "a reasonable and moderate meal each day is better than an austere fast over several days."[29] The one daily meal had become, from before the end of the fourth century, a universal

---

[19]HM 15, 4.
[20]N 73.
[21]HL 22, 3.
[22]VA 7.
[23]Cassian, Inst. 5, 26.
[24]N 467.
[25]A 536, 835 (Ward, pp. 149, 219).
[26]A 448 (Ward, p. 122).
[27]A 102 (Ward, p. 23); Eth 14, 63.
[28]A 605 (Ward, p. 171).
[29]Cassian, Inst. 5, 9.

custom. An elder said: "If a man eats once a day, he's a monk; if he eats twice a day, he's a carnal man; if he eats three times a day, he's a beast."[30]

Bread, The Essential Food

The frequency of meals is one thing, another is the menu, the quantity and quality of food consumed. From time immemorial, as today, bread is the Egyptian's essential food. It seems that Egypt is actually the country where the average consummation of bread per capita is the highest. With the Desert Fathers, bread was the main food, often the only one. Antony on his mountain, as in his tomb where he first lived, ate bread brought to him at rare intervals.[31] These were the small, round, thick loaves that are still baked in Upper Egypt and in the Coptic monasteries — loaves which can be dried and kept for months. Before eating them, one soaks them in water. They are about four and three-quarters inches in diameter and weigh a bit more than six ounces. Two loaves weigh approximately twelve ounces, that is, one Roman pound (about forty grams). Palladius speaks about these six-ounce loaves. In one well-known story, Antony took one and gave three to Paul.[32]

In Cassian's time, two loaves made up the daily ration for most anchorites.[33] They ate one at the ninth hour and kept the other to share eventually with a visitor. The monk who had not received a visitor ate this second loaf at night. But some contented themselves with one loaf a day; they took two only when they hadn't eaten the night before.[34] According to an apothegm, this was Abba Moses' practice since his arrival in the desert,[35] while Palladius says he ate his two each day.[36] His disciple Zacharias and Poemen, when young, were satisfied with one loaf

[30]Eth 14, 1.
[31]VA 7-8 and 50.
[32]HL 22, 6.
[33]Cassian, Conf. 12, 15.
[34]*Ibid.*, 2, 26.
[35]Eth 14, 35.
[36]HL 19, 6.

each.[37] Megethius ate only one loaf every two days. An elder advised him to eat a half-loaf each day.[38] For others, the two daily loaves were insufficient and they ate more, but this was not looked upon with favor. A brother asked Abba Xoius if eating three loaves was too much. The elder replied, "If the devil did not exist, that would not be too much."[39] An apothegm tells of an elder who used to eat three and could not "persevere in his asceticism," because he had judged a brother who ate six a day.[40]

It is written that one day in Cellia some elders first took two small loaves and then, at their guest's insistence, ate ten more.[41] In this same desert of the Cells, Evagrius ate his two small loaves each day.[42] Palladius tells the story of a possessed monk who ate enormous quantities of bread and then threw them up as steam. Because the demon in him was "of the species they call fiery." Macarius wanted to heal this poor soul and asked his mother how much she wanted him to eat. "Ten pounds of bread," she replied. After fasting and praying for him for seven days, Macarius set his ration at three pounds.[43] The anecdote gives an idea of how much an Egyptian could eat in a day and the austerity of the anchorite diet.

An expert on modern Egypt, Father Ayrout, says a fellah can eat an average of a dozen loaves a day, over three pounds.[44] One understands how a young monk could sometimes be tempted to steal a loaf to increase his ration. This is what Serapion, Theon's disciple, did for a time.[45] Cassian tells how he himself was received one day by an elder and at the end of the meal, his guest urged him to eat more. He replied that he couldn't. The elder then said, "As for me, this is the sixth time

---

[37]Eth 14, 24.
[38]A 536 (Ward, p. 149).
[39]A 566 (Ward, p. 158).
[40]N 20.
[41]N 155.
[42]HL 38, 10.
[43]HL 17, 13.
[44]H. Ayrout, *The Egyptian Peasant*, p. 83.
[45]Cassian, Conf. 2, 11.

today that I've eaten with visitors and I'm still hungry, yet you who eat now for the first time say you can't take any more!"[46]

Bread and Salt

In Scetis, as everywhere else, one would normally add salt to the bread.[47] Paphnutius declared that bread without salt made one sick.[48] Bread and salt were also on the normal menu for Pachomian ascetics.[49] The custom of pouring salt on bread is often mentioned in sources such as the *Lives of Pachomius*.[50] They tell about Theodore of Pherme who had eaten two loaves a day for six years. He would put them out to soak in the morning with a sprinkling of salt and eat them in the evening with a spoon like soup.[51] One day when the heat was especially intense, Isaiah had the idea of doing the same so that the bread would be easier to swallow. But arriving at that moment, Achilles reprimanded him severely, "Come see how Isaiah gulps down soup in Scetis! If you want to eat soup, go to Egypt."[52] Another anecdote describes two monks from Scetis traveling and eating their bread on the banks of the Nile. One soaked his bread in water but the other refused to do so.[53] Apparently the custom was not universal. But to honor a visitor, one could improve the ordinary fare and pour a little vinegar on the salt.[54]

Supplies of Bread

Some monks purchased their bread by trading baskets or mats in exchange. They kept their bread supplies in a special hutch or basket.[55] Like Antony, Arsenius had enough for several

---

[46]Cassian, Inst. 5, 25 = A 429 (Ward, p. 113).
[47]A 143, 226, 344, 486 (Ward, pp. 34, 62-63, 91, 134); Ch 248, Ch 254.
[48]HL 47, 14.
[49]Veilleux, p. 170.
[50]N 149; Veilleux, pp. 79, 104, 277 n. 59
[51]Eth 14, 48.
[52]A 126 (Ward, p. 29).
[53]Bu I 72.
[54]N 229.
[55]N 281; Ch 256.

months or even a year.[56] In Nitria, then in Scetis when the number of monks increased, they set up bakeries where each one came to make his bread. One day Theodore helped several brothers prepare their loaves and only after that did he bake his own two batches.[57] In Cassian's day, each anchorite on Saturday placed his week's food in a basket (that is to say, fourteen loaves) so that if he should forget his refectory supplies, he would surely notice it. Moreover, when the basket was empty, Sunday had arrived and they had to go to the brothers' assembly.[58]

Abba John, who tells us about this custom, was himself often so absorbed in God that he didn't always remember at night if he had eaten.[59] Sisoes also often forgot to eat his meals but he had his disciple to remind him.[60] Other anchorites were sometimes so wrapped up in prayer or a spiritual conversation that daybreak arrived without their having eaten.[61]

The custom the monks from Scetis had of keeping a reserve of loaves in their cells had become so widespread that one Scetis monk, staying in the Thebaid, always observed it. To the local monks who reproached him for breaking the evangelical precept to "give no thought for the morrow," and who, themselves, went to the market each day to buy their food, he replied, "My market is my cell."[62] He was against a hermit leaving his cell too often.

Bread was usually made of wheat but could, in exceptional circumstances, be of barley or lentils.[63] A brother told Poemen of an elder who ate only unleavened barley bread.[64] But barley bread was not restricted to monks; in some areas there was no other kind.[65] Even today barley bread isn't hard to find in Egypt.

---

[56]A 55 (Ward, p. 11); VA 8 and 49-50.
[57]A 297 (Ward, p. 79).
[58]Cassian, Conf. 19, 4.
[59]Ibid., 2, 23.
[60]A 807 (Ward, p. 213).
[61]N 149, 150.
[62]Bu II 279.
[63]A 191 (Ward, p. 55).
[64]Eth 13, 5.
[65]Ch 249.

Amoun could make do for two months with a small quantity of barley.[66] They could also make flour with chick peas.[67]

Vegetables and Fruit

Along with bread, lentils and chick peas were among the most common foods in Egypt. Many monks fed themselves with these. Anchorites who, like Antony, cultivated a garden, could harvest vegetables and fruit.[68] Mark knew a brother who found a few vegetables growing near his cell but who had yanked them out.[69] In general, the texts distinguish between green vegetables and those with pods. Green vegetables, salads, lettuce and different herbs were usually eaten raw, fresh or preserved in vinegar with salt.[70] Vegetables with pods — peas, lentils and beans — were normally cooked or roasted, though one could occasionally soak them.[71] Paul used to spend his entire Lenten season with one measure of lentils but it isn't said that he cooked them.[72] As for Isaiah, he would remove the lentils from the fire as soon as they began heating up, and say to his companion, "Isn't it enough to have seen the flame? This is already a great satisfaction."[73]

Some anchorites such as Dorotheus ate a little bread and a few vegetables.[74] Elias in his old age ate three ounces of bread and three olives each evening.[75] But most who ate vegetables or fruit deprived themselves completely of bread. Abba Or, Theon, Apollo, Patermuthius and other heroes of the *History of the Monks* were content eating herbs and wild plants.[76] In Nitria, many anchorites ate neither bread nor fruit, only sour chicory.[77] John of Lycopolis took only fruit and abstained from bread and any

---

[66]A 135 (Ward, p. 31).
[67]A 274 (Ward, p. 74).
[68]VA 50.
[69]A 60 (Ward, p. 12).
[70]HM 2, 5; Cassian, Inst. 4, 11.
[71]N 149, 150.
[72]A 796 (Ward, p. 205).
[73]A 253 (Ward, p. (70).
[74]HL 2, 2.
[75]HM 7, 3.
[76]HM 2, 4; 5, 4; 8, 9; 10, 6.
[77]HM 20, 17.

cooked food.[78] Another ate no bread, only soaked chick peas.[79] Sisoes also normally deprived himself of bread.[80] Postumianus knew an elder in Egypt who ate nothing more than six dried figs a day.[81] Such examples contradict Cassian's assertion that among the famous elders, none had stopped eating bread—the usual food and the easiest to obtain—and that "none of those who instead fed themselves vegetables and fruit had ever been among the most esteemed, and had not even obtained the grace of knowledge or discretion."[82]

Austerity of Diet

Certainly everything depends upon the quality and quantity of the food eaten. Regardless of their dispositions, we see that all the Desert Fathers wanted to practice food restrictions in quality as well as quantity. To be forever happy with two small loaves of bread a day was undoubtedly the most austere diet, as Cassian has Abba Moses put it.[83] And Cassian also reports the remarkable description by Isaac of the monk tortured by greed: "My spirit dreams of dishes unknown in the desert; in the midst of a ghastly solitude, I inhale the aroma of meals served on the tables of kings.... The regular meal hour arrives and it is time to eat my food, but I loathe bread...."[84] Now one understands the recommendation of Moses: "It is advisable, when the hour comes, to eat this food, however repugnant it might appear."[85] And Moses told Cassian and his companion Germanus, who, as part of their abstinence, wished to deny themselves the daily two small loaves: "Do try to faithfully follow the amount indicated, without adding anything cooked on Sundays or Saturdays, nor when a brother comes to visit...and you'll see!"[86] In the Cells,

---

[78]HM 1, 17.
[79]N 527.
[80]A 855 (Ward, p. 221).
[81]Sulpicius Severus, *Dial*, I, 20.
[82]Cassian, Inst. 5, 23.
[83]Cassian, Conf. 2, 19-21.
[84]*Ibid.*, 10, 10.
[85]*Ibid.*, 2, 17.
[86]*Ibid.*, 2, 21.

Amoun admitted how hard it was to leave the table still feeling hungry.[87]

Some Fathers still found a way to make this menu, already so restricted, even more difficult. For instance, Isaiah mixed into his bread some ashes from the censer.[88] And it isn't out of the question to think that the monks who ate herbs, and who are mentioned in the *History of the Monks,* found any more pleasure in chewing their sour chicory than the others did with their dry or soaked bread. Surely one didn't enter the desert in order to eat fine meals, but we know that such a diet could not be kept up in all its rigor for very long. Excavations in the Cells have unearthed the presence of stoves and ovens in most of the hermitages. Throughout the fourth-century texts we already find a certain mellowing showing up, especially in an increasingly frequent use of cooked food. Sisoes told a brother, "Eat your bread with your salt and you won't have to cook anything."[89] Despite the efforts of the rigorists, cooking spread little by little among the anchorites, along with different "sweets" mentioned by Cassian: "leek stems, fried salt meat and fish, olives, small fish in brine...."[90]

Mitigations for Invalids and Guests

Early on, some dispensations from the strict diet were allowed for sick or worn-out monks. Despite his former "very soft, delicate and opulent" life, Evagrius lived in the Cells for fourteen years, eating just his daily pound of bread and a little oil, "without ever touching lettuce or any other green vegetable, and no fruit or meat...." But at the end of his life, with his stomach in a bad state, he had to give up bread and eat nothing but cooked vegetables.[91]

---

[87]Eth 14, 17.
[88]A 377 (Ward, p. 100).
[89]PA 1, 1.
[90]Cassian, Inst. 4, 22.
[91]HL 38, 10-13.

According to Cassian, some Fathers advised others not to relax their diet when receiving guests.[92] Also Evagrius in his *Outline on Asceticism* warns the monk against looking for better food under the pretext of fulfilling his duties of hospitality.[93] Bread, salt and water are enough. To the monk from Scetis who apologized for offering only these to a bishop, the latter, who visited the Fathers every year, said that on his next trip he did not even want to find salt.[94] And yet, little by little, charity prevailed over austerity and the monk receiving a guest had to do a little cooking. One day, during the strict fast period, a scandal erupted in Scetis: smoke was rising over Abba Moses' cell. He had welcomed a few brothers from Egypt and was cooking them something. He was eventually praised by the elders for "having not kept the commandment of men but instead kept that of God."[95]

To start the fire, cells were equipped with "flints"[96] and, when needed, one would fetch fire from a neighbor. Helle used to carry some of these stones in the folds of his tunic to his neighboring brothers.[97] But was it not possible to make do with the heat of the Egyptian sun to cook something?

This is what Postumianus maintains telling, upon returning from Egypt, of a saintly monk who served him a dish of vegetables "cooked by the sun," so hot is the sun in this country — something unbelievable to Gallic people![98] — but confirmed by the testimony of war veterans in the Leclerc Division. In the course of their 1944 North Africa campaign, they cooked eggs on the steel of their tanks, by the heat of the sun.

Visitors to the desert were usually well-treated. They occasionally wanted to express their gratitude by giving the monks food they had brought with them — vegetables, pumpkins or

---

[92]Cassian, Conf. 2, 21.

[93]Evagrius, *Outline Teaching on Asceticism and Stillness in the Ascetic Life*, 3, *The Philokalia*, vol. 1, London, 1979, p. 32.

[94]N 28.

[95]A 499 (Ward, p. 139).

[96]Cassian, Inst. 8, 19.

[97]HM 12, 1.

[98]Sulpicius Severus, *Dial*, I, 13.

fruit, for example. These were left at the church and the monks could help themselves.[99] Some elders categorically spurned what they considered to be the food of greed. Thus Achilles did not accept the apples offered to the elders.[100] During the fruit season, Arsenius would only taste each type of fruit once.[101] One day he complained at having been overlooked when some small bad figs were distributed.[102] We know the famous story about grapes offered to Macarius, which the brothers dutifully passed from one to the other without eating any, until they came back intact into the hands of Macarius.[103]

It doesn't appear as if meat ever was on the menu of the anchorites,[104] even when needed to give strength to a sick brother or to honor a guest. The fellahs themselves rarely ate any and this is still the case today with many of them. Meat was so unknown among the Desert Fathers that, when they were served some at Archbishop Theophilus' table, they thought they were eating vegetables![105]

To see just how far the favorable treatment accorded by the anchorites to their guests could lead, one must read Cassian's savory description of the feast served to him and Germanus by Serenus:

> Rather than brine with a drop of oil, which he usually served himself for his daily meal, he created a little sauce which he sprinkled more copiously…. Then he served us browned, grilled salt with three olives each. He also gave us another basket with toasted chick peas—what the recluses call delicacies. We took only five each, we also took two plums and a fig each. In the desert, anything beyond this number would be sinful.[106]

---

[99]N 481.
[100]A 125 (Ward, p. 29).
[101]A 57 (Ward, p. 11).
[102]A 54 (Ward, p. 11).
[103]N 494.
[104]VA 7.
[105]A 306 (Ward, p. 81); N 162.
[106]Cassian, Conf. 8, 1.

Use of Oil

As Serenus explains it, the drop of oil which the anchorites never fail to put in their pittance is intended to repress conceit without arousing greed in any way because "such a small amount would never be enough to grease the passages of the gullet; instead, it disappears before it even gets there."

In the pioneering days of the first desert hermits, their diet had no oil whatsoever. It was only after Antony had become very old that the brothers began taking him olives, vegetables and oil every month.[107] To celebrate Easter, the young Pachomius thought it a good idea to add a little oil to the crushed salt. When Palamon saw that, he started to lament, "The Savior was crucified and here am I eating oil!"[108] In the cells of the anchorites there was almost always oil for the lamps and this was the same oil added now and then to their food. As Herodotus noted, the Egyptians used "castor oil which is just as good as olive oil for the lamps, but gives off a strong odor."[109] There was also linseed oil and a brother, mistaking it for honey, put some in a portion of vegetables served to a sick elder. Despite his repugnance, the elder ate it but couldn't finish the dish and to encourage him, the brother ate some too and noticed his mistake.[110] A few words from Chaeremon shed light on this error, which strikes us as incredible: "I declare it possible to extract from wheat a kind of honey or a very mild oil, similar to that obtained from rapeseed or linseed."[111]

Benjamin reports that, after the harvest work, the monks from Scetis each received, as remuneration, a sealed earthenware jar containing a pint of oil and at the following year's harvest, each took back to the church what he had left. Benjamin, who hadn't opened the jar but had only pierced it with a needle to take his daily drop of oil, assumed he had done something great. When he saw the other brothers returning their unopened and

---

[107]VA 51.
[108]Veilleux, p. 33.
[109]Herodotus, *Hist.* IV, 94.
[110]N 151.
[111]Cassian, Conf. 12, 8.

intact jars, he was "so ashamed, as if he had committed an act of fornication."[112]

The same Benjamin tells about visiting an elder with some brothers. The elder served them horseradish oil. When they asked their host if he didn't have a somewhat better oil, he replied, "Is there some other kind of oil? I don't know of any."[113]

Oil, Cassian used to say, is the only sweet for desert monks and their guests.[114] But from the meager usage at the beginning, abuses evolved which were deplored by Abba John:

> In the early days, we used to forget about oil, or a pint was enough for a whole year of receiving guests. Now we have doubled, tripled, the ration and it is scarcely enough to live on. We're far removed from the drop of oil of the first anchorites. We go so far as to freely sprinkle oil on Egyptian cheese: two foods with their own culinary charms and which could easily provide the monks with two different treats at various times.[115]

Contrary to Pachomian customs,[116] cheese doesn't appear to have figured in the Desert Fathers' meals. Only two mentions are found in the apothegms and one could be interpreted as a criticism of the cenobites. It comes from Poemen who is asked by a superior of the community, "How can I acquire a fear of God?" and who replies, "How can we acquire a fear of God when we have stocks of cheese and pots of salt, fish and meat?"[117] The one time we see an anchorite eating cheese is when Simon took bread and cheese in order to shock a great personage who arrived with his suite to visit him.[118] Then where did this cheese come from? Perhaps Simon kept some to offer the guests he received.

---

[112]A 168 (Ward, p. 43).
[113]A 170 (Ward, pp. 43-44).
[114]Cassian, Inst. 4, 25.
[115]Cassian, Conf. 19, 6.
[116]Veilleux, p. 335.
[117]A 755 (Ward, p. 192).
[118]A 869 (Ward, p. 225).

Wine and Water

According to an axiom of Poemen, quoted by St Benedict in his Rule, "Wine is in no way suitable for monks."[119] The elder says this to justify the conduct of a brother who never drank any, obviously because the majority of monks did not do the same. We find some fifty mentions of wine in the apothegms and almost all attest to the fact that, even if it was not generalized, the use of wine in the desert was nonetheless not as rare as one would be led to believe. Antony, like his ascetic companions, never drank wine.[120] But we can scarcely quote other names which the anti-alcohol brigades might claim as role models. One might suppose that the anchorite in his cell never touched wine. He could keep a small reserve for eventual visitors and then drink some with them.[121]

The main occasion for drinking wine was the banquet which preceded the Eucharist on Saturday and Sunday. On this occasion, it was considered both charitable and humble to do like everyone else. Sisoes, for instance, sipped two portions but declined the third.[122] Anyhow, this is the order he gave to a brother — to avoid the third glass.[123] Macarius also drank wine with the brothers, who were delighted to do so, until the day he found out that an elder would then deprive himself of as many glasses of water as he had drunk of wine. He then stopped offering him any.[124] It was therefore not an absolute rule to drink wine during a meal taken in common. Isaac the Theban used to go hide in his cell right after the liturgy without waiting for the small portion of bread and wine which was part of the brothers' *agape*.[125] In the Cells, at the moment of the distribution, a brother fell down, and a vault collapsed on top of him. The accident was interpreted as divine punishment for the brother's obvious vainglory. But his elder took up his defense and forbade any re-

---

[119]A 593 (Ward, p. 169).
[120]VA 7; A 22 (Ward, p. 6).
[121]A 217 (Ward, p. 61).
[122]A 811 (Ward, pp. 213-214).
[123]A 805 (Ward, p. 213).
[124]A 463 (Ward, p. 129).
[125]A 423 (Ward, p. 110).

building of the vault during his lifetime.[126] Again in the Cells, on Easter Sunday, they gave a glass of wine to a brother and insisted he drink it. He asked to be excused because, he said, "you did the same last year and it afflicted me for a long time."[127]

In Scetis, some elders were stricter. One day an elder, who had been offered a glass of wine, turned it down, saying, "Rid me of this mortal poison." On the spot, the brothers eating with him abstained also.[128] All these anecdotes amply show that abstinence from wine had become, at a certain period, right after the death of Macarius, a practice left to each one's judgment. An apothegm praising the virtue of the monks from Scetis says that, among them, one ate no bread and another drank no wine.[129] The Fathers sometimes advised total abstinence and sometimes, to drink only a little.[130] Even when old or sick, many elders couldn't bring themselves to take any.[131] Pior the Pionite accepted only a little bit of it in order to redden his water.[132] Another sick elder began weeping when he saw them bringing him a glass of wine and said, "I never thought I'd be drinking wine before death."[133] On the other hand, Piamoun, who had spent twenty-five years without drinking any, accepted the glass offered him without hesitation.[134]

Like Christ who drank wine and freed those possessed, Xanthias chased away a demon by drinking a glass of wine.[135] As for Paphnutius, he converted a whole band of thieves by agreeing to drink wine while threatened with a sword.[136] While claiming wine to be unsuitable for the monk, Poemen must nevertheless have kept wine in his cellar, because he had, in fact,

---

[126]N 148.
[127]N 60.
[128]N 144.
[129]N 467.
[130]N 130; Bu II 378; Am 22, 14.
[131]A 523, 799 (Ward, pp. 145, 209).
[132]A 782 (Ward, p. 200).
[133]N 157.
[134]Cassian, Conf. 17, 24.
[135]A 569 (Ward, p. 159).
[136]A 787 (Ward, p. 202).

taken some to a jealous elder he sought to mollify, and to a monk who had taken a wife who had just had a child.[137] The Desert Fathers thus knew that wine could be used to exercise charity and humility. As Palladius judiciously put it, "It's best to drink wine with discernment than water with pride."[138]

Even in the use of water which was the anchorites' usual drink, the Fathers advised moderation. Antony is supposed to have said that the monk must no more fill himself with water than abstain from wine.[139] Because, according to Evagrius and Cassian, water in excess could also favor carnal movements and nocturnal fantasies.[140] This had already been taught by Hippocrates.[141] But furthermore, according to the *History of the Monks*, Evagrius often advised against drinking water to satiety because the demons, he said, constantly frequent watery places.[142] And Evagrius quotes Macarius as saying that he measured his water as he weighed his bread.[143] In the heat of the desert, it is surely a great mortification to sip water sparingly. Paul spent an entire Lenten season with a set amount — "one small jug."[144] In one week alone, Chaeremon would normally drink twice as much.[145] One should add that desert water had a bitter taste and could not have been very pleasant to drink.[146]

A General Rule

As can be seen, there were in the desert a great variety of observances concerning food and drink. This matches the diversity of temperaments, ages and states of health as well as places and circumstances.[147] All monks did not have the same oppor-

---

[137]A 578 (Ward, p. 165); Sy 9, 20.
[138]HL Pr.
[139]N 490/1.
[140]Cassian, Conf. 12, 11.
[141]Hippocrates, *Regimen I*.
[142]HM 20, 15. Cf. Texts quoted by A. Guillaumont in SC 171, pp. 542-545.
[143]Evagrius *Praktikos* 94, SC 171, pp. 698-701.
[144]A 796 (Ward, p. 205).
[145]A 932 (Ward, p. 244).
[146]HL 39, 3.
[147]Cassian, Inst. 5, 5.

tunities or difficulties in obtaining certain foods. And all were not inspired by God to the same dietary restrictions. However, a general rule had been, little by little, favored by the Desert Fathers as a result of their experience: regardless of the frequency of meals, the quantity and quality of the food and beverages taken, one must take what is needed to sustain the body, while avoiding satiety at all costs and always leaving the table hungry.[148] This is the fundamental principle, the golden rule: "Take what's required to sustain the body, never enough to satisfy it." An excess of abstinence is as much to be avoided as an excess of food and drink.[149]

Abba Moses told Cassian how the Devil had egged on the famous John of Lycopolis to excessive fasts.[150] Alone with God, the anchorite adjusted his own diet, while often accepting the control of the elders. One recalls St Antony saying that, if possible, he had to tell the elders the number of drops of water he drank in his cell.[151] The demons of greed and vainglory are very clever at deluding us, first by having us reduce our abstinence, then by having us increase it. We have earlier mentioned Dorotheus saying about his body, "It kills me, I kill it."[152] The formula shouldn't be taken literally and applied to all the Desert Fathers. Poemen declared that even if he gave himself up to great excesses during his youth, "he did not kill the body, but restrained it only to the point where this was enough for the just moderation of the Lord."[153] Faced with such a declaration, have we the right to reproach the desert monks for their abstinences which strike us as exaggerated? The key word is "restraint," accepted by the Fathers so as to remain faithful to their vocation.

Sensing they were called to higher pleasures, they refused to allow themselves to be carried away by the pleasures of the stomach. This is surely why they sometimes adopted special

---

148*Ibid.*, 5, 5-8.
149Cassian, Conf. 2, 22.
150*Ibid.*, 1, 21.
151A 38 (Ward, p. 9).
152HL 2, 2.
153Eth 14, 24.

ways of eating. Helladius, like Bane, often ate standing up.[154] Pior ate his meals while walking.[155] Another elder ate with one hand, while extending the other in prayer, never ceasing to think about the judgment of God.[156]

Body and Soul

While Athanasius said Antony would be ashamed to be seen eating or sleeping, it is a trait repeated in the *Life of Plotinus* who was, said Porphyry, "ashamed to be in a body." Nevertheless, the Father of monks often ate with the brothers.[157] Abba Daniel said, "As much as the body flourishes, the soul vegetates; as much as the body vegetates, the soul flourishes."[158] Such turns of phrase could be dangerous and lead to the excesses Antony was the first to denounce: "Some have crushed their bodies in asceticism but, lacking wisdom, they found themselves a long way from God."[159] We must, he declared, give all our spare time to the soul rather than the body; put aside a little time needed for the body, but dedicate the rest to developing the soul's well-being, so that it isn't attracted to the sensual delights of the body, but rather that the body be made a servant of it; this is what was taught by the Savior.[160] In fact, in the spirit of the Gospel, as Palladius explains in the prologue to his *Lausiac History*, "what counts for Christians is neither eating nor abstinence, but rather the work done in charity."[161]

Some pagan ascetics and philosophers were able to lay down dietary restrictions so as to maintain a strict continence and a perfect mastery of their passions. This viewpoint was not overlooked by the Christian monks but such was not for them

---

[154]A 226 (Ward, p. 63); Ch 248.
[155]A 778 (Ward, p. 199).
[156]N 146.
[157]VA 45; *Life of Plotinus* 1.
[158]A 186 (Ward, p. 52).
[159]A 8 (Ward, p. 3).
[160]VA 45.
[161]HL Pr 10-14.

the main objective of their fasts and abstinences.[162] These practices were part of their general intentions for austerity with
a view to imitating Christ and associating themselves with his
passion. We already quoted Palamon's thought: "The Savior was
crucified and here I am eating oil." We also read in the apothegms: "Fixing the eyes on Jesus who, instead of the joy that
was proposed to him, endured a cross." "It takes a lot of toil;
without toil one cannot possess his God, because for us, he was
crucified."[163]

The texts don't always explicitly tell us the motive which
inspired the Desert Fathers, but one must know how to read between the lines when we come across an anecdote such as this:

> One Saturday feast day, the brothers happened to be
> eating in a church in the Cells. As they were served
> a plate of boiled, mushy vegetables, Helladius began
> weeping. James asked him, "Abba, why are you crying?"
> He replied, "Because now we are finished with the soul's
> joy — the fast — and now it is time to satisfy the body."[164]

Such a simple and spontaneous reaction clearly shows the
state of soul of this anchorite who certainly found in his fasting
much greater spiritual joy than in the pleasures of eating.

---

[162]Contrary to the opinion of Aline Rousselle, for whom the dietary
restrictions the anchorites imposed on themselves were only aimed at repressing
the sex drive, leading men, as she says, "from abstinence to impotence" and
women "from virginity to frigidity." These are the titles of the last two chapters
of her book *Porneia*, pp. 160-193.

[163]A 438, A 265 (Ward, pp. 116, 72).

[164]A 949.

SEVEN

Life in the Cell

The Anchorite's View of the Cell

In current speech, the word "cell" immediately evokes a room where, in a prison, a criminal is locked up, isolated and cut off from all contact with others. And, in fact, for the Egyptian who really enjoys fresh air and relations with others, the hermit's cell must look like a veritable dungeon. The Desert Fathers were aware of this and drew from it salutary thoughts. Ammonas suggested to a brother that he think of himself as an imprisoned lawbreaker, asking himself when the judge will come and how he will defend himself.[1] John Colobos decided that the monk who remains in his cell with the constant thought of the Lord's presence puts into practice the words of Christ: "I was in prison and you visited me."[2] Contrary to the prisoner locked up against his will, the anchorite locks himself in a desert cell so as to better know Christ. And it is for this same reason that he stays there as long as he can. To Palladius who complained to Macarius about his being tempted to leave, the elder replied, "Tell your mind: 'As far as I'm concerned, I remain within these walls for Christ.' "[3] It isn't that life there is always pleasant and comfortable. During a persecution, a hermit was tortured to the point where he was forced to sit on a white-hot iron seat. Finally set free, he

---

[1]A 113 (Ward, p. 26).
[2]A 342 (Ward, p. 91).
[3]HL 18, 29.

returned to his cell crying out, "Woe is me because here I am, back to a lot of evil!"[4]

We see that the Desert Fathers did not harbor delusions. The cell is not always "the furnace of Babylon where the three children found the Son of God and the pillar of cloud where God spoke to Moses."[5] The monk could be cruelly burned in the furnace or believe himself lost in the cloud. The periods of boredom and disgust often alternated with moments of fervor and elation.[6] However, one had to always remain steady and persevere in the cell.

Sitting Down in the Cell

This fundamental requirement of life in the desert is expressed in Greek by a verb which signifies at the same time being seated, staying and "holding oneself correctly" in the cell. The anchorite often sat down in his cell to eat, work, read and write, and even to sleep. At the time, the posture in Egypt was to sit on the ground with legs bent and the head on the knees or between the knees. In a painting of a pharaoh's burial, the courtiers are shown sitting like this. It was also an attitude familiar to the Pachomian monks.[7] Normally one did not lean against the wall. Theodore was criticized by Pachomius for allowing himself to relax in this position.[8] Even today the Copts sit this way in their churches, like Moslems in mosques. And experience proves that one can sleep very well like this during the lengthy services of the Coptic liturgy. However, in the fourth century, the monks sometimes sat upon low seats made of papyrus bales called "embrimia." These seats, described by Cassian, also served as pillows.[9] In addition, they could be used for writing. While working as a scribe, Dioscorus had an "embrimion" beneath him.[10]

---

[4]N 469.
[5]N 206.
[6]Cassian, Conf. 4, 2-6; 6, 10.
[7]Veilleux, pp. 132, 135, 174. Cf. p. 282, n. 5.
[8]Veilleux, pp. 102-103.
[9]Cassian, Conf. 1, 23.
[10]Ch 256.

Staying in the Cell

The anchorite could also remain standing in the cell and even stroll back and forth. What counted was to stay there, keep resisting the perpetual temptation to go out to amuse himself, and escape the pain of solitude and, indeed, boredom — what the monks called "acedia." We must understand that the temptation was frequent and strong, sometimes even compelling, for the elders speak so often about it in all the collections of apothegms. We might even call it the hardest battle the monk had to wage.[11] We find frequent examples of the Fathers' advice to remain in the cell: Arsenius, Hierax, Macarius, Isidore, Paphnutius, Moses, Rufus, Sarmatas, Serapion, Sisoes, without counting the anonymous ones.[12]

All these recommendations were given at a time when the desert was well-populated. Under these circumstances, the only way to be alone with God was to remain confined in the cell. The temptation to leave arose with all sorts of often specious pretexts. Wouldn't it be charitable to go visit the brothers, especially the sick ones?[13] Aren't we advised to go consult an elder?[14] If I have the impression that I'm doing nothing and losing myself in the desert, isn't it best to go live in a cenobitic monastery?[15] The less dangerous way of falling prey to temptation was to leave the cell to go confide one's thoughts to an elder, whose reply would always be, "Stay in your cell." But this was often accompanied by additional advice we can find astonishing: "Go, say a prayer in the morning, another in the evening and one at night; eat, drink, sleep and don't work, but don't leave your cell."[16] This often astonished the brother who heard it and thought it best to go consult another elder. This second one gave the same kind of

---

[11]Bu I 23.

[12]A 49, 399, 480, 494, 495, 500, 790, 801, 874, 878 (Ward pp. 10, 104, 133, 138, 139, 203, 210, 226, 228); N 147, 195, 202, 207, 278, 443; Sy 11, 66.

[13]A 49, 874 (Ward, pp. 10, 226).

[14]N 278, 394, 443.

[15]A 790 (Ward, p. 203); N 202.

[16]A 49 (Ward, p. 10).

reply but went so far as to say, "Don't pray at all. Just remain in your cell."[17]

Cassian had come across these kinds of replies and, through the teaching of Abba Serenus, saw in them a sign of laxity. Some monks had become half-hearted. "They think they've gained a lot if they can only keep themselves in solitude, whatever their apathy; and for a single cure, the elders have the habit of telling them: 'Stay in your cells; eat, drink, sleep as much as you want, as long as you stay there constantly.' "[18]

Despite all the esteem one has for Cassian, people have a right to ask if he has here really grasped the Desert Fathers' psychology and not rallied instead to the opinion of that great expert on the monks of the Orient, Irénée Hausherr. According to him, the Fathers knew

> what courage, what heroic endurance was needed to tolerate the demon of *acedia*...the most oppressive of all, whose specialty it is to cause people to take a dislike to stability in one place. All things considered, this commonplace advice to stay in the cell, even without working or praying, concealed a fearsome demand under a conciliatory appearance, and the conviction that the fight against the "noonday demon" would sooner or later... lead the monk...spontaneously to perform this prayer or that work which was not imposed upon him.[19]

An elder would tell a brother, "Remain in your cell and God will grant you relief."[20] Abba Moses put it better: "Remain in your cell and your cell will teach you everything,"[21] including the secret of staying there successfully. The Fathers were psychologists and also had an implacable logic. One goes to the desert to seek God in solitude. Cost what it might, one had to remain in the solitude of the cell to persevere in the desert. They

---

[17] A 790 (Ward, p. 203).
[18] Cassian, Conf. 7, 23.
[19] I. Hausherr, *Spiritual Direction in the Early Christian East*, Kalamazoo, MI, 1990, p. 73.
[20] N 147.
[21] A 500 (Ward, p. 139).

understood it well, these brothers, who used every means—sometimes ingeniously—not to flee the cell. For nine years a brother was tempted to leave the hermitage. Each day he got his coat ready to leave and, when night came, he would say to himself, "I'll leave here tomorrow." The next morning he would say, "Let's get our act together and stay another day for the Lord." When he had done this for nine long years, God removed all temptation from him and he found peace.[22]

Another brother was tempted to go visit the sick. After three days, he was bored in his cell. He took palm branches, hung them up, and the next day plaited them. After work, he said, "Here are more small branches. I'll get them ready, then I'll eat." After reading, he said, "I'll recite my little psalms, then I'll eat without a care." Thus, little by little, he progressed with the help of God and finally regulated his life. Having tackled his thoughts with assurance, he triumphed over them.[23]

As we have said, the most subtle temptation was the one suggesting to a monk that he go visit an elder, if only to admit to him that he wanted to leave his cell. Was it not laudable to go confess to the elders all the thoughts assailing one? And yet sometimes it was only a pretext whispered by the Devil to get the anchorite out of his cell. Experienced monks did not allow themselves to be seduced. One of them, to rid himself of such a temptation, would take his coat, walk around his cell outside, then re-enter right away, imagining that he came as a visitor.[24] Another, without even leaving, would mentally visit an elder, playing alternatively the role of the elder and that of the visitor, and so overcome the temptation.[25] But some didn't notice the trap and only became aware afterwards, such as this brother from Cellia, whose story is worth telling:

> A brother in the Cells had put some palm tree leaves to soak and, as he sat down to plait them, his mind told him, "Go find such and such an elder." Then he told

[22]N 207.
[23]N 195.
[24]N 394.
[25]N 443.

himself, "I'll go in a few days." Again, his mind told him, "And if he dies, what will you do? Go talk to him. It's time." Again he said to himself, "No, it's not the right time." Then his mind suggested, "But since you're cutting the canes, the moment has come." And he said, "I'll finish with the palm leaves, then I'll go." He then said to himself, "My, the air is wonderful today." And he arose, left the palm tree leaves soaking, took his coat and left. It happened that in the neighborhood there was an elder gifted with clairvoyance. When he saw him running, the elder shouted, "Captive, captive, where are you running to? Come here." When he approached, the elder told him, "Return to your cell." The brother told him about his inner battle and returned to his cell. Once inside, he prostrated himself on the floor. The demons shouted, "You've defeated us, monk, you've defeated us!" And the mat on which he lay spread out was consumed as if by fire, while the demons vanished like smoke. This is how the brother learned of their tricks.[26]

The Mid-Day Devil

In the apothegms, we catch a glimpse of the anchorite in his cell as he falls prey to acedia, that painful boredom intrinsic to monastic life. The cure is certainly not to go out, say the theoreticians Evagrius and Cassian:

> One must not desert the cell at the hour of temptation, as plausible as the excuses we concoct might be; but one must remain inside, hold up and valiantly face the assailants, all of them, but especially the demon of acedia who, since he is the most burdensome of all, makes the soul suffer to the utmost. Because to run from such struggles and to avoid them leads the spirit to become inept, lazy and a runaway.[27]

---

[26]N 278.
[27]Cassian, Conf. 24, 4-5; Evagrius, *Praktikos*, 28.

Evagrius and Cassian each describe in remarkable fashion the manifestations of this fearsome demon, which they identify as "the mid-day devil" referred to in a psalm, because he mounts his attack upon the monk at noon, when the heat is most oppressive. The anchorite finds the time long, the sun appears to have stopped, the day seems never to end. He's forever on the lookout at the window, hoping a visitor will drop by to take his mind off things and make a somewhat earlier meal hour possible. But, he muses, the brothers have no charity, none come to comfort me. And if anyone ever saddened him lately, the demon seizes this to increase his aversion. He dreams of going to other places where people and things would be more pleasant, where he could more easily find what he needs and work at something less wearisome and more profitable. Where he is, everything is repugnant: work, lectures, this monastic life in which he has the feeling he's wasting his time, when he could be off doing good for his dear ones and friends — neglected sick people, even such and such a woman, devout and dedicated to God…. And how many more years will he have to spend in this gloomy state? Finally, he thinks that to get out of this depression he has no choice but to quit the cell or fall asleep.[28]

Keeping Oneself Well in the Cell

Staying in the cell isn't everything. There's also the manner. Ammonas said, "This man spends a hundred years in a cell and doesn't even know how to keep himself in the cell."[29] One can waste one's time there, but "keeping oneself well in the cell fills the monk with good things."[30] In fact, the Greek word for "being seated," "keeping oneself" and "staying" also indicates the state of peace and contemplation which the anchorite strives to maintain for himself in the cell with a whole series of physical and spiritual observances. This state was also called *hesychia* in Greek and in this sense, the "keeping of the cell" is more a disposition of soul than a position or posture of the body. For the pioneer

---

[28]Evagrius, *Praktikos*, 12; Cassian, Inst. 10, 1-3.
[29]A 670 (Ward, p. 180).
[30]N 116.

88

Desert Fathers, nothing had yet been firmly established for the use of cell time, as we'll see; yet for them, what Abba Moses was quoted earlier as saying was already being accomplished: "Stay in your cell and the cell will teach you everything." This sentence, in which one recognizes an echo of the words of Christ in St John's epistle, really means, "In your cell the Holy Spirit will teach you everything."

Led to the desert, as was Jesus by the Holy Spirit, the Fathers learned from him how to remain there and, in the light of their experiences, they had little by little elaborated a code of *savoir-vivre* for the anchorite in the cell, of doing things which became customs and then sacred traditions. The ABC's of this code were to persevere in the initial deprivation assumed by the monk upon reaching the desert. The cell must have none of the worldly things he had given up and left, and he must not reconstitute and surround himself with them ever again.

Keeping in the Cell Only What is Strictly Needed

When Melania, visiting the monks of Egypt, reached the cell of a holy man named Hephestion, "she walked around the cell, examining his things." She noticed that he owned nothing in the world "but a mat, a basket containing a few small loaves of dry bread and a small container of salt."[31]

Of all the furnishings to be found in the cell of an anchorite, the mat is the object most frequently mentioned in different documents. To underscore the destitution of the Egyptian monks Cassian says they own nothing but the previously mentioned clothes and a mat upon which they sleep and sometimes sit.[32] Antony "made do with a mat for sleeping and even slept most of the time on the bare ground."[33] Even Dioscorus who, like Antony, slept on the bare ground without a pillow, at least had a mat in his cell, if only to use as a table or to offer to a visitor for sitting on.[34] The mat is usually made of plaited rushes. We have

---

[31]*Life of St. Melania* 38, SC 90, p. 198.
[32]Cassian, Inst. 4, 13.
[33]VA 7.
[34]Ch 254, 258, 262. Cf. Cassian, Conf. 18, 11.

already mentioned the "embrimia" serving as seats or pillows. A bed was a luxury reserved for the sick.[35]

Apart from this rudimentary furniture, no text gives an inventory of the objects to be found in the cell. But by collecting details scattered throughout the various documents, we can list the elementary supplies of the anchorites. None could do without a container for the indispensable water: jug, amphora, jar or pitcher. The excavations at Cellia brought to light a large quantity of diverse pottery, but it is from an era (sixth-seventh centuries) when there were many hermitages on this site. Some containers were used to fetch water from the wells, others to transport it, and still others to keep a reserve.[36] It was undoubtedly this kind of pottery the Desert Fathers had, but in small quantities. The apothegms several times mention *the* jug of a hermit,[37] which leads one to suppose they each had only one. It was often made of fragile earth and could easily be knocked over and broken. Rarer still is the mention of a large jar. Amoun had one brought to him so as always to be able to offer a drink to his many visitors.[38] These jars were sometimes large enough to hold a man or a woman, indeed two women. It is in a jar that a monk hid his concubine when Ammonas came for a visit. The latter went and sat on the jar, which must therefore have had a cover.[39] In John Colobos' parable, which was mentioned earlier, there are two naked women a man brought with him in a large jar on a ship.[40] But the texts most often emphasize the small capacity of the container, since Paul goes through a whole Lenten season with a small three-quart jug.[41] We also know that in all Egyptian periods, amphoras and jars were used to protect food from insects and rodents. Bread most especially, which the anchorites kept for months in reserve, was protected like this. And most of these containers had a narrow neck so that they could be corked

---

[35]A 83, 132 (Ward, pp. 20, 30).
[36]F. Bonnet, in *Dossiers Histoire et Archéologie*, No. 133, pp. 47-57.
[37]N 201; Cassian, Inst. 4, 16.
[38]HM 22, 5-6.
[39]A 122 (Ward, p. 28).
[40]A 330 (Ward, p. 88).
[41]A 796 (Ward, p. 205).

more easily. A child, wanting to take some nuts from this kind of vase, couldn't overload his hand.[42] This is also what Macarius of Alexandria used to do with his bread—he contented himself with what little he could grab and remove with his hand.[43]

So long as the anchorite ate only bread and salt, he needed no dishes, but for the times when he had to cook—if not for himself, then at least for the guests he was receiving—he required a cooking pot with a cover, a stove and something with which to light a fire.[44] To the brother who boasted about letting grass grow in his home, an elder replied, "So you've banished hospitality from your abode."[45] And for service, a plate or bowl was needed.[46]

Night-time called for a lamp,[47] one of the small ones of which many specimens were found in the excavations at Esna and the Cells. All these utensils were made of baked clay and were no doubt somewhat crude. We can understand the admiration aroused by the "seven senators who, like Arsenius, had become monks in Scetis and used worthless earthen utensils,"[48] having dined until then from precious dishes of gold or silver.

Every anchorite also needed a knife to split reeds and palm tree leaves, or to prepare a fish.[49] Agathon had only this kind of knife but gave it to a brother who wanted it.[50] One day, bandits who had plundered Dioscorus' cell gave him back his knife.[51] The making of mats, baskets and nets also called for bodkins, spindles, pins.[52] When a monk had a small garden to cultivate, he also needed a few tools. Thus Antony had someone bring him

---

[42]Sy QRT 58.
[43]HL 18, 2.
[44]A 685, 253 (Ward, pp. 183, 70); Eth 13, 58.
[45]N 385.
[46]A 184 (Ward, p. 51).
[47]A 574 (Ward, p. 161); N 151, 189.
[48]N 14.
[49]A 776 (Ward, p. 198).
[50]A 89, A 107 (Ward, pp. 21, 24).
[51]Ch 261.
[52]A 168, 180, 535 (Ward, pp. 43, 49, 149); N 58, N 577; Sy 3, 52; Eth 13, 93.

a hoe and an ax.[53] The ax is often mentioned in the apothegms; it served to cut wood or carve stone.[54]

Books

Books surely didn't clutter up the anchorite's cell in the fourth century. They were expensive, as much due to the material of which they were made — papyrus or parchment — as for the length of time needed to copy the texts. Some monks were copyists and could set up a small library for themselves or make copies for others.[55] It is to one of these book-lovers, in whose place he saw an alcove full of books, that Serapion said, "You have taken the living of widows and orphans and put it on your shelves,"[56] or, in other words: Instead of helping the poor with your alms, you acquired a quantity of books. Was this the same Serapion who had given all he had, including a small gospel book, to the poor? "I even sold," he said, "the book that told me to sell everything and give the money to the poor."[57] Theodore of Pherme, had three beautiful books which he gladly loaned to the brothers but, on the advice of Macarius, he sold them and gave the money to the poor.[58] The same Theodore also had other books which thieves took from him.[59]

In the Cells, a brother used to read day and night. One day, he sold all the books he had and went further into the desert, no doubt to Scetis. Meeting Abba Isaac, he told him, "For all of two years, Father, I've heard nothing but the words of the gospel, and now I want to put into practice what I learned from Holy Writ."[60] This apothegm suggests that the books of the anchorites were scriptural ones. Only once is it another book — the treatise by Athanasius against the Arians — that Sisoes owned and had

[53]VA 50.

[54]A 35, 486, 534 (Ward, pp. 8, 134, 149); Arm 19, 53; SP, New Collection, p. 273 (II 498).

[55]A 142 (Ward, p. 34). Cf. Isaiah 3, 23.

[56]A 876 (Ward, p. 227).

[57]N 392, N 566; Evagrius, *Praktikos* 97.

[58]A 268 (Ward, p. 73).

[59]A 296 (Ward, p. 78).

[60]N 541.

his disciple read to Arian visitors.[61] In Scetis, Isaiah always took his book to the weekly liturgy.[62] Could he have been a reader?

The earliest Desert Fathers probably had no books at all or had only one, such as Isaiah's. A brother in Scetis went one day to hide his book in Paphnutius' cell.[63] Fervent anchorites like Bessarion never allowed themselves to collect books.[64] But as the pioneer days receded, monks piled books in their cupboards[65] and an elder could then sadly note, "The Prophets wrote books, then our Fathers came and put them into practice. Those who followed learned them by heart. And now comes this generation, which copied and stored them, useless, in alcoves."[66] This unknown censor is probably a bit too severe since Ammoes speaks of monks who used to leave their cells "with the cupboards full of parchment books, without closing the doors,"[67] demonstrating their detachment. His disciple Isaiah ordered a monk departing from a cell to leave everything behind that he had found there.[68]

Persevering with Total Detachment

Whenever and wherever people put down roots for awhile, it's certain they will amass, little by little, a thousand items they could do without. It was like this with books as well as with furnishings and tools. For monks who had given up everything, it was a formidable peril and the elders warned them to be on the watch for it, first of all by making themselves examples of perfect detachment. One had to be ready at all times to give a brother what he had and never keep in the cell a useless object or one he would not want to give or even simply to lend.[69] Since every anchorite had to look after himself, some could be tempted to put a bit of money aside for illness or old age. Several apothegms

---

[61]A 828 (Ward, p. 217).
[62]Eth 13, 79.
[63]Cassian, Conf. 18, 15.
[64]A 167 (Ward, p. 42).
[65]A 134 (Ward, p. 31).
[66]N 228.
[67]A 134 (Ward, p. 31).
[68]Isaiah 4, 62.
[69]Isaiah 4, 26; 30, 5F; Cassian, Conf. 19, 12.

(including many from Cassian) denounce this avarice,[70] stressing how sad it is for monks, who gave up riches that were sometimes considerable, to allow themselves to be again trapped by lust for worldly goods, often becoming attached to such trifles as a mat, a basket, a bag, a manuscript, a scraper, a bodkin, a needle, a stalk of reed to write with....[71] On the contrary, there was an admirable detachment among others, such as Archebius who, on several occasions, gave up his cell with its furnishings and utensils,[72] or the brother who constantly got rid of everything he had, "a small piece of money or a bite of bread," by taking it to his neighbor's cell.[73]

One anecdote shows the need for the monk who wants to persevere in his cell not only to abandon everything but to become detached from everything. A newcomer to the desert had kept a hundred coins. Scarcely had he entered his cell when he saw that the door was in bad shape and said to himself, "The door is old and has to be replaced." His elder advised him to truly renounce the world, so the brother now kept only ten coins. Soon he noticed that the roof needed to be repaired. On the elder's advice, he went and gave away the ten coins and returned to his cell, imagining that he had finally renounced the world for good. But then other thoughts cropped up: "Heavens, everything here is old. The lion will come and devour me." This time the elder told him, "I'd like everything to collapse on me and the lion eat me so that I be freed from life. Go, stay in your cell and pray to God."[74]

The Fathers also knew that by accumulating lots of things in the cell, one could have a rather pleasant and comfortable life. John Colobos used to say, "If a man has anything in his heart from God, he can remain in his cell, even without owning a single thing of this world. And again, if a man has the things of this world without those of God, he, too, remains in his cell, thanks to the things of this world. But he who has neither the things

---

[70]N 258, N 262.
[71]Cassian, Inst. 7, 7; Conf. 1, 6 and 4, 21.
[72]Cassian, Inst. 5, 37.
[73]N 6.
[74]N 17.

of God nor the things of this world can absolutely not stay in a cell."[75] The implicit conclusion is that if one wants to remain in the cell and have the things of God, he must not have the things of this world. And vice versa, the monk who, in the cell, has the things of God, finds it hard to keep the things of this world.[76] In fact, as an elder put it, the man who has sampled the sweetness of owning nothing is weighed down and oppressed even by the garment he wears and his jug of water. For his spirit from now on is busy elsewhere.[77]

---

[75]A 959 (Ward, p. 95).
[76]N 464.
[77]N 578.

EIGHT

❧✠❧

A Day in the Life
of the Anchorite

It isn't advisable to define the anchorite's day as confined
to the hours between the rising and the setting of the sun, since
for most of the time the appearance and disappearance of the
divine star which figured so greatly in the life of the Egyptians
of Antiquity, did not greatly affect the occupations of the Desert
Fathers. At midnight, some had not yet ended their day; others
at that time had already begun theirs. It is therefore best to
consider the twenty-four hour day and the usual day, with the
exception of Saturday and Sunday, which, from the earliest time,
had separate roles in the unfolding of the semi-anchoritic life in
the desert.

A Life of Prayer and Work

In the beginning, the totally isolated hermits each had their
own system and timetable, depending on divine inspiration or
individual whims. For those, in the East as well as in the West,
there was neither a liturgical Sunday or year. On Easter Sunday
St Benedict, in his Subiaco solitude, didn't know that this was the
great Christian feast day. The same was true for the first Desert
Fathers.

Antony, in the ruins of his small fort or his Mount Colzim
grotto, led, day after day, a life of prayer and work which continued unabated with the passage of the weeks, months and
years. Undoubtedly this life was more fervent and intense during the nocturnal darkness, since the saintly hermit sometimes

deplored the rising of the sun: "Oh, sun, why do you trouble me? You only get up so early so as to yank me away from the clearness of the True Light."[1] From the daily life of these first mystics of the desert, we can say only that they lived continuously in union with God and that everything else had scarcely any importance for them. And yet we already see the appearance of what Poemen would present many years later as the visible observance of the anchorite in the cell: to work with the hands, eat only once a day, keep silence and "meditate," that is, to recite by heart the word of God.[2] Prayer is not mentioned, either because it is included in this "meditation," or forms the monk's first and essential activity, which must be continuous and accompany all occupations[3] or, finally, because prayer is more a part of hidden, intimate and personal activities, in which Poemen sees "the hidden progress in the cell." Isaiah would say, "When you keep yourself in your cell, concentrate always on these three things: manual work, meditation and prayer."[4]

When living the ascetic life on the outskirts of his village, Antony himself worked with his hands and prayed all the time. His work provided a living as well as alms to give to the poor.[5] We know that in the desert he continued these two activities and so did all the anchorites who followed in his steps. The sources reveal a few exceptional cases of loners who only prayed and did no work (but this was for good reasons and not on principle) as did certain heretics called, because of this, "Messalians" or "Euchites" (words derived from "prayer" in Syriac and Greek).[6] For example, Apollo at Scetis didn't work but prayed all the time because he had, he said, to catch up on forty years spent without praying.[7] Paul of Pherme did barely enough to earn his liveli-

---

[1] Cassian, Conf. 9, 31.
[2] A 742 (Ward, p. 190).
[3] Bu II 191 and 493.
[4] Isaiah 9, 20.
[5] VA 3.
[6] A 446, A 860 (Ward, pp. 120-121, 223); N 440.
[7] A 150 (Ward, p. 36).

hood.[8] As for Achilles, he worked as much as he could day and night, "for fear of incurring God's wrath."[9]

Some didn't have to work in order to live but did anyway so as not to be idle and to avoid being bored,[10] also to have enough for alms for the paupers,[11] or simply to have something to offer as refreshments to eventual visitors.[12] Isaiah said, "Look after your manual work so that the poor have bread, because idleness is the death and ruination of the soul." Cassian tells the story of an Abba Paul who lived in the depths of the desert, seven days' walking distance from the populated areas. He had a garden which provided him with food, but he also made baskets, which he piled up in his grotto and burned each year, because he had no one to sell them to.[13]

Alternation of Prayer and Work

As long as the hermit lived alone, he had no need to establish a timetable. He strove only to reduce the needs of the body to a minimum in order to dedicate as much time as possible to his soul and to God.[14] He could therefore go several days without eating or sleeping, constantly applying himself to prayer and work. However, man is not an angel and the greatest mystics are still human beings who not only need to refresh their bodily strength regularly, but also to invigorate from time to time their spiritual energy in order to overcome the boredom, which can arise, fatally, from the routine. This was the lesson given one day to Antony by an angel and recounted in an apothegm placed at the beginning of an alphabetical collection, no doubt because of its importance in any monastic life.

In his desert, Antony was disgusted and discouraged. He pleaded with God to show him what he must do

---

[8]HL 20, 1.
[9]A 128 (Ward, pp. 29-30).
[10]A 781 (Ward, p. 200); N 424.
[11]A 643, A 864 (Ward pp. 176, 224).
[12]Cassian, Inst. 10, 22.
[13]Isaiah 16, 95; Cassian, Inst. 10, 24.
[14]VA 45.

to be freed from his confusion. He then saw "someone like himself sitting down to work, then getting up to pray, sitting down again and plaiting cord, then getting up again to pray some more. It was an angel of the Lord sent to lead and reassure him. And he heard the angel declare, 'Do this and you will be saved.' Upon hearing this, Antony was overjoyed and filled with new courage."[15]

This formula from an angel, which Antony passed on to his disciples, would spread throughout the desert, so much so that any traveler or pilgrim venturing to surprise an anchorite in his cell at Scetis in the fourth century, had every chance of finding him sitting down to plait his cord or standing up to pray. It was the very stuff of his everyday life. If the practice isn't always mentioned in the apothegms, it is because it had become something of a rule. When it is said of a brother "that he never left his work and that his prayer rose continually to God," it is because he was a laudable exception, because this monk "was also very humble and very stable in his state."[16] One more exception: Bane never sat down but worked and ate standing up, so had no need to stand up to pray.[17]

Before his vision, Antony probably already plaited cord while praying. What the angel taught him was to interrupt his work from time to time and get up to pray. Modifying the bodily posture, tied to the change of routine, breaks the monotony of remaining in the cell and constantly forces the monk to stay physically and spiritually awake.

Work of the Monk in the Cell

It seems that basketry was taken up very early by the monks as the ideal solitary work in their cells. It was the work Pachomius had learned from his first master Palamon.[18] In the Scetis desert, they found near the marshes reeds and palm tree

---

[15]A 1 (Ward, pp. 1-2).
[16]N 415.
[17]Ch 248.
[18]Veilleux, p. 32.

branches.[19] They would harvest a supply, then pile them in the cells to dry. It was behind this kind of pile that one of Moses' disciples hid and escaped the massacre when barbarians made a foray into Scetis.[20] First, the palm tree leaves were removed from the branches and put to soak in water to soften them. They were then split with a knife and plaited into a long cord which was sold as is or fashioned into baskets and mats. They could also be made into straps for draught animals. When a new recruit reached the desert, an elder would teach him the techniques of the craft.[21] Each one plaited and sewed at his own speed and ability. In a single night, Achilles would make no fewer than twenty lengths of cord, or about eighty feet.[22] Paul the Simple, in a day of up to fifteen hours, used to make fifteen lengths but, to test him, Antony once made him undo what he had plaited and start over before eating.[23] During a visit by Macarius to Antony, each of them plaited all night long. Macarius' cord wound from the window right down to the grotto. Antony admired its length and said, "A great strength comes from those hands."[24]

When the cord was meant for a basket, they would calculate beforehand the length required to make the right size. The end of the plait was tied to the wall. One day, John Colobos, absorbed in contemplation, ended up making a single basket from what he had prepared for two, and only noticed when he reached the wall.[25] Megethius made three baskets a day, the value of his food.[26]

This basketry work was, in fact, carried out automatically and left the spirit free for prayer. It could even be done at night in the dark. Dorotheus, who spent the day gathering stones to build cells, spent the night plaiting cord.[27] When a monk who

---

[19] A 325, A 464, A 486 (Ward, pp. 87, 129, 134).
[20] A 504 (Ward, p. 140).
[21] A 288, A 486 (Ward, pp. 76, 134); HL 22.
[22] A 128 (Ward pp. 29-30).
[23] HL 22, 5.
[24] A 457 (Ward, p. 128).
[25] A 326 (Ward, p. 87).
[26] A 535 (Ward, p. 149).
[27] HL 2, 2.

was busy sewing dropped his needle, the Devil could intervene and create light, which happened to the presumptuous Valens.[28]

The making of mats from branches was a more tedious work. Hands were often scratched.[29] Macarius would take three days to make a mat.[30] Some anchorites also worked with flax, especially in Nitria,[31] but elsewhere too.[32] The raw material apparently varied with the seasons. An apothegm mentions an elder who "doesn't work for the time being; at the net season, he works with straw, and when we look after the nets, he works with flax, so that his spirit would not be troubled by the jobs."[33]

Another found that flax weaving was unsuitable for a monk because, by selling beautiful cloth, he risked being lured by gain: "If, in fact, they see someone coming with baskets, mats or sieves, they say, 'He's a monk,' but if they see someone selling fine linen, they say, 'Oh, here comes a merchant.' "[34] Literary criticism proves that monks weaving flax were not that rare and, while handling the spindle, they could have salutary thoughts. One said, "I drop the spindle and envision death before picking it up."[35] And another: "I spent a long time letting go of the spindle and wondered if I would live long enough to pick it up, awaiting death."[36] The words of Agathon were also quoted: "I don't allow a single bad thought to enter my heart while lifting my spindle from the hole."[37]

The making of fishing and hunting nets was also a monastic job. Achilles devoted himself to it but we also know that he made cord, at least at night.[38] Some monks worked with papyrus but this involved more delicate work.[39]

---

[28]HL 25, 2.
[29]N 375; Sy QRT 31.
[30]Am 221, 13.
[31]HL 7, 5.
[32]A 64, A 110 (Ward, pp. 13, 24).
[33]N 59.
[34]N 375.
[35]Sy 3, 52.
[36]N 58.
[37]Eth 13, 93.
[38]A 124, A 128 (Ward, pp. 28-30).
[39]N 614.

Another form of labor should be mentioned also: calligraphy. Evagrius was especially gifted in this field.[40] We know the names of two other copyists who lived at Scetis: Mark, Silvanus' disciple, and Paphnutius.[41] But the elder we heard criticizing flax weaving also warned the calligrapher monk, saying he "needed to humble his heart because he had a task which leads to pride."[42] Such was not the case with the hermit from Sinai who accepted orders for copies but who died without writing anything for anyone because he spent his time thinking about death and shedding tears.[43] At Scetis an elder copied out books but, since he had ecstasies now and then, he would "jump lines and omit the punctuation." To his client who pointed this out, he simply remarked, "Go, do first what's written; then come back and I'll copy the rest."[44]

Recitation of Divine Words

Whatever work one had to do in the desert, the essential object was not to become attached to it and to keep the spirit free for spiritual things. This is why one must not, Sisoes used to say, choose a work that pleases.[45] One could even find charm in weaving. Manual labor should be real work but it should never become the monk's main activity to the detriment of the essential one, the work of God.[46] This was a danger one must guard against, and it is with this in mind that a Father said, "The love of manual work is the ruination of the soul, but its peaceful practice is rest with God."[47] This is why the Desert Fathers insisted so much upon linking manual labor with recitation of words almost always taken from Holy Writ. It could be the same short verse repeated indefinitely or long passages, because most knew by heart a good part of the Bible. Daniel could recite 10,000 verses a

---

[40]HL 38, 10.
[41]A 526 (Ward, p. 145); Eth 13, 36.
[42]N 375.
[43]N 519.
[44]A 142 (Ward, p. 34).
[45]A 842 (Ward, p. 220).
[46]A 277-278, A 401 (Ward, pp. 75, 105).
[47]Bu II 333.

day.[48] While plaiting his cord, Lucius would recite, over and over again, the beginning of Psalm 50 (51): "Have mercy upon me, O God, according to thy loving kindness: according unto the multitude of thy tender mercies blot out my transgressions." [49]

Paul the Great was happy with the first words: "Have mercy upon me."[50] To Cassian, Isaac suggested especially a verse from Psalm 69 (70): "Make haste, O God, to deliver me; make haste to help me, O Lord."[51]

The work of copying did not prevent this recitation. Isidore of Nesarius, while copying, would frequently look upwards and say from his heart without moving his lips, "Jesus, have mercy on me; Jesus, help me; I bless you, my Lord."[52] Out of habit, when the anchorite was alone in his cell, he recited out loud and a visitor approaching the door might overhear his voice. For instance, Macarius heard a brother crying and saying, "Lord, if your ears don't hear me crying towards you, have mercy on me because of my sins, because for me, I never get tired of calling for your help."[53] Arsenius' disciples overheard their master crying towards God, "O God, don't abandon me. I have done nothing good in your presence, but in your kindness help me to start doing so."[54] Ammoes, coming to see Achilles, heard him repeating for a long time a verse from Genesis, "Fear not, Jacob, to go into Egypt."[55] When a monk had visitors, the rule then was to recite silently, as did Isidore, Zeno, Theodore of Pherme and Macarius' two young disciples.[56] Isaiah speaks of the monk in the cell "carrying out his liturgy towards God in silence."[57]

---

[48]Ch 250.
[49]A 446 (Ward, pp. 120-121).
[50]A 795 (Ward, p. 205).
[51]Cassian, Conf. 10, 10.
[52]Eth 13, 43.
[53]N 16.
[54]A 41 (Ward, p. 9).
[55]A 128 (Ward, p. 29).
[56]A 242, A 373, A 486 (Ward, pp. 67, 99-100, 134).
[57]Isaiah 26, 29.

Reading

During the anchorite's long day, was there a chance to read? Among the Pachomian cenobites, reading was reserved for specific periods, but no proof exists to affirm that it was the same with the hermits.

Many an apothegm gives a precise timetable for the day of a monk from the Cells. He would work all morning until noon. Afterwards, from noon until three p.m., he read and split palm leaves.[58] In the Armenian translation of this apothegm, the three midday hours are devoted exclusively to the reading of Holy Writ, but this isn't mentioned in the Syriac version.[59] Another fragment preserved in Latin enumerates the activities of John Colobos upon his return from the harvest; reading is mentioned, but this is missing in the Greek text[60] so one can assert that reading is never mentioned in any categorical manner as a regular and common anchorite occupation. As mentioned earlier, we know that, in general, the Desert Fathers had very few books in their cells. However, the apothegms sometimes talk of reading done in the cell. For instance, a brother was reading aloud from the Book of Genesis to a sick Agathon.[61] Amoun of Rhaithou read the Scriptures and Sisoes, the New Testament.[62] Tempted to leave his cell, a brother said to himself, "I'll read for awhile."[63] It was said that an elder's cell was miraculously lit up so that he could read as well at night as during the day.[64] The brother from the Cells who spent twenty years reading night and day finally sold all his books and vanished into the desert.[65]

All these testimonials allow us to suppose that the monks read in their cells, especially at Cellia, but it wasn't a universal and indispensable practice. Evagrius and Cassian felt they had to recommend reading, yet it is significant that these two learned

---

[58]Sy 20, 14.
[59]Bu II 526; Arm 19, 52; SP, New Collection, p. 273 (II 498).
[60]CSP I 2; A 350 (Ward, p. 92).
[61]A 104 (Ward, p. 23).
[62]A 820, A 838 (Ward, pp. 216, 219).
[63]N 195.
[64]N 425.
[65]N 541.

monks each emphasized its secondary and relative importance.[66] Nesteros exhorted Cassian to learn the Scriptures by heart but added that we learn less through reading than "by a painstaking experience."[67] Among the nine apothegms quoted by Evagrius at the end of his *Praktikos*, two show that we can very well do without books.[68] Apart from Serapion's story about selling his bible to feed the hungry, there's the question posed to Antony by a philosopher: "Father, how can you hold private the consolation of books?" Antony told him, "My book, oh philosopher, is nature, where I can read when I want the word of God." His biography shows us clearly that Antony was always very attentive to the reading of the Scriptures in church, "that he let nothing slip his mind and that his memory took the place of books."[69] The other desert anchorites could also keep in their hearts the biblical readings they heard during Saturday and Sunday liturgies. Thus they had for the entire week something to nourish and uphold their recitations and meditations of Holy Writ.

Prayer

Reciting Gospel verses while working was not always an explicit prayer, but the habit of doing so had to be anchored in the heart of the monk. St Epiphanius said "the true monk must always have psalmody and prayer in his heart,"[70] and Evagrius declared, "We were not given a prescription to constantly work, watch and fast, but for us it is a law to pray without ceasing."[71] Prayer became explicit and more fervent when the monk interrupted his work and stood up, often lifting his arms to heaven after having knelt and prostrated himself on the ground. The frequency of this prayer could vary depending on the individual and circumstances, in accord with each one's inspiration and the resolution to say a predetermined number of prayers each day.

---

[66]Evagrius, *Praktikos* 15; Cassian, Inst. SC 109, Index, p. 521.
[67]Cassian, Conf. 14, 13-17.
[68]Evagrius, *Praktikos* 96 and 97.
[69]VA 3.
[70]A 198 (Ward, p. 57).
[71]Evagrius, *Praktikos* 49.

For example, Moses used to say fifty, Evagrius 100,[72] Paul of
Pherme, 300. The latter was very upset to learn that a certain virgin said 700, but Macarius comforted him by telling him that, as
far as he was concerned, he'd stick to 100. But Paul, we know,
did not work and counted his prayers according to the number
of small pebbles he had collected and then threw away as he
prayed.[73] Apollo, who also didn't work and "devoted his time to
the worship of God in prayer, used to bend his knees a hundred
times a night and as many times a day."[74] For those engaged
in weaving, they could easily calculate the intervals between
prayers by how fast the work went. Referring to the customs of
Scetis, John of Gaza in the sixth century would advise an anchorite: "When you've done three rows of meshes on your net, get
up to pray. Having knelt down and also stood up, do your praying." This prayer could be the "Our Father" or any other formula
asking to be redeemed and delivered from the old person. "After
that, you sit down again for manual labor."[75]

Concerning an elder living in Rhaithou, the following practice is reported: "He would keep to his cell, grave and bent over
towards the ground, constantly shaking his head and saying
while moaning, 'What will happen to me?' Then keeping quiet
for about an hour. he worked on his cord...."[76] His groaning, a
form of prayer, would therefore take place every hour. Another
apothegm counsels to interrupt work and stand up "every hour
on the hour, to pay God this debt which is prayer."[77]

The Hours of the Office and Meals

We can ask ourselves whether this practice of praying
hourly day and night was the foundation for the morning and
evening "offices," made up of twelve psalms and as many silent
prayers. As Isidore said one day, "When I was young and stayed

---

[72]HL 19, 6; 38, 11.
[73]HL 20, 1-3.
[74]HM 8, 5.
[75]Barsanuphius and John, *Correspondence*, Letter 143, Solesmes, 1972.
[76]N 531.
[77]N 592/47.

in my cell, I had no way of keeping track of the divine offices; both night and day were for me times for the offices."[78] In fact, at the beginning, many Desert Fathers did not know of these morning and evening offices of twelve psalms, because they prayed continuously day and night. We don't know the origin of these offices which would later be called "Lauds" and "Vespers." According to Cassian, they go back to apostolic times and came from an angelic revelation.[79] Palladius said this revelation was made to Pachomius for his cenobites.[80] What is certain is that the custom of praying morning and evening existed for a long time in all of Christendom, but it was only in the fourth century that the double daily measure of twelve psalms became widespread. Among the anchorites, the morning office was recited during the second part of the night and the evening one at sunset. When two or three monks were together at the office hour, each took turns chanting parts of the twelve psalms while standing up, the other, or other two, being seated and joining in silent prayer.[81]

Fervent monks like Pambo ate only at day's end.[82] Paësius could declare that the sun had never seen him eat.[83] Such was the universal practice at Lent. Outside of Lent, most Desert Fathers took their meal at the ninth hour, that is, at about three p.m., but recited the twelve psalms at night, before going to sleep.[84] However, Palladius said that in Nitria, towards the ninth hour, the chanting of psalms was heard coming from each cell.[85] Were these psalms recited before eating, in addition to the twelve of the evening office? For the Pachomian monks, Palladius mentions an office of three psalms at the ninth hour.[86]

According to Abba Moses in Cassian, the ninth-hour meal has certain advantages, especially that of freeing the spirit

---

[78] A 360 (Ward, p. 97).
[79] Cassian, Inst. 2, 5-6.
[80] HL 32, 6.
[81] A 486 (Ward, p. 134); N 229.
[82] A 724 (Ward, p. 188).
[83] A 430 (Ward, pp. 113-114).
[84] A 799 (Ward, p. 209); N 229.
[85] HL 7, 5.
[86] HL 32, 6.

for prayers in the evening and at night.[87] It seems that for a long time the ninth-hour meal was, in the daily timetable, the observance most commonly practiced. In particular instances, a certain monk could have a reason to postpone his meal until evening. For a monk assailed by temptations, who normally ate at the ninth hour, Macarius advised him to wait until evening.[88] Antony who, according to the *Life* and the apothegms, took his meal at the ninth hour after having prayed standing up,[89] put his new disciple Paul to the test by having him wait until after the evening office.[90]

Both morning and evening prayer seem to have become the general rule by the end of the fourth century, but the time could still vary enormously because, as we pointed out, some had already begun their day while others, at the same hour, had not yet finished the previous one. The time spent sleeping could also vary greatly.

Nocturnal Occupations

In the Thebaid, Pachomius had learned from Palamon three ways to spend the night: "Either you pray from evening until midnight and then sleep until the worship hour; or else you sleep until midnight and then pray until morning; or, finally, you pray a little, then sleep a little, doing this from evening until morning."[91] The three ways were probably followed by the anchorites of Lower Egypt with, however, one difference. Antony and many others would often spend the whole night in prayer.[92] Elpidius in his Scetis grotto would thus recite the entire psalter every night.[93] Bessarion spent forty days on his feet without sleeping.[94] Moses, tormented by evil desires, spent, according to Palladius, six years in his cell, standing up praying all

---

[87]Cassian, Conf. 2, 26.
[88]A 456 (Ward, p. 127).
[89]VA 65; A 34 (Ward, p. 8).
[90]HL 22, 6.
[91]Veilleux, p. 77.
[92]VA 7; A 486 (Ward, p. 135).
[93]N 627 A.
[94]A 161 (Ward, p. 42).

night without closing an eye. So as not to be overcome by sleep, he would make the rounds of the elders' cells, quietly picking up their jugs and filling them with water.[95] Dorotheus, Palladius' master, had never voluntarily slept at a predetermined hour, but it happened sometimes that he was overcome by sleep while working or eating.[96] Sarmatas, for his part, often fasted for forty days nonstop and said he could sleep whenever he wanted.[97] Arsenius habitually spent all night praying and only slept a little in the morning.[98] He declared that "if he's a fighter, the monk can do with an hour's sleep."[99] This surely represents an uncommon performance. Chaeremon advised Cassian to be content with three or four hours.[100] The monk from the Cells for whom an apothegm gives a timetable slept for four hours.[101]

To sleep, the anchorite would usually lie on a mat or on the bare ground, but here again there were numerous and varied exceptions. In the early pioneer days, Pachomius and his brother John slept sitting down in the middle of their cell, without leaning their backs against the wall.[102] Several Scetiots, for example Bessarion and Macarius, never lay down to sleep.[103] Several would lean on bales of papyrus, the "embrimia" mentioned by Cassian. Macarius, who had to stop and spend a night in an old temple, used a mummy as a pillow.[104] Bane slept by leaning his chest against a low wall he had made just for that purpose.[105]

Dawn of a New Day

In the inconvenient postures in which they found themselves, the Desert Fathers must have found it easy to wake up to

---

95HL 19, 7-8.
96HL 2, 3.
97A 872 (Ward, pp. 225-226).
98A 52, A 68, A 81 (Ward, pp. 11, 14, 19).
99A 53 (Ward, p. 11).
100Cassian, Conf. 12, 15.
101Sy 20, 14.
102Veilleux, p. 40.
103A 163 (Ward, p. 42); Eth 14, 29.
104A 466 (Ward, p. 130).
105Ch 248.

pray. Isaiah said frankly, "When the Lord wakes you up, do your office with zeal."[106] The Lord could call upon the guardian angel always beside the sleeper, "When your heart tells you day and night, 'Up and pray!' realize that this is the angel right beside you speaking. And so, when you arise, he stays beside you and prays with you."[107] But sometimes the demons, in the guise of angels, also came to awaken a monk for prayer.[108] The plan could be to exhaust him through repeated bouts of sleeplessness.[109] But they didn't always succeed and the praying monk could take his revenge on them. One demon didn't want to take the risk because, as he told another, "Once after I woke him up, he burned me with his psalms and prayers."[110] For lack of an alarm clock, it happened that a monk stayed sound asleep until daybreak. He then had to close the windows and door to recite his office.[111] For anyone finding it hard to get up, a few dietary restrictions are recommended.[112]

Regardless of the hour one awakens, the first thing to do is glorify God and chant because "the first preoccupation to which the spirit becomes attached as soon as day breaks will continue to grind it like a millstone all day, whether it be wheat or rye grass. So always be the first to throw in some wheat before your enemy throws in the rye grass."[113] Another elder gave this advice: "Up and at it early; tell yourself, 'Body, work to feed yourself; soul, be vigilant to receive the heritage.' "[114]

But even before they had learned the office of twelve psalms, the anchorites already had to be used to chanting after as well as before sleeping, as Antony advised his visitors.[115] But they could also pray in other ways, and more freely. What counted was to stir up the soul's fervor right away so that the

---

[106]Isaiah 4, 45.
[107]N 592/45.
[108]N 224.
[109]Cassian, Conf. 10, 10.
[110]N 36.
[111]N 230.
[112]N 592/18.
[113]N 592/43.
[114]N 269.
[115]VA 55.

entire day would go well. Isaiah said, "Each day, when getting up in the morning, recite the word of God; remember that you will render to God an account of all your acts and you mustn't sin against him."[116] St Antony also advised, "Each day, when we arise, let's assume we won't live until nightfall, and at night, when going to sleep, let's assume we won't awaken."[117] The Fathers especially took to heart the maintenance of their élan, or spirit, by the thought that each day they were only starting out. At the beginning of a whole list of practices and virtues to be observed, John Colobos said, "Each day, when you get up at dawn, make sure you start out with all the virtues and commandments of God...."[118] Poemen liked to recall Abba Pior who "each day made a new beginning."[119] Silvanus even declared to Abba Moses that one can not only start over each day, but at every hour."[120] But this no longer concerns exterior activities which succeed each other in the anchorite's day, it deals with the much more important work carried out continuously in secret, visible only to God and his angels.

---

[116]Isaiah 3, 42; 16, 34.
[117]VA 19.
[118]A 349 (Ward, p. 92).
[119]A 659 (Ward, p. 179).
[120]A 866 (Ward, p. 224).

NINE

❧✝❧

The Hidden Activity

The Anchorite's Inner Life

The entire day—and night—of the anchorite was spent working and praying, with a rigid minimum of time set aside for eating and sleeping. But this is only the tip of the iceberg, not the principal part. Even what the elders called "meditation" was not today's mental prayer but formed a part, along with vocal prayer, of corporal practices, since it consisted of repeating, more or less out loud, the words of Holy Scripture. The desert monk's essential activity was invisible and inaudible, being carried out within his being, and was what the Fathers called inner activity or "the hidden activity," embracing all of the thoughts, desires, wishes, sentiments and inner words which lodge in the spirit and the heart, what we mean by "the inner life."

The Desert Fathers have often been depicted as beings who regressed to the wild state, the condition of an animal or plant, carrying out like robots their monotonous work and reciting their continuous invocations like prayer mills. It isn't absolutely impossible for there to have been a few old men "vegetating" like this for long years, but most probably these didn't wait too long to return to the world. If the Fathers were able to colonize the desert and make it so fertile, it wasn't done simply by weaving baskets while reciting verses of psalms or other words of Holy Scripture; it is that at the same time, they had a depth and intensity of spiritual life we find hard to imagine. What we can grasp and say about it has little to do with the reality, since the Egyptian anchorites were always very concerned about not allowing anything to be seen which could draw the slightest praise and fame. They said that Poemen had the habit of doing everything in secret,[1] but this was everyday practice in the desert. The Fathers hid from others as much as they could of their corporal and visible observances. So there was even more reason to do what they could to hide their secret life! Happily they weren't entirely successful, they opened up in their words — or their silences — and, thanks to the apothegms handed down to us, we can know something about it.[2]

This inner life was not an intellectual one, the effort of a thinker or philosopher to reflect, nor even of a theologian. Nevertheless the privileged conditions of solitude and silence enjoyed by the anchorites in the desert greatly favored the attention, reflection and activity of the spirit, so much so that even on a purely human level, the thinking of the Desert Fathers could refine and enrich itself in an exceptional manner. They have often been considered fierce adversaries of intelligence and intellectual work. Certainly they were not the ones who developed theological science — this was not their vocation — but they nevertheless played a key role in the history of Christian spirituality and of spirituality in general. Their apothegms testify to a deep wisdom and a remarkable psychology. As Henri Brémond rightly noted, this is why they had "the most extensive, the most profound and the most durable influence on the morals of the Christian people, on civilization itself."[3] Did not the forerunners of our modern psychologists and psychoanalysts promote, even further than their predecessors had, the exploration of "self,"[4] of all this inner world where the strictly human activity is carried out and where the true destiny of the person is fulfilled?

[1] A 712 (Ward, p. 186).
[2] I. Hausherr, *The Name of Jesus*, Kalamazoo, MI, pp. 169-171.
[3] H. Brémond, *Les Pères du desert*, Paris, 1927, p. xx.
[4] I. Hausherr, *Spiritual Direction*, pp. 87ff.

A Single and Many-Sided Undertaking

As one of the Fathers said, "Man must necessarily have an activity within himself."[5] The monk coming to the desert to be completely united with God will try to dedicate to the Lord not only his exterior acts but all his inner activity. Arsenius said, "With all your might, strive to put your inner activity in tune with God...or concerning God,"[6] meaning not only to conform with divine will, but to be turned towards God, given to God. In other words, the monk must constantly attend to God's work. "The bee, wherever it goes, makes honey; the monk, wherever he finds himself, carries out God's work."[7] This is "the spiritual undertaking for which he came to the desert"[8] or "the work of the soul."[9] Such is the essential undertaking of the monk and even, one might say, his unique work, "the work of the monk."[10] Not that it be specifically the monk's—Antony spoke of "man's great activity,"[11] that of everyone—but the monk makes of this work his whole life.

The apothegms about this inner activity are very numerous, and also extremely varied in the sense that the descriptions or definitions given differ somewhat one from the other. This activity is at once a singular and many-sided one. John Colobos said, "The saints are like a garden where the trees have different fruits, even if sprinkled by the same water. In fact, one is the work of such-and-such a saint, another that of such-and-such other person, but it is the same Spirit working in all of them."[12] Another elder declared, "The heart of the palm tree is but one, it is white and encompasses the whole activity of the palm tree. This is akin to what we find among the just: their heart is unique and simple, looking only towards God."[13] But each of the Fathers

---

[5]N 241.
[6]A 47 (Ward, p. 10).
[7]N 399.
[8]N 240.
[9]A 277-278 (Ward, p. 75).
[10]A 243 (Ward, p. 67).
[11]A 4 (Ward, p. 2).
[12]A 958 (Ward, p. 95).
[13]N 362.

had his own way of viewing this activity, bringing out such-and-such an element according to his own dispositions and those of the person he was addressing. We will therefore try to gather together and synthesize all these elements a little so as to get an accurate portrait, and one that is as complete as possible, of the Desert Fathers' inner life.

Remembrance of Sins Committed

In this complicated set of thoughts, images and sentiments, there are first of all memories of the past, especially the remembrance of sins committed. At least this is what appears to hold, almost exclusively, the attention of the desert anchorite. This takes up so much space in the texts that one would be led to think that the monks had all been out-and-out crooks obsessed by this heavy liability. In reality, as has been seen, apart from a few real brigands, the majority of the anchorites were honest and honorable folk. But their unremitting contact with God in solitude had made their consciences so pure and delicate that they blamed themselves for the slightest faults of human frailty. As Matoes put it so well, "The more man gets closer to God, the more he sees himself a sinner."[14]

It is with this perspective that we must read all the texts where it is said that the monk must cry over his sins and/or where it is seen that the Fathers practiced what they taught others: "Remain in your cell and cry over your sins."[15] The order is often given by Macarius and Poemen. Arsenius, especially, cried all the time and, while doing his manual work, had to always keep a cloth on his chest to wipe away the tears.[16] Poemen said, "He who would make amends for his sins must do so by his tears. In effect, crying is the way given to us by Scripture and the Fathers when they said, 'Cry,' because there's no other way."[17]

---

[14]A 514 (Ward, p. 143).
[15]A 455, A 480, A 495 (Ward, pp. 126, 133, 138); Sy 115, 52; Ch 107.
[16]A 79 (Ward, p. 18).
[17]A 693, A 696 (Ward, pp. 184, 185).

The Fathers also knew that the important thing was not the visible demonstration, which is not always possible nor desirable, but the mood of the heart for which tears are but the outward expression of what they call mourning, this grief one feels constantly when one has lost a loved one. Each one has his own death to weep over.[18] And it seems that, for these monks, bereavement never ends and lasts until death.

However, all of them did not hold the same views. For example, St Antony's spirituality on this point appears to be quite different from that of Macarius and Poemen. In the desert as elsewhere, there could be many ways of repenting. The story is told of two brothers who had each quit the desert to take a wife. They repented and the Fathers gave them both the same penance: one year in seclusion with nothing to eat but bread and water. At year's end, one was pale and glum, the other, in great health and happy. This was because the first one had spent his year in fear, thinking of his faults and the punishment incurred, while the other had done nothing but thank God for having extracted him from his impurity, and he was filled with joy thinking about God.[19]

Custody of the Heart

Yet what counts more than regret for past faults is the care one now takes to avoid them. This explains why the anchorites assiduously practiced what they called "custody of the heart," meaning the surveillance and discernment of all thoughts that spring to mind. Antony pointed out that the monk who withdraws to the desert is freed from three battles: "that of hearing, that of the lips and that of sight. He has only one left, that of the heart."[20] In giving up the world he has freed himself from every-

[18]A 512 VII, A 580 (Ward, pp. 142, 165).

[19]N 186.

[20]A 11 (Ward, p. 3), reading *kardias* and not *porneias*: such is the exact meaning of Antony's words according to the majority of Greek manuscripts and of ancient Latin and Syriac versions. Aline Rousselle (*Porneia*, pp. 185-186) chose (for the sake of her argument) to adopt a translation by J.C. Guy, done hurriedly and based upon a faulty text by Cotelier reprinted in Migne's *Patrology*. She was no doubt unaware of what I. Hausherr wrote on this subject in 1956: "What

thing which, from the outside, could lead him into sin. All he has to do now is keep himself from the dangers within. And this is an important part of his hidden activity.

The Desert Fathers didn't completely ignore the examination of conscience at particular times, morning and evening,[21] and on certain occasions—for example, before leaving or re-entering the cell.[22] But they speak much more often of the continual vigilance to which they subjected themselves in the cell and everywhere. The anchorite lives constantly on his guard, "attentive to himself,"[23] to quote an expression dear to the Stoics, but which takes on a much different meaning among Christians than among pagan moralists.[24] In effect, the monk watches himself so as not to displease God by trying always to "keep the Lord before his eyes."[25] This is the basic disposition of "fearing God" in the biblical sense, which doesn't exclude love but expresses above all the conviction of living always under the gaze of the Lord. With humility, his inseparable companion, the fear of the Lord is, for Poemen, as necessary to the monk as air entering and leaving through the nostrils.[26] The same Poemen also said that it is both the principle and the end,[27] the beginning and the completion of the monk's every work.

Thus anchored in the Lord, the anchorite watches over the thoughts which inevitably come to the door of his heart. As Isidore put it, "If we did not have thoughts, we would be like wild animals."[28] And Moses told Cassian, "It's impossible for the spirit to avoid being pierced by multiple thoughts, but we are

---

should we think henceforth of these 'critical minds' who jump on this *porneias* to insinuate that the desert monks were subject to an exaggerated libido?" (*Orientalia Christiana Periodica* XII, 1956, p. 34.)

[21]VA 55, A 560 (Ward, p. 155).

[22]A 340, A 350, A 606 (Ward, pp. 91, 92, 172).

[23]A 2 (Ward, p. 2).

[24]I Hausherr, "L'Hésychasme," *Orientalia Christiana Periodica*, XXII, 1956, pp. 273-285.

[25]A 3 (Ward, p. 2).

[26]A 623 (Ward, p. 173).

[27]N 647.

[28]VP VI 4, 21 in SP, New Collection, p. 206.

free to welcome or reject them."[29] To a brother who complained of being assailed by thoughts, Poemen gave a concrete lesson.

> He dragged him out of his cell into the full wind — and God knows how the wind can sometimes blow in the desert! — and told him, "Fill your chest and hold the winds there."
>
> "Impossible," replied the brother.
>
> "Well, then," said the elder, "if you can't do that, neither can you prevent thoughts from entering, but you must resist them."[30]

"The work of the monk," said another elder, "is to see thoughts coming from afar."[31] To every thought that arises one must ask, "Are you of us or of the enemy?" and it will surely admit it.[32] Normally, with the fear of God and vigilance, the monk obtained the charism of discernment,[33] but this was more often only after a long apprenticeship in the school of an elder to whom he submitted all his thoughts.

Rejection of Bad Thoughts

As soon as a thought is recognized as bad or vain, it must be rejected right away without coming to terms with it. Otherwise it will settle in and soon become impossible to dislodge.[34] Bad thoughts are like mice who penetrate a house; if we kill them one by one as soon as they enter, we don't have any trouble. But if we let them multiply, we'll have lots of trouble exterminating them.[35] Yet a single thought, of lust, for instance, could torment an anchorite for a long time, up to nine years or more.[36] Ordinarily different thoughts would succeed each other and one had always to be careful not to allow an intrusive one in. A momen-

---

[29]Cassian, Conf. 1, 17.
[30]A 602 (Ward, p. 171).
[31]N 64 in SP, New Collection, p. 214.
[32]N 99.
[33]Eth 13, 7; 13, 18.
[34]N 169.
[35]N 535.
[36]N 210.

tary error could prove fatal. Some elders, including Evagrius and Cassian, advised their experienced disciples to allow the thoughts in so as to fight them more energetically, in a hand-to-hand fight, and thus make more progress.[37] This is what Abba Joseph told Poemen one day. But to other less-hardened monks, the same Joseph said to repel the thoughts as soon as they arrive.[38]

It is said of a brother from Rhaithou that he was so vigilant that, when walking about, he'd stop at each step and question himself: "What gives, brother? Where are we?" And when he found his spirit busy chanting psalms and praying, he would say, "That's good, that's great." But if he found himself thinking of anything, right away he would take charge and say, "Come back from there, you scatterbrain, and do your work!"[39]

In the eyes of the desert monks, all these strategies were good to train and stimulate oneself for the ceaseless battle. One monk found an ingenuous method. He worked with a small pile of pebbles in front of him and two baskets, one on his left side, the other on the right. Each time he had a good thought, he would toss a stone in the right-hand basket; if it was bad, he would toss one into the left-hand basket. When evening came, he would count his stones and, if there were more in the left-hand basket than the right-hand one, he wouldn't eat that day. And the next morning, if he still had a bad thought, he'd tell himself, "Be careful what you do, because you won't eat again today."[40] It doesn't appear that such a practice had become widespread and we are inclined to find it somewhat naive. However, it does show the especially delicate care that an anchorite had for keeping his heart pure.

St Antony advised his disciples to write down the actions and movements of the soul so as to understand both and "Be sure," he would say, "that for the shame of being found out, we will stop sinning and harboring any evil thought in the heart."[41]

---

[37]Cassian, Conf. 19, 14.
[38]A 386 (Ward, p. 102).
[39]N 529.
[40]N 408.
[41]VA 55.

The brother with the pebbles probably could neither read nor write and so used his own unique method. The meticulousness of the procedure used shows how much importance the Desert Fathers placed on the complete and deep purification of their hearts for the Lord. All did not have the same strength of soul and felt obliged to use somewhat bizarre stratagems.

Sometimes they give the impression of spending all their energy fighting bad thoughts, but in reality they spent as much time entertaining good ones. The thing is, we know more about their bad thoughts because these were the ones they would speak about more freely. Of the others, they were much more discreet. Thus Poemen: "As long as the pot is on the fire, a fly can't land on it. And likewise, if the monk perseveres in his spiritual practices, the Enemy, the Devil, has no hold on him."[42] According to another comparison put to Cassian by Moses, the soul is like a millstone, forever turning. One must always supply it with wheat to grind; otherwise, it'll start grinding rye grass.[43]

This is precisely why the continual recitation of Holy Scripture is prescribed and takes up, as we noted, the anchorite's entire day. It keeps alive in his heart the thought of God, the "remembrance of God," as the Fathers often put it.

Recourse to God

Prayer, which we have seen had an important place in the lives of the Desert Fathers, was for them the mightiest weapon of spiritual warfare because they were conscious of the need they had of God's assistance in this battle against evil. Contrary to pagan ascetics, they counted most of all on divine grace.[44] At the same time, prayer was the shield that protected them and the spear used to attack the Enemy. The verse of the psalm suggested to Cassian by Moses ("Come, O God, to my aid; make haste to help me, O Lord") suits especially the monk struggling with his thoughts.[45] To repel the assault, another elder tells his

---

[42]A 685 (Ward, p. 183).
[43]Cassian, Conf. 1, 18.
[44]A 512 (Ward, p. 143); N 342.
[45]Cassian, Conf. 10, 10.

disciple, "Get up and pray saying: 'Son of God, help me.' "[46] And still another, "Get up, pray and bow low while saying: 'Son of God, have mercy on me.' "[47] All these invocations must surely have been said out loud, but prayer could still be implicit and secret, such as the words of the publican in the Gospel which Ammonas suggested should be kept in the heart always: "O God, be favorable to me, a sinner."[48] The cry for help could also be just a simple glance towards heaven. Macarius declared that it wasn't necessary to say a lot, "He only has to extend his hands and say: 'Lord, according to your will and wisdom, have mercy,' and in battle: 'Lord, help!' He knows what is useful and will grant us mercy."[49] He also told a brother, "If a thought comes to you, never look down, but always upwards, and immediately the Lord will come to your rescue."[50]

One expression recurs several times to show the best thing to do to achieve victory: "To cast out one's helplessness" or "to cast oneself before God."[51] Poemen uses it willingly. "In the struggle against thoughts," he says, "it is like a man with a fire on his left and a pitcher of water on his right. If the fire burns too fiercely, he takes some water and puts it out. The fire is the Enemy's seed and water is casting oneself into the presence of God."[52] Abba Isaiah also frequently repeated the same expression, and for him it is the main work of the monk in his cell: "To cast himself into the presence of God and do all he can to resist any thought seeded there by the Enemy."[53]

The expression designates especially an attitude of soul but is often accompanied by a bodily gesture: the monk prostrates himself completely on the ground to mark at the same time his humility, his worthlessness and his powerlessness before God, but also his confidence and total submission.

---

[46]N 167.
[47]N 184.
[48]A 116 (Ward, p. 26).
[49]A 472 (Ward, p. 131).
[50]A 456 (Ward, pp. 126-127).
[51]A 103, A 610 (Ward, pp. 23, 172).
[52]A 720 (Ward, p. 187).
[53]Sy 2, 15, Sy 15, 25; Isaiah, Intro. pp. 29-30.

Blaming Oneself in All Circumstances

In all the different confidences and recommendations of the elders, we always find the same disposition to humility which can be described by different negative or positive expressions. The most commonly used are "not to esteem oneself" and "to blame oneself,"[54] the two being linked and correlative. "Not to esteem oneself," meaning not to justify oneself, not to believe oneself just. "To blame oneself," on the other hand, is to judge oneself to be responsible and guilty. When Poemen, describing life in the cell, comes to that which cannot be seen, he puts at the top of the list "to carry everywhere the blame of self."[55] This assumes the monk is anchored in this essential disposition which puts him at peace with God, with himself as much as with others. In this, there is no guilt-complex since the *me* being blamed and accused is in no way the authentic me, the deep me, but the apparent me. It is this latter which prevents the monk from placing himself in truth before God. Insofar as he effaces himself, the real me is in its place facing the Lord, and this explains why Poemen can say, "When the soul blames itself before Him, the Lord loves him." Real justice is "to accuse oneself constantly."[56]

One day the Archbishop of Alexandria, Theophilus, on a trip to Nitria, asked an elder what he found best in the lifestyle of the desert monks. The elder replied, "To never stop accusing and blaming oneself."[57] Every Christian must see himself as a sinner before God, yet he can often forget it, while the anchorite in the solitude of his cell is, as it were, forced to remember this always. And, again, as Poemen put it, this is the secret progress in the cell,[58] simultaneously the condition and mark of progress.

---

[54] A 165, A 708 (Ward, pp. 42, 186).
[55] A 742 (Ward, p. 190).
[56] A 645, A 672 (Ward, pp. 177, 181).
[57] A 304 (Ward, p. 80).
[58] A 742 (Ward, p. 190).

A Laborious Rest

Another elder declared that "the monk who blames himself in all circumstances finds rest by the grace of God."[59] Rest is a word often used in the apothegms but it has different meanings. There is rest of the body, physical well-being, always detestable in the eyes of the Desert Fathers.[60] There is also spiritual rest, the peace of soul, which doesn't necessarily exclude combat. Following Antony, Poemen affirmed that temptation is required for salvation and that one must expect it until the final breath.[61] We see several monks who, having wished for and obtained a cease-fire in the battles, later asked for them back,[62] among them John Colobos who understood better than anyone the benefit of the struggle and who defined the monk by the word "toil." For him, it was enough that the Lord gave him patience and endurance.[63] Sometimes God, taking our weakness into account, removes temptation, but we must then become even more humble and remain on guard.[64] This apparent peace could be nothing more than a temporary truce. Even after being completely freed from certain temptations — greed and lust, say — the monk can still be attacked on other fronts and by even more subtle suggestions, especially pride. To a brother abandoned by the demon of lust, a thought arose: "You cry well, don't you?"[65]

There are more troublesome temptations, spoken of very seldom by the Fathers: these are what they call the temptations of blasphemy, that is, very strong doubts concerning faith and hope. After having hesitated and shilly-shallied for a long time, a brother admitted to Poemen his horrible thought: "Father, I'm in danger of losing myself through the action of the spirit of blasphemy, because it almost tries to convince me that God does not exist, which the pagans neither do nor think."[66] About these

---

[59]N 416.
[60]A 612 (Ward, p. 172).
[61]A 4-6, A 699 (Ward, pp. 2, 185).
[62]N 170, N 584.
[63]A 328, A 352 (Ward, pp. 87-88, 93).
[64]A 164 (Ward, p. 42).
[65]N 582.
[66]A 667 (Ward, p. 180); Sy 10, 63.

kinds of temptations, we learn much more from Evagrius who, according to Palladius, had dealt with them himself[67] and who pinpoints it in his *Antirrheticos*, concerning the spirit of greed:

> From the heart of the soul blasphemous thoughts continually spring forth: God doesn't exist, at least, He pays no attention to me. His grace counted for nothing in the victory I had over the other demons. The angels? What good are they? The Fathers! What more have they done than me? The commandments? Even the very knowledge of Christ? Fiddlesticks! How can I believe God is in me? Sin? But free will is a joke and judgment, an injustice. We speak of the goodness of God and I want to laugh. And there's worse yet. I want to shout to God the worst things, unimaginable blasphemies that I couldn't write down, for fear of making heaven and earth shake. Because it is a hot-tempered demon who does not pull back from the worst contempt for God and His holy angels. Those who've been tempted by him know what I mean.[68]

Irénée Hausherr, who thus summarizes Evagrius' notations, adds that they would be enough to convince us that the Fathers had gone through the same spiritual trials which more recent saints, such as John of the Cross, have described and analyzed at length. Thérèse of Lisieux, when confiding to Mother Agnes the hideous thoughts of doubt which obsessed her, held back, like Evagrius, and didn't want to say more for fear of blaspheming.[69]

It would be as false to portray the Egyptian anchorites continuously enjoying intimacy with God as to paint them being ceaselessly tortured by doubt, discouragement, indeed despair. After spending 69 years in the desert, Theodore of Pherme admitted he had never found there a single day's rest.[70] But another

---

[67]HL 38, 11.

[68]I. Hausherr, "Les Orientaux connaissent-ils les Nuits de saint Jean de la Croix?" *Orientalia Christiana Periodica* XII, 1956, p. 28.

[69]Saint Thérèse of Lisieux, *Story of a Soul*, trans. by John Clarke, OCD, Washington, 1976, p. 213.

[70]A 269 (Ward, p. 74).

elder declared, "Even if the saints had a hard time down here, they had already been given a bit of peace and quiet."[71] In the desert, more than anywhere else, the friends of God encountered the greatest sorrows and the greatest joys. We will see how the wonders performed through them by the Lord proves how he favors those who abandon everything for his love.

---

[71]N 235.

TEN

※✝※

Elders and Disciples

"If man does not say in his heart, 'I alone and God are in this world,' he will have no peace."[1] This maxim from Abba Alonius is really the key which opens to us the universe of the Desert Fathers. It explains their withdrawal from the world, their total renunciation, their love of solitude and silence, their life in the cell, their secret preoccupations. Their whole existence was, as it were, polarized by this unique objective: to disappear from the eyes of the world, to live simply and constantly under the gaze of God alone.

Most of them undoubtedly carried out this objective, yet not always in the fashion they had foreseen. In fact, the documents which tell us about them show them much more in relationships with one another than exclusively with God. Among these reports are privileged ones to which we've often alluded but which deserve a special chapter of their own; these concern relations between elders and disciples.

The First "Elders"

Among the first monks who set out for the desert, a few were able to accomplish what they had hoped to do: to live and die alone, unknown by all the others. They were certainly the exceptions. Those we know became famous because their influence attracted to their sides many courageous and generous men who wanted to live like them and follow their example.

---

[1] A 144 (Ward, p. 35).

Thus came into being the monastic agglomerations of Nitria, the Cells and Scetis, and very soon one could distinguish, among the monks living there, the elders and the disciples. The former were called "Old Man," "Father" or "Abba" while the others were "the young ones," "the brothers" or "the beginners." As the earth became peopled little by little through the propagation of life from generation to generation, so the desert came to be filled with inhabitants through a process of spiritual generation which was truly remarkable and original.

The monks who live in a community, the cenobites, gather around a father who founded the community—for example, Pachomius in Upper Egypt—who exercises upon all the members a sovereign authority. At the death of the founder, another superior, appointed by him or the community, succeeds him.

In the anchorite or semi-anchoritic areas, there is no hierarchical superiority, only the spiritual and moral authority of the "elders" upon the others, an authority freely exercised and freely accepted. Those who will receive priestly ordination are chosen due to the holiness of their lives and if they enjoy special prerogatives, it is more as elders than as priests.

Necessity of Consulting Elders

In keeping with a law common to all professions, beginners are trained in a school by those who already know the trade and have practiced it for a certain time. This is how Antony did his apprenticeship in asceticism in his village, near those who had practiced it before him.[2] His biography even mentions "his elder," whom he consulted before departing for the desert.[3] Afterwards, in the total solitude he found there, Antony had no one he could consult for his initiation into such a new life. It was necessary for God to take charge of training him either through His Spirit or an angel. It is in this sense that Athanasius called him "self-taught" or *theodidacte*.[4] But as soon as this "column of

---

[2]VA 4.
[3]VA 11.
[4]VA 66.

light," as Hilarion called him,[5] loomed in the desert, he became a beacon towards which were turned the eyes of all the monks who wanted to follow in his steps. It is significant that the most well-known of the early anchorites thought it advisable to consult Antony: Macarius and Amoun in particular.[6] Saint Jerome himself pays tribute to this exceptional "seniority" through his heroes Paul and Hilarion. Antony would become known and honored as the Father and Patriarch of all Christian anchorites.

Antony's situation is unique among the Desert Fathers. All the others were, in some way, disciples before becoming masters. The apothegms make this clear for several elders: Poemen, John Colobos, Theodore of Pherme, Moses and Longinus.[7]

In the desert, the need to consult an "elder" isn't motivated simply by natural wisdom which leads the beginners to profit from the experience of the elders. The monastic profession is not a trade like others, but a situation which grasps and possesses all of life. For twenty-four hours out of twenty-four, the anchorite must, in body and soul, live the Gospel completely, that is, he must, with all his strength, renounce evil, drive back the evil spirits and the thoughts they suggest, give up himself, all his goods and earthly pleasures to dedicate himself fully to the search for God in the steps of Christ. Whether dealing with asceticism or a spiritual struggle, prayer and all the corporal and spiritual practices, he needs to be advised, helped and encouraged. In the early days, newcomers to the desert could settle into a grotto or cell without getting any training from an elder. But the results were sometimes disastrous, as Antony himself pointed out: "I saw some who had crushed their bodies through asceticism and who, for lack of discernment, ended up far from God." And again: "I saw some monks who, after much labor, fell and even went insane for, having been deceived by their own works, they impugned God's commandment which says: 'Question your father and he will teach you.' "[8]

---

[5]A 425 (Ward, p. 111).
[6]A 34, 135, 457, 479 (Ward, pp. 8, 31, 128, 133).
[7]A 268, 316-317, 449, 495, 575 (Ward, pp. 73, 85-86, 122, 138, 164).
[8]A 8, A 37 (Ward, pp. 3, 8-9).

Later, when anchoritic life was organized in the great centers of Nitria, Cells and Scetis, the elders watched carefully to make sure such calamities did not happen. A story tells of a brother who put on the habit and immediately shut himself up in a cell declaring, "I am an anchorite." The elders made him go out and do the rounds of the brothers' cells, prostrating himself and saying, "Forgive me for I am not an anchorite but a beginner."[9] During this period, the novice could confide in someone through the elders. Arsenius, upon reaching Scetis, was handed over to John Colobos, who treated him somewhat harshly. John had been trained the same way by Ammoes.[10] Palladius says he himself was entrusted to Dorotheus by Isidore.[11]

Reception of a Disciple by an Elder

Most candidates for the eremitic life were well aware of this need to be initiated and trained for a life so different from the world's normal one. This is why they sought out an elder who would take charge of their apprenticeship. In the early days, it could not have been easy to find a master. We've seen the anchorite alone in his cell or grotto, praying or working, living his life under divine inspiration in a very simple setting. He asks only to persevere in this solitude without distraction or diversion. It is easy to understand that the arrival of an intruder would not be welcome. But in fact what most newcomers asked was to live with an elder. A brother went to find Helle to ask the favor of living with him.[12] Another showed up at Agathon's cell to beg: "Let me live with you."[13] Even when the request is couched in more general terms—"I want to become a monk" or "Turn me into a monk,"[14] as Paul the Simple told Antony, or Pachomius said to Palamon—it implicitly asks to live with the elder. The two little strangers who came to Macarius asked him, "Where is

[9]N 243.
[10]Regnault, pp. 39 and 42.
[11]HL 2, 1.
[12]HM 12, 12.
[13]A 94 (Ward, p. 22).
[14]HL 22, 3.

Abba Macarius' cell? Having heard talk of him and of Scetis, we've come to see him." After he told them, "It is I," they bluntly declare, "This is where we want to live." The inference being: "next to you."[15]

In most instances, the elder begins by deterring the new-comer and trying to discourage him by pointing out the difficulties of desert life. "You are too old," Antony told Paul, "you cannot endure the trials of the desert."[16] No anchorite worthy of the name would immediately accept a disciple. This would have compromised his vocation as a recluse and his humble and hidden life. But even his resistance was proof that he deserved to become a master in turn. And after having thoroughly tested the postulant's firmness and courage, he could agree to take on the burden sent to him by God. And, for that matter, he did it only while striving to safeguard the essential requirements of his vocation of solitude and silence, of renunciation and abnegation of his own will.

Intermittent Relationships

The elder and the disciple usually lived apart. So Helle, who lived in a grotto, settled his young disciple in another grotto.[17] Sometimes the elder gave the newcomer the monastic habit,[18] then contented himself with showing him how to build a cell and obtain food. If he agreed to take him in, it was most often for only a few days or a few months, after which they lived apart in the neighborhood. Antony only kept Paul the Simple with him for a few months. Macarius showed the two young strangers where and how to build a cell and make baskets. After that, he didn't see them again for three years.[19]

Interviews between elders and disciples could be more or less spread out according to the wishes and needs of the subjects. Three brothers used to visit Antony once a year to question him

[15]A 486 (Ward, p. 134).
[16]HL 22, 3.
[17]HM 12, 12.
[18]Bu II 385.
[19]A 486 (Ward, pp. 134-135).

about his thoughts.[20] For his part, Paphnutius called on Anoub
and Poemen twice a month.[21] When beset by temptations, a new
monk could go see his elder several times a day or at night.
There was no rule. We've seen how sometimes the wish to go see
an elder could be a demon's temptation, but in general the most
frequent temptation was, on the contrary, not to go, due to a feeling of independence or embarrassment at having to admit faults
or humiliating thoughts. Little by little there developed a law
requiring them to tell the elders not only their sins and temptations but even apparently indifferent actions. Already Antony
was saying, "If possible, the monk must confide in the elders
about all the steps he takes and all the drops of water he drinks
in his cell, to see if he isn't sinning by this."[22] Poemen would
say, "In everything you do, seek advice, because acting without
advice is folly."[23] "Even a man like Adam in the garden still
needs to ask for advice,"[24] said Abba Abraham.

If we have so many apothegms from the Fathers, it is precisely because many monks consulted their elders. Before asking
for anything else, what the disciple sought from the elder was his
prayer. The prayer of an elder accompanied the disciple everywhere and protected him from all danger.

A Community of Life

Even after lodging the disciple in his cell and letting him
live there, the elder did not stop observing silence. And most of
the time, he did not want to give orders. Such was the case with
Cronius, Theodore of Pherme, Sisoes and many others. "Do what
you see," Sisoes would say.[25] And Abba Or: "What you see me
do, do likewise."[26] Isaac tells of living successfully with Cronius,
then with Theodore, and that neither one gave him orders. To a
remark by the elders on this subject, Theodore replied, "Am I

---

[20]A 27 (Ward, p. 7).
[21]A 788 (Ward, pp. 202-203).
[22]A 38 (Ward, p. 9).
[23]Eth 350.
[24]Ch 246.
[25]A 848 (Ward, p. 220).
[26]A 940 (Ward, p. 247).

then a community superior, to order him around? I tell him nothing but, if he wants, let him do what he sees me doing."[27] This anecdote shows there were nevertheless some elders giving orders to their disciples, though this could not have been the rule. It seems that, in the desert, authority was only exercised grudgingly, each being afraid to impose his will and hinder the freedom of the Spirit. To a brother who asked him what must be done, Poemen says, "Go, live with someone who says, 'What do I want?' and you'll find rest."[28] In other words, go live with someone who doesn't want to impose his will on others.

To another, Poemen said, "Go, attach yourself to a man who fears God, and he will teach you to fear God too."[29] Among the Desert Fathers, what counted most was not words but practice. The disciple learned more watching the elder live, and living with him, than listening to drawn-out speeches. It is said several times in the *Life of Antony* that many visitors came "just to see him"[30] and this was enough to encourage them to do good. Of the three brothers who visited Antony regularly, one never asked any questions. "It is enough for me to see you, Father," he'd say.[31] And this happened only once a year.

What would we say then of the disciple who lived constantly in the intimacy of an elder? The relations between them had to be stamped with reserve and solemnity. The case is mentioned of an elder who, at the end of two years, still didn't know his disciple's name. The sacrosanct law which forbade monks to abandon themselves to a lack of consideration for others, to casualness, to shocking ways and chattering applied first of all, to be sure, to relations between elders and disciples. The closeness to God in which they lived gave their whole life a dignity and seriousness which must have been marvelous but also, sometimes, terribly demanding.

---

[27] A 373 (Ward, pp. 99-100).
[28] A 717 (Ward, p. 187).
[29] A 639 (Ward, p. 176).
[30] VA 46, 62, 67, 70, 84, 88.
[31] A 27 (Ward, p. 7).

Families in the Desert

It was like this especially when two members of the same family—or more—came to the desert together. They could be brothers, or a father and son. Normally it was the older brother who took on the role of elder and the younger one obeyed him. We see, for instance, John Colobos and Pachomius each submitting to their elder brother.[32] In Poemen's family circle of seven brothers, the eldest one, Anoub, directed the group and all shared the renunciation as if strangers one to the other.[33] It would also happen that a father came to the desert with his son for whom he took the place of an elder. In the Cells, James had as his spiritual father his real one.[34] Zacharias, while still a child, had joined his father Carion in Scetis and lived under his guidance. Carion, a great ascetic but not well versed in the mystical world, soon found himself unable to usefully guide his son, who had progressed rapidly in the ways of holiness and contemplation.[35] Likewise, Anoub withdrew little by little when the young Poemen showed exceptional gifts as a pastor of souls. Generally, the elder was not jealously attached to his title and rank. He was more disposed to reverse the roles, which sometimes happened.

In the desert there circulated the story of an elder with an excellent disciple named Peter. One day, in a fit of temper, he chased him out of the cell and Peter stayed outside near the door. Two days later, the elder found him there and told him, "Come, come in, and from now on you be the elder and father and me, the young disciple."[36]

Criterion of Seniority

Two brothers could also live together on an equal footing for years on end without the slightest disagreement or quarrel, even if the Devil used all his shrewdness to sow discord between

---

[32]A 317 (Ward, p. 86); Veilleux, pp. 41-43.
[33]A 138 (Ward, pp. 32-33).
[34]A 926 (Ward, p. 240).
[35]N 171, N 173.
[36]A 800 (Ward, p. 210); CSP IV 15.

them.[37] They tried to outdo each other in patience and humility. If one day God manifested in some special manner the holiness of one with regard to the other, the latter recognized his superiority and from then on considered him to be the elder, no longer calling him "Brother" but "Father."

Neither great age nor a long time spent in the desert were, in themselves, a measure of "seniority." As Cassian remarked, "The young are not always equally fervent, wise or virtuous. And we don't find among all the old ones the same degree of perfection, the same proven virtue. Many grow old in half-heartedness and backsliding."[38] Some monks while still young are given the title of Abba because they have great wisdom and the charism of the Word,[39] but one also finds elderly anchorites who don't deserve the title because they don't have the discernment needed to guide others. However, Cassian shows us other elders who were more than 100 years old and "whose holiness shone forth just from their appearance,"[40] such as Chaeremon who didn't want to keep any more disciples near him fearing, he said, that his example would have the effect of causing others to relax their austerity.[41] In Egypt, senior citizens have always been honored and respected. This was a country where, a historian noted, "it was good to live in old age."[42] But in the desert, these considerations were reserved especially for the "elders," old in wisdom and saintly living.

Continuity of Relationships

The common life of an elder with his disciple could last for long years and constitute a tough school for patience, if on top of it all there was between them a certain incompatibility of humor, or one fell into some vice. Every day, an elder went to the nearby

---

[37]A 565 (Ward, p. 157); N 352.

[38]Cassian, Conf. 2, 13.

[39]A 635 (Ward, p. 175).

[40]Cassian, Conf. 11, 2.

[41]Ibid., 11, 4.

[42]P. Montet, *Everyday Life in Egypt in the Days of Ramesses the Great*, Philadelphia, 1981, p. 302.

village to sell the two mats he and his disciple made. He would drink away almost all the money and return to his disciple with nothing but a chunk of bread.[43] Another "extremely bilious" one each day insulted his disciple, covering him with spit and showing him the door.[44] Sometimes the elder's patience was put to the test. That of Nisterus and his disciple has remained notorious in the annals of the desert.[45] Another elder, who had admonished his young disciple, found himself abandoned, with an empty stomach, with no supplies for thirteen days and, to a neighbor who helped him out, simply said of the imp, "Bah! He'll return when he can!"[46]

A disciple could leave his elder on the advice of another elder, when it was decided his soul would be jeopardized by staying there,[47] but the case was rare. Most of the time, elder and disciple remained faithful to each other until death. When the elder, advanced in age, became handicapped and unable to look after himself due to physical or mental infirmity, the disciple then became mostly the elder's "servant." It is said that John the Theban spent twelve years next to Ammoes on his mat, looking after all the old man's needs without the latter showing him the least sign of gratitude. Just before dying, only then, did Ammoes praise his disciple-servant: "He's not a man, he's an angel!"[48] He was later able to show his gratitude to his disciple by interceding on his behalf before God, as Arsenius had promised his disciple Daniel as a reward for the trouble he had caused him.[49]

Arsenius' chief disciples were Alexander and Zoïlus, who were very attached to him. One fine day, he decided to get rid of them and live in total solitude. It didn't take long for him to regret it and he went back to them. All three shed abundant tears and remained together until the old one's death.[50]

---

[43]N 340.
[44]N 551.
[45]A 705 (Ward, p. 186).
[46]N 341.
[47]A 968 (Ward, p. 193).
[48]A 420 (Ward, p. 109).
[49]A 73 (Ward, p. 16).
[50]A 70 (Ward, p. 15).

135

Many of the toughest and most solemn elders had hearts of gold. When Poemen would notice his disciple dozing off during the chanting of the psalms, he would take the younger one's head and rest it on his knees.[51]

When the elder was pleased with his disciple's virtue, we can understand that he would not wish to change it. This was true of Sisoes in regard to his faithful Abraham.[52] But Longinus acted the same way with his disciple who, they said, wasn't known for his irreproachable conduct.[53]

After the elder's death, the disciple could stay alone or place himself under the guidance and service of another anchorite. Isaac had been a disciple of Cronius and then of Theodore of Pherme before becoming an elder when his own time came.[54] Alexander and Zoïlus had been disciples of Agathon before they lived with Arsenius. After the latter's death, they stayed together and had as a disciple Daniel, who had also been at the service of Arsenius.[55] Some apothegms allow us to determine lines of disciples who became, in turn, elders with their own disciples.

We know how strong family traditions have been in Egypt since Antiquity. To distinguish between namesakes, the father's name is always added. For instance, the apothegms speak of a Joseph, Abba Lot's disciple; of another Joseph, Alonios'; of a John, Abba James'; of an Isaac, Abba Bes'; Nisterus, Abba Paul's and of Sisoes, the one with Antony.

The Anchoritic Groups

An elder could have several disciples. Agathon, Arsenius and Milesius each had two,[56] Silvanus had twelve,[57] another, five.[58] But the most well-known Fathers saw a large number of young or less-than-young men come to them for training with-

---

[51]A 666 (Ward, p. 180).
[52]A 849 (Ward, p. 220).
[53]N 708.
[54]A 373 (Ward, pp. 99-100).
[55]A 110 (Ward, p. 24).
[56]A 70, A 102, A 532 (Ward, pp. 15, 23, 147).
[57]A 526 (Ward, p. 145).
[58]N 419.

out, however, remaining in constant touch with them. In dying, Moses left seventy disciples.[59] Antony had many but when he died, there were only two companions with him.[60] Without being able to give numbers, it is certain that other elders such as Macarius, John Colobos and Poemen already had, while living, a countless number of spiritual descendants. They said of John Colobos: "Who is this John who, through his humility, has lifted up all of Scetis by his little finger?"[61] And yet John had only "his" disciple with him.

One or two disciples usually lived with the elder and the others had their cells in the neighborhood. And so it was that, among elders of great renown, there arose clusters of hermitages, revealed lately by excavations in the Cells but which certainly also existed in Nitria and Scetis. At the end of the fourth century, according to Cassian, Scetis counted four churches for four communities of which the primitive hub must surely have been set up by disciples of a great elder.[62] In the same era, Palladius tells us about a Cells "fraternity" gathered around Evagrius and his friend Ammonius.[63]

In our own day, the Coptic monasteries with their cells and churches surrounded by walls, could be mistaken for monasteries similar to those of Western ones. In reality, all are groups of disciples around one or several elders. The manner in which the monastery of St Macarius was restored in the last twenty years truly reminds us of the early fourth-century phenomenon in the Wadi Natrun as well as in Nitria and the Cells. A great elder, Abouna Matta-el-Meskin, already well-known, arrived there in 1970 with a dozen disciples who had gathered around him. The number of disciples grew bit by bit and today, the community has more than a hundred monks, all anchorites, even if communal life is somewhat more advanced than that of other Coptic monasteries. As the St Macarius monks readily admit, the impressive development of new buildings is nothing "but a facade"

---

[59]HL 19, 11.
[60]VA 19.
[61]A 351 (Ward, p. 93).
[62]Cassian, Conf. 10, 2.
[63]HL 24, 2.

on the desert. In their eyes, true monastic life is the eremitic one fully lived by a few disciples of Father Matta-el-Meskin in their grottoes next to the monastery. And between the spiritual Father and his sons there reigns today the same climate of freedom which characterized the mutual relations of the fourth-century elders and their disciples. The Spirit of God who brought the monks to the desert is still the one and only Master who inspires and propels the conduct of all.

ELEVEN

❧✝❧

Welcoming Visitors

Doing Good Unto Others

Abba Poemen used to say, "There are three fundamentals: fear God, pray without ceasing and do good unto others."[1] The Desert Fathers were not the old bachelors we imagine, happily withdrawn into themselves in the isolation of their cells and uniquely preoccupied with their personal sanctification in some "one-on-one" privacy with God, whom they had gone to seek in the desert. Poemen's words would suffice to convince us of the importance they placed on the effective practice of charity towards their brothers. "To do good to others" is as indispensable as the fear of God and continual prayer.

And again, they had to have relations with others. It wasn't necessary to leave their cells to do good. Some monks — but these were rare, as we've seen — lived in inaccessible places and saw no one. A few others, in spots easier to reach, barred their doors and greeted no visitors.[2] All of these, however, did the greatest good for others by interceding on behalf of all people and, as the prologue to the *History of the Monks* puts it: "It is fully evident that through them the world is kept in being, and because of them human life is preserved and honored by God."[3]

But while fulfilling before God this first duty of charity, the majority of the anchorites had visible and direct relations with their fellow creatures. Most were not alone in their cells and all

---

[1] A 734 (Ward, p. 189).
[2] A 82 (Ward, p. 19).
[3] HM Pr 9.

139

had more or less frequent occasions to receive visitors. The great ascetics, who are now famous, were flooded with so many that they sometimes had to defend their solitude by taking refuge in a back-cell or secret place. Others, seized by boredom in their cells, waited in vain for the arrival of providential visitors who would allow them to break their fast a little sooner.[4] Most did not have visitors every day. In the bulk of the apothegms, visits seem frequent, but this should not delude us since many apothegms were created precisely because of a visit.

Visits Between Monks

There were first of all visits between monks. The visits of an ancient to a young one appear to have been rare. One apothegm says, "Our Fathers had the habit of visiting the cells of the young brothers and checking up on them,"[5] but this must have been written much later, since in all the documents, the fact seldom shows up. We know the case of Macarius who went each day for four months to see a brother and who never found him loafing but always busy praying.[6] Cassian tells of receiving an impromptu visit from Abba Theodore who found him stretched out on his mat and reproached him for it.[7] Even when invited by a brother to come see him, the elder found it hard to accept.[8] Usually it was the young one who visited an elder, the disciple to his master and spiritual father. And the latter was always ready to greet the brother who needed to be comforted, appeased, or advised. Poemen even received visits during Lent.[9] Several times John Colobos received a brother who, each time, forgot what he wanted to tell him.[10]

We understand that young monks would visit elders to ask their advice or that elders would visit each other for mutual edification. But visits between the young were not recom-

---

[4]Cassian, Conf. 10, 2.
[5]N 351.
[6]A 545 (Ward, p. 152); N 16.
[7]Cassian, Inst. 5, 35.
[8]N 482.
[9]A 632 (Ward, pp. 174-175).
[10]A 333 (Ward, pp. 89-90).

mended.[11] These could be undertaken in cases of need but one had to avoid falling into gossip or talk of vain things. They were also advised not to disturb a brother in his cell before the ninth hour. However, this applied only to monks who knew each other and didn't live too far apart. In fact, the orders are only mentioned in connection with Nitriots who visited the Cells or vice-versa.[12] Those coming from a great distance could not determine the time of their arrival in advance.

Rituals of Welcome

From the sources at our disposal, it is possible to reconstitute the ceremonial generally followed for welcoming guests. When a monk noticed visitors approaching his cell, he would pray in advance for the interview to go well, saying, for instance, "Lord Jesus Christ, deliver us from malicious gossip and insults, and escort them from here in peace."[13] But the visitor usually arrived without being announced or seen. He would then knock on the door.[14] The door would open, he would be greeted and brought into the cell.[15] (In the Nile Valley, there were some recluses who never opened their doors and who conversed with visitors through the window, as did Theon.[16] There were no known cases like this in Nitria, the Cells or Scetis.) Once inside, the monk would take the visitor's coat and baggage, then pray.[17] Often, it seems, it was the new arrival who was invited to say a prayer. Antony, for instance, when visiting Didymus, agreed immediately to his request, while Palladius declined.[18] Due to false modesty, a brother greeted by Serapion also declined to say the prayer and have his feet washed; the elder then taught him a lesson.[19] So it was an honor rendered the visitor. As described by

---

[11]A 136 (Ward, pp. 31-32).
[12]A 34 (Ward, p. 8)
[13]N 592/9.
[14]A 346 (Ward, p. 91).
[15]N 280.
[16]HM 6, 1.
[17]A 356, A 486 (Ward, pp. 96, 134ff.).
[18]HL 4, 3.
[19]Cassian, Conf. 18, 11.

Apollo, it is in fact the Lord being received in the person of
the guest, who must then be given every consideration.[20] The
washing of feet was one of the marks of respect inspired by the
example and the commandment given by Jesus on the evening
of Maundy Thursday.[21] One willingly requested of an elder or a
younger brother the honor of washing his feet.[22] John the Persian
wanted to carry out this ritual when thieves came to rob him;
they were converted on the spot.[23]

One day an elder told Evagrius, "When you go visit someone, don't make the first move to talk before being questioned."[24]
It was a general principle never to talk before being questioned,[25]
but still one of the two monks present had to start the conversation. If each considered himself inferior to the other and unworthy to speak, there would be no dialogue at all. Most often it
was undoubtedly the visitor who spoke first, in order to put forward the purpose of his visit. For example, the brother visiting
an elder to receive a good word might say, "Father, tell us about
life, how to find God, and pray for me, because I have many
sins."[26] But the elder sometimes guessed what he would be
asked and answered without waiting for the question.[27] The dialogue imagined by the brother tempted to leave his cell to go
visit an elder must show pretty clearly how to start an interview:
"Suppose you go to an elder and say to him, 'Are you well,
Father? I've wanted to see Your Holiness for a long time.' Then
he takes a basin, washes himself and, playing the role of elder,
says, 'You've done well to come, brother; forgive me for tiring
yourself on my behalf. May the Lord make it up to you!' "[28] In
Abba Isaiah's recommendations, the brother receiving a foreign

[20]A 151 (Ward, p. 37); HM 8, 55-56.
[21]A 253 (Ward, p. 70).
[22]N 482.
[23]A 418 (Ward, p. 108).
[24]A 224 (Ward, p. 62).
[25]A 479 (Ward, p. 133).
[26]N 592/28.
[27]A 384 (Ward, pp. 101-102).
[28]N 443.

monk must first of all greet him cordially, then invite him to pray and sit down. He will then ask him, "How are you?"[29]

The Meal Offered to Visitors

After the usual introductions, the first duty of the one receiving a visitor is to serve him something to eat and eat with him, breaking, if he must, his habitual fast, even if it is still morning.[30] Several times in the apothegms, we see the visitor excusing himself before leaving for having obliged his host to break his rule. The latter replies with a kind remark: "My rule is to give you some refreshment and let you go in peace."[31] Some brothers asked an elder, who had been forced to eat before time, "Abba, did you not feel distressed?" And he told them, "My distress is to do my own will."[32] "Thus," said another, "I have double merit—I give up my own will and carry out the precept of charity."[33] To Cassian and Germanus, the elder who had received them said pleasantly, "The fast is always with me but as for you, I can't always keep you with me.... Receiving Christ in you, I must treat you right, but once I have seen you go, I can resume my fast. In fact, the sons of the bridegroom cannot fast while the bridegroom is with them...."[34] If a monk had several visits on the same day, he could and even had to renew the sacrifice of his fast and of his own will. Evagrius suggested he not be upset but instead rejoice and give thanks to God.[35]

The anchorite with only bread and salt couldn't offer anything else to his guests, but most of the Desert Fathers had a reserve of things to improve the menu. We're already noted the "extras" sometimes offered to Cassian and Germanus on their visits to the elders in Scetis. Cassian also reminds us that, in the desert, a visitor must always be satisfied with what he is offered

---

[29]Isaiah 3, 46.

[30]A 518 (Ward, p. 143); Cassian, Inst. 5, 24-25.

[31]N 283.

[32]N 284.

[33]N 288.

[34]A 427 (Ward, p. 113); Cassian, Inst. 5, 24.

[35]Evagrius, *Outline Teaching on Asceticism...*, 10, *The Philokalia*, p. 36.

without asking for "any other seasoning."[36] Neither was it considered good form to refuse any dish, under the pretext of mortification.[37] One could only be excused for declining wine. However one Abba Piamoun, who hadn't had any for twenty-five years, didn't hesitate to accept grapes and wine offered by a brother,[38] since humility is always preferable to abstinence.

Corporal and Spiritual Nourishment

The *History of the Monks* states that it was the custom among the great ascetics "not to give the body any nourishment until the soul had been given its spiritual food, that is, the communion of the Body of Christ."[39] The remark concerns Abba Or who did not live in the full desert but in the Thebaid, near populated places, surrounded by thousands of monks But we have no documentary proof of this custom among the monks of Nitria and Scetis. The only spiritual nourishment offered visitors by the Desert Fathers consisted of words or an edifying discourse which could be quite lengthy.

One evening, John Colobos received a brother who was in a hurry to return home. The next morning they were still conversing and it was only at noon, after the meal, that the brother left.[40] Most of the time, visitors came mainly for a spiritual conversation. If they came from afar, they were invited to spend the night with their host and they'd chant psalms together for evening and morning offices.[41]

According to Palladius, Antony used to make a choice of visitors to receive. If they were simple and boorish, he'd tell his disciple to prepare some lentils and have them eat. Then after a prayer, he would dismiss them. But when their minds were more astute, he would sit with them and spend the night talking about spiritual matters.[42] Often visitors arrived in groups, and each one

---

[36]Cassian, Conf. 5, 11.
[37]N 592/48.
[38]Cassian, Conf. 17, 24.
[39]HM 2, 8.
[40]A 341 (Ward, p. 91).
[41]A 486 (Ward, pp. 134ff.); N 229.
[42]HL 21, 8-9.

questioned the elder in front of the others without shame. If someone wanted to speak in private, he would arrange to see the elder alone. This is what Daniel did with Poemen one day during the siesta.[43] Sometimes a brother would visit an elder simply to request a service or to render one — for example, to beg him to teach him how to weave[44] or to carry his baskets to market.[45]

Visits from People "of the World"

But visitors were not only monks. From the time an anchorite first became famous, lay people also came to him for a word of salvation or, occasionally, to seek a physical or spiritual cure. It also happened that an ordinary person visiting an elder would be invited to give an edifying exhortation, such as the vegetable merchant Poemen allowed to speak before several brothers.[46] Peddlers sometimes came to barter with the monks. They would exchange onions for wheat[47] or other items for bread.[48]

Another category of visitors was represented by persons of some importance. Generally, whether they were civilians or ecclesiastics, they didn't receive a hurried welcome, even when a top civil servant showed up at Arsenius' cell with Theophilus, the Archbishop of Alexandria. It was to them that an elder spoke some memorable words after having them promise to keep it to themselves: "If you discover where to find Arsenius, don't go near."[49] Abba Simon was a worthy emulator of Arsenius. The only two apothegms we have from him describe two kinds of strategies to get rid of important persons. When they arrived, he would be sitting at the cell door, wearing rags and munching on bread and cheese. To the question, "Where's the anchorite?" he'd reply, "There's no anchorite here!"[50] Theodore also took pleasure in shocking, by his slovenly attire, a count who had come to visit

---

[43] A 712 (Ward, p. 186).
[44] A 288 (Ward, p. 76).
[45] A 345 (Ward, p. 91).
[46] A 683 (Ward, pp. 182-183).
[47] A 289 (Ward, p. 77).
[48] A 346, A 862 (Ward, pp. 91-92, 224).
[49] A 45-46 (Ward, p. 10).
[50] A 868-869 (Ward, pp. 224-225).

him.[51] To the governor who came to Scetis to see him, Moses, without being recognized, snapped, "What do you want with that fool?"[52] And neither did Poemen receive the governor, not even to obtain the release of his imprisoned nephew.[53]

The axiom of the Fathers reported by Cassian, saying one must flee from bishops as much as from women,[54] was nevertheless not always observed. Sisoes amiably greeted Adelphius, Bishop of Nilopolis.[55] And we know that Athanasius was well received by the monks, because he hid among them to escape the imperial police.

As for women, if a Roman matron got a cool reception from Arsenius despite the recommendation of Theophilus,[56] other highborn Roman ladies were cordially welcomed, especially Paula, who was brought along by Jerome, and Melania who was accompanied by Rufinus.[57] Monks were formally forbidden to receive women in their cells, but Nitria had an inn and Melania spent six months there. Pambo, feeling near death, sent for her and gave her the last basket he was weaving. After this he died and it was the saintly moniale who dressed and prepared the great anchorite for the funeral.[58]

Generally speaking, pagan priests appear to have been better received than bishops by the Desert Fathers. One of them spent the night in the cell of Olympius, who gave him an uplifting word before they parted.[59] Another, forced to seek shelter with an anchorite, was astounded at being so well treated, converted on the spot and became the elder's disciple.[60] Heretics could also visit the desert monks. Poemen received some but as they set about denigrating the Archbishop of Alexandria, the

---

[51]A 295 (Ward, p. 78).
[52]A 502 (Ward, p. 140).
[53]A 579, A 583 (Ward, pp. 165, 167-168).
[54]Cassian, Inst. 11, 18.
[55]A 818 (Ward, p. 215).
[56]A 66 (Ward, pp. 13-14).
[57]Evelyn White, pp. 75-77, 86-87.
[58]HL 10, 5.
[59]A 571 (Ward, p. 160).
[60]N 289.

elder gave them something to eat and sent them away.[61] When some Arians came to see him, Sisoes asked his disciple to read out loud in their presence Athanasius' treaty against the Arians, then bade them go in peace.[62]

Undesirable Visitors

We mention a final category of visitors as an aside: thieves or bandits who came to strip the monks and even sometimes to massacre them. From time immemorial in Egypt, nomadic desert bands came to plunder populated areas. It is not surprising that they would sometimes target anchorites, more so because they usually offered no resistance. Some, like Macarius for instance, even helped the plunderers load up their booty on the camels.[63] As we've seen, John the Persian was so kind that he wanted to wash the bandits' feet.[64] It was a good way of converting them but one that didn't always succeed. An elder in Scetis surprised some bandits plundering his cell. He simply told them, "Hurry up before the brothers get here."[65] When some plunderers arrived at the hour of prayer, another elder told the brothers, "Let them do their work and let's do ours."[66] Even so, some monks could hold their own against the thieves and not let them take everything. In one case, Theodore insisted on keeping his Sunday tunic which he wore to the *synaxis* (congregational liturgy).[67]

Yet occasionally the bandits wanted not only the monks' meager possessions but their lives, too. During the fourth century, several raids caused the deaths of numerous monks at Scetis. Remembering his previous crimes, Moses was thus happy to be assassinated. He refused to flee and joyfully welcomed the barbarians who would allow him to fulfill the warning of Christ: "Those who live by the sword shall perish by the sword."[68] Not

[61]A 652 (Ward, p. 178).
[62]A 828 (Ward, p. 217).
[63]A 471, A 493 (Ward, pp. 131, 137-138).
[64]A 418 (Ward, p. 108).
[65]N 554.
[66]N 607.
[67]A 296 (Ward, p. 78).
[68]A 504 (Ward, p. 140).

all Desert Fathers were such resolute partisans of non-violence. Concerning this point, one brother had a question of conscience which he submitted to Sisoes: "If a barbarian should come with the intention of killing me and I'm stronger than he, should I kill him?"

"No," answered the elder, "instead, abandon yourself to God. Because in any trial forced upon him, a man must say, 'This is happening to me because of my sins.' If it's a good thing happening, let him say, 'This is by the providence of God.' "[69]

Desert Hospitality

Regardless of the rank and intentions of the visitor, the monk greeted him as an envoy from God. He treated him as best he could and when the visitor was ready to leave, it was good form to invite him to stay a bit longer.[70] When leaving, the visitor would ask, "Pray for me,"[71] and the one who had received him would accompany him to the door and sometimes even go a little way on the road with him.[72] But afterwards, the anchorite had to take up his regular and contemplative life once again. If he had the feeling that he had not benefited from the visit — having slipped into distraction, curiosity, gossiping, impatience, scandal-mongering or greediness — then, according to Poemen's advice, he had to examine himself and find the cause of this backsliding.[73] It probably was a case of not having the right frame of mind, even before the visitor arrived. While maintaining his heart in a state of devotion, the monk could, without risking anything, be happy and playful with his guests. Other than the benefit to be obtained from exercising charity, visits had the advantage of rousing the monk and allowing him see if his solitary life was progressing well. So on this point, says Cassian, one must not await with impatience the visit of a brother nor fret

---

[69]A 837 (Ward, p. 219).
[70]A 486 (Ward, p. 134); N 229.
[71]A 486, A 487 (Ward, pp. 134, 136).
[72]HL 17, 3-4; Sulpicius Severus, *Dial.* I, 14 and 15.
[73]A 749 (Ward, p. 191).

about it.[74] We're not in the desert to receive visits, but all those brought to us by the Lord are graces which, far from hampering spiritual progress, really boost it.

Such were the rules and customs usually followed when greeting visitors to the desert. In practice, there were certainly many variations depending on the anchorite's temperament and humor and also the caliber and intentions of the visitor. John Colobos had a reputation for showing unselfishness and kindness to everyone who visited him.[75] On the other hand, Theodore of Pherme was the most rigid — "like a sword" — in dealing with visitors.[76] Moses, the repentant bandit, was much friendlier than Arsenius, the former dignitary of the imperial court.[77] The former had to make up for his brutalities; the other had to cut off worldly relationships and atone for his frivolous attachments.

Generally the Desert Fathers gave warmer receptions to those who had shown them hostility or had bad reputations. This was so with Poemen.[78] The elders always showed discernment and when their customary friendliness left something to be desired, it was for a good reason.

As the monks became more numerous in the desert, hospitality was programmed, special structures were built and set aside for guest monks and lay people and some brothers were appointed to receive and lodge them, much as is done in the Wadi Natrun monasteries still in existence today.[79] From then on, anchorites could, without causing any inconvenience, bar their doors on certain days or periods of the year. Some only received visitors on Saturday and Sunday,[80] others didn't open their doors during Lent.[81] For all that, they did not think it necessary to post notices on their cell doors. The arrangements were well known and generally respected.

---

[74]Cassian, Conf. 19, 12.
[75]A 618 (Ward, p. 173).
[76]A 69, A 270, A 288 (Ward, pp. 14-15, 74, 76).
[77]A 76, A 475 (Ward, pp. 17-18, 133).
[78]A 644 (Ward, p. 176).
[79]Evelyn White, pp. 173-188.
[80]Eth 13, 7.
[81]A 632 (Ward, pp. 174-175).

TWELVE

❧✝❧

Outings and Trips

Outings Away from the Cell

While keeping the rule to remain in his cell, the anchorite might have an occasion and even the necessity of leaving it. The fact that sources mention some exceptional cases of monks who never left, proves that almost all of them left their cells from time to time. It is said that Arsenius did not readily leave his cell;[1] so he obviously left it sometimes, if only to take a breath of fresh air nearby. We'll see that almost all the monks of Nitria, the Cells and Scetis gathered together on Saturday and Sunday for the celebration of the Eucharist. Apart from these weekly liturgical meetings, there were ample legitimate reasons for leaving the cell, either for several hours or several days, depending on the distance to the destination in mind. For that matter, it was a sign of pride for an anchorite to boast about never having left his cell. If a brother was tempted, Poemen used to advise taking a night's stroll around the village.[2]

First of all, one could go a distance from the cell and still be in the desert. Brothers went to the wells to fetch water[3] or to the marsh to cut reeds for mat and basket making.[4] One would go to visit an elder or a brother,[5] especially an invalid or a brother

---

[1] A 59, A 66 (Ward, pp. 12, 13-14).
[2] A 684 (Ward, p. 183).
[3] A 290 (Ward, p. 77); N 49, N 50.
[4] A 334, A 873-874, A 788 (Ward, pp. 90, 226, 202-203).
[5] N 443, N 471, N 613.

150

requiring some service.[6] Relations between Nitria, the Cells and Scetis were frequent. The trip took a day or two. Sometimes a disoriented recluse would suddenly go on an adventurous outing in the desert only to have an unexpected meeting there.[7] But the most important reasons for leaving the cell, and also the rarest, were those which forced a monk to return to the populated world, the towns and villages of the Delta. A much graver motive was required for undertaking these trips because of the inevitable distractions and frequent temptations they entailed.[8]

Business Trips

In the early days in the desert, each anchorite had to provide for his own living. To do so, he sold mats, baskets and other wickerwork he made, or bartered them for provisions. Contrary to many monks who lived near their villages, the Desert Fathers could not live off alms from their relatives and acquaintances.[9] At the most, one might benefit from the services of a pious layman who took care of worldly business for them.[10] But most of the time the Fathers or their disciples looked after indispensable errands entirely by themselves. Many apothegms tell of anchorites going to the nearest small town to sell their merchandise. This is how an elder met a demon who spirited away the baskets he was carrying.[11] One day Macarius, exhausted by his load of baskets, prayed and was miraculously transported all the way to the Nile.[12] Often the merchandise went by camel. We are told of an elder who sent his disciple to fetch a camel to carry his baskets to town.[13] Cassian reports that in order to test a disciple of noble blood, the elder sent him to market with ten baskets,

---

[6]A 835 (Ward, p. 219); N 195.

[7]N 5, N 132 ABD, N 490 A.

[8]Evagrius, *Outline Teaching on Asceticism...*, 8, *The Philokalia*, p. 34; Cassian, Conf. 6, 15; 24.

[9]Cassian, Conf. 24, 12.

[10]N 293.

[11]N 49.

[12]A 467 (Ward, p. 130).

[13]N 344.

telling him to sell them one by one.[14] So as not be distracted from their contemplation, monks at the market were urged not to haggle over prices, whether buying or selling. This is what Agathon used to do.[15] To a brother going to market, Poemen said, "Sell your merchandise quietly."[16] Some monks took advantage of their village trips to give alms or do different works of charity.[17]

Meeting Women

During these trips, the monks might meet women and be tempted to seduce them or be seduced by them. Several accounts mention temptations resisted by the monks or the woman, others where they succumbed, but in general the monk repents and returns to the desert.[18] One brother was miraculously rescued from danger by the intercession of his elder from a distance.[19]

It could also happen that an anchorite, tormented by violent desires, went to town or took advantage of a trip there to satisfy his passion in a place of ill repute. But this was rare. We're told of a brother who went every night for three years to sleep with a woman. While on the way, going and coming, he recited the psalter, especially the psalms of penitence, which finally earned him the grace of repentance.[20] As noted, certain monks had withdrawn to the desert after a wild life and it is not surprising that the demons relentlessly tried to return them to their old habits. One monk heard them screaming in his ears with rage, "Aren't you going to get up and get out of here? Aren't you going to return to your old habits with us? The whores, the innkeepers are waiting for you."[21]

Some anchorites also visited prostitutes to convert them. The apothegms recount a few beautiful stories about this where

---

[14]Cassian, Inst. 4, 29.
[15]A 98 (Ward, p. 16).
[16]A 737 (Ward, p. 189).
[17]N 287.
[18]N 52, N 179.
[19]A 137 (Ward, p. 32).
[20]N 44; Arm 5, 15; SP, New Collection, p. 256 (I 622).
[21]HM 1, 39.

the heroes were a Timothy,[22] Serapion and John Colobos. The latter was sent to the famous Paësia. Orphaned as a child, this young woman had converted her house into an inn for Scetis monks coming to shop in town. But impoverished by her generosity, she had fallen on hard times and the monastic inn had become a brothel. Coming there as a client, John Colobos touched Paësia's heart by his words and she asked him to guide her to a place where she might do penance. Traveling together in the desert, they had to stop for the night and during his sleep, John saw the soul of his penitent transported to paradise by angels.[23] The story of this conversion had so moved St Thérèse of Lisieux that she wanted to mention it at the end of her autobiography.

The story of Serapion's penitent is entirely different but also very uplifting The elder, passing through a village, noticed a prostitute at her doorstep. He made an appointment to spend the following night with her. Upon returning, he entered, closed the door and advised the woman that he had some practices to do first. He began reciting the psalter and went right through to the end, stopping only to pray to God for her conversion. He then read a good part of St Paul's Epistles and, finally, the woman was converted and became an exemplary moniale.[24]

Over-Night Visitors

Anchorites overtaken by night in the desert simply went to sleep in the sand, using a bit of it to make a pillow. If they came upon a tomb or an old temple, they could find shelter there and this explains why Macarius, walking from Scetis to Terenuthis, entered a pagan temple to rest.[25]

Pagan tombs and temples were also where demons stayed, and the anchorite would go there not only to confront them but to pray. Pachomius, like his master Palamon, would often spend a night in the tombs.[26] One day, a monk had a very special rea-

---

[22]A 917 (Ward, p. 237).
[23]A 355 (Ward, pp. 93-94).
[24]A 875 (Ward, p. 226).
[25]A 466 (Ward, p. 130).
[26]Veilleux, p. 32.

son for going to a tomb. Tormented by the memory of a very beautiful lady he had known, he one day learned of her death. Immediately he went to her tomb, soaked his tunic in the pus dripping from the corpse and then returned like this to his cell. He kept the stench next to him and fought his thoughts by saying, "This is what you wanted, you have it, now be done with it."[27] This procedure is certainly not meant for everyone but it must have been effective!

Normally an anchorite never went back to see his parents or any family members. On episcopal authority, Pior had to go visit his elderly sister, saw her, but did not agree to look at her.[28] We also know of a moniale who refused to see her brother before she died.[29] Pachomius always refused to see his sister who had come to dedicate herself to God near him in Tabennesi,[30] while Antony, it seems, visited his sister at her monastery of virgins.[31]

Trips to Alexandria

Alexandria was the great port and gateway for all the commerce between Egypt and the other provinces of the empire. It was a cosmopolitan city of sailors and soldiers, merchants and traffickers but also of well-read people and scholars.

At the end of the third century, pagans and Jews still formed the bulk of the population. But it was also the religious metropolis where Christianity had first sprouted and where the main dignitary of the Coptic church, the Patriarch or "Pope" of Egyptian Christians, resided. If the desert monks were not drawn to the Greek city, noisy and dissolute, nor to intellectual circles, they could have sound motives for visiting the Patriarch, whose authority they recognized. He occasionally summoned them: for instance, Pambo by Athanasius[32] or, later, the Nitria monks were called by Theophilus to destroy the pagan temples.[33] Isidore, the

---

[27]N 172.
[28]HL 39, 2.
[29]N 153.
[30]Veilleux, pp. 49-50.
[31]VA 54.
[32]A 765 (Ward, p. 196).
[33]A 306 (Ward, p. 81).

priest from Scetis, also went to see Theophilus one day but the reason is not known.[34]

From his faraway mountain, Antony had visited Alexandria at least twice: once to encourage the confessors of the faith during the persecution by Maximin (308-313) and another time to refute the Arians.[35] The apothegms tell of the special case of a former slave who became a monk in Scetis and every year took what he had earned to his masters in Alexandria.[36] We're told that Macarius returned one day to his native city to find some small treat for an elder who was ill.[37] But for their regular things, the Desert Fathers had no need to go as far as the capital. In the Delta villages they found what little they needed plus a large enough market for their products.

Harvest Outings

When their numbers in the desert increased, the anchorites could not always earn their living just by selling objects made in the cells. They then started going out to work in the fields at harvest time. Numerous texts mention this unusual work and the travel involved.[38] Most of the time the monks were paid in kind, with wheat[39] or oil.[40] We know that a monk could earn twelve *artabas* (about ten bushels) of wheat.[41] The Scetiots each received a pint of oil.[42] Three brothers went to harvest one day and agreed to do one and a half acres together. One of them being ill, the other two did all the work but wanted him also to receive his share.[43]

---

[34]A 364 (Ward, p. 97).
[35]VA 46, 69.
[36]A 540 (Ward, p. 150).
[37]A 461 (Ward, p. 129).
[38]A 375, A 880 (Ward, pp. 100, 228); Ch 227.
[39]A 252 (Ward, p. 70).
[40]A 168 (Ward, p. 43).
[41]HM 18, 1.
[42]A 168 (Ward, p. 43).
[43]N 350.

Under the boiling Egyptian sun, the work was really tough. At midday, a siesta was needed.[44] Women would often glean behind the reapers and one day Macarius took pity on one of them who was crying because she was poverty-stricken.[45] The presence of these women could give some monks troubled thoughts. Recall the one who thought he spotted a brother sleeping with a woman in a field: they turned out to be two sheaves of wheat.[46]

This work outside the cells among secular people was not accepted unreservedly by the Desert Fathers. A few were absolutely opposed to it. So an elder, seeing a brother leaving one day for the harvest, sidetracked him from his purpose.[47] Such outings were sources of temptations and distractions. John Colobos, overhearing two brothers arguing at work, fled back to his cell. Once there, he took care to purify and calm his mind.[48] He also practiced more abstinence to make up for the more copious meals he had had to eat during the difficult harvest days.[49]

Outings in Search of Holiness

One exceptional reason for an outing remains to be mentioned: a revelation given to an elder of the eminent saintliness of some person living in the world. It is a recurring theme in our sources. The great old fathers who achieved a high degree of perfection risked thinking themselves superior to all others. God took care to protect them from this pretension by letting them know that there were lay people as virtuous as they.[50] For instance, Antony learned of a doctor in a certain town "who gives all that he has left over to the poor and who sings every day with the angels,"[51] or of another lay person, a courier in

---

[44]A 460 (Ward, pp. 128-129); CSP I 2.

[45]A 460 (Ward, p. 128).

[46]A 688 (Ward, pp. 183-184).

[47]N 291.

[48]A 321 (Ward, p. 86); CSP I 2.

[49]A 543 (Ward, p. 151).

[50]Cf. K. Ware, "The Monk and the Married Christian," *Eastern Churches Review*, VI, 1974, pp. 72-83.

[51]A 24 (Ward, p. 6).

Alexandria, so perfect that he surpassed Antony himself.[52] In his youth, near his village, Antony visited all the ascetics who distinguished themselves by their virtues.[53] So no one was surprised to see the old fellow take his stick and go to be edified by the courier.

Paphnutius was especially anxious to meet all the saints who were the most distinguished in virtue. He learned about a flute player, a "municipal councilor," and even a pearl merchant who competed with him by their asceticism and piety. And he went to visit each one, but it was to bring them all to the desert with him.[54]

Two other elders learned that in a village, Eucharistus and his wife Mary were far ahead of them in spiritual matters, but they lived like a monk and a moniale in celibacy and good works.[55] Macarius heard a celestial voice telling him he hadn't yet reached the spiritual perfection of two married women living in a certain town. He went to see them and found them living normally with their husbands after having wanted to join a monastery. Even though they lived in the same house, they had never argued or uttered any vain words.[56]

Another anchorite learned from an angel that he wasn't as saintly as a certain layman who cultivated and sold vegetables. He, too, immediately went to visit him and was uplifted by the horticulturist's remarks.[57] Apart from Paphnutius who took advantage of his "missions" to do recruiting, all the great old men were content to admire the beautiful examples they discovered and returned to the desert filled with new fervor.

How the Anchorites Traveled

In the desert, the anchorites traveled on foot. When a donkey[58] or a camel[59] is mentioned in the apothegms, it isn't as a

---

[52]N 490.
[53]VA 3.
[54]HM 14, 2-22.
[55]A 216 (Ward, p. 60).
[56]N 489.
[57]N 67.
[58]A 12, A 372, A 392, A 862 (Ward, pp. 3, 99, 103, 224).

mount but as a beast of burden to carry luggage, except for visitors coming to the desert to visit a famous elder.[60] Whether alone or in a group, getting lost in the desert was easy, more so when a sudden fog made it impossible to see anything or a sandstorm erased every trace of footsteps. Many anecdotes mention lost monks. On a trip to see Antony, Ammonas lost his way.[61] Paphnutius found himself in a strange village.[62] Even a guide leading a group of brothers could get lost.[63] The gravest danger facing the lost ones was to die of hunger or thirst, which is what happened to two young monks sent to bring two figs to an elder who was sick.[64] Two others, completely exhausted, were rescued by nomads.[65]

In the delta and valley of the Nile, the monks as well as lay people often got around in small boats, and could use ferries to cross rivers and streams.[66] On such occasions, the monks would meet together and discuss the Fathers, Scripture or their manual labor.[67] Arsenius took a ferry down to the region of Alexandria.[68] The ferries advanced under sail or by oars. Agathon, when taking a ferry, was always the first to grab an oar.[69] Along river banks, boats could also be towed by men.[70] Usually the monks paid the fares for their boat trips. One day Isaac lamented that his manual work had not brought him enough to pay the fare for the boat he had to take to visit the elders.[71] At this time the elders were dispersed throughout the delta.

---

[59] A 346, A 493, A 584 (Ward, pp. 91, 137, 168); N 192, N 344, N 439.
[60] A 66 (Ward, p. 13); N 176.
[61] A 119 (Ward, p. 27).
[62] A 786 (Ward, p. 202).
[63] A 332, A 833 (Ward, pp. 89, 218).
[64] Cassian, Inst. 5, 40.
[65] Cassian, Conf. 2, 6.
[66] A 117, A 118 (Ward, pp. 26-27); Sy 20, 19; Eth 13, 35; 13, 39.
[67] A 18 (Ward, p. 5).
[68] A 70 (Ward, p. 15).
[69] A 111 (Ward, p. 24).
[70] A 719 (Ward, p. 187).
[71] A 374 (Ward, p. 100).

When the monk set out, he always took with him his coat and staff.[72] This staff, frequently mentioned in the texts, was not just for the elderly. It was indispensable for walking in the desert. It was also used to prod a stubborn donkey or camel, to chase away or kill a serpent, or indeed to get rid of a woman or revive a dead person.[73] The traveler also carried a pouch with some food and a water skin.[74] However, this is seldom mentioned and one may wonder if the Desert Fathers, accustomed to doing without food and drink, couldn't walk for several days like the camels without eating or drinking. Heron used to travel like this for thirty-five miles in the desert.[75] Once they reached the populated area, the anchorites might be invited by pious lay people to eat, but they preferred to be housed and fed by other hospitable monks. It was not proper for a monk to enter a tavern. A Scetiot, spotting a brother entering one, reproached him for it and the other replied, "Now look, dear fellow, God expects only purity of heart."[76] We see that all the monks were not as straight-laced as the Scetis anchorites.

During their travels, the monks happily recited psalms or verses of Holy Writ. Isaiah advised the brothers walking together to keep some distance one from the other so as to observe silence and pray from the heart.[77] According to the apothegms, it seems that an elder traveling with a disciple gladly let the other go ahead in order to continue contemplating.[78]

On the road, the monks could have unexpected encounters, not only with women, as we've seen, but with hunters[79] and more or less wild beasts, which we also find in the desert bestiary. Macarius often met a demon on his way; it didn't disturb

---

[72]A 317 (Ward, p. 86); Cassian, Conf. 11, 3.

[73]N 431, N 459, N 490 B.

[74]A 156 (Ward, p. 40); HL 26, 3.

[75]HL 26, 3.

[76]J. Moschus, *Pratum spirituale*, 194.

[77]Isaiah, 3, 4.

[78]A 130, A 492 (Ward, pp. 30, 137).

[79]A 13, A 810 (Ward, pp. 3, 213).

him anymore than when he came across a skull which began talking to him.[80]

Relocations, Expulsions and Emigrations

An elder said the monk is like "a bee that makes its honey everywhere."[81] As much as the monk insists on staying in his cell when he has no sound reason to leave it, he's equally detached when necessity dictates that he abandon it.

Among reasons causing an anchorite to move were first of all personal ones. If a certain elder decided he had become too well-known and famous, he either moved somewhere else in the desert or went to live incognito in a monastery in the Thebaid. This is what John and Pinufius did, as mentioned by Cassian.[82] Soon spotted and recognized, Pinufius then left for Palestine. Many other anchorites also went to the Holy Land, in particular Isaiah, Porphyry, the future bishop of Gaza, Silvanus and his disciples. All it sometimes took to make him move was for an elder to notice "something not very edifying" in the neighborhood of his cell. This happened to Agathon who left a brand new cell, and Ammoes who left behind a large supply of bread he had just sun-dried.[83]

Often it was constraints, sometimes brutal ones forced upon them, which obliged all the anchorites in a group of hermitages to pack up and emigrate. In 399, several hundred monks, followers of the doctrines of Origen, were expelled from the Cells by a troop of roughnecks hired by Patriarch Theophilus. Exiled, they found refuge in Palestine, then in Constantinople and it was only several years later that they were able to return to their desert.[84] In the first half of the fifth century, we know that Scetis was devastated several times by barbarian hordes and the monks were massacred or dispersed.[85] Poemen and his brothers, and

---

[80]A 456, A 464, A 488, A 491. (Ward, pp. 126, 129, 136ff.)
[81]N 399.
[82]Cassian, Conf. 19, 2-3; 20, 1.
[83]A 88, A 134 (Ward, pp. 21, 31).
[84]Evelyn White, pp. 125-144; Chitty, pp. 124-129.
[85]Chitty, pp. 143-144.

later Arsenius and his disciples, had to settle for some time near the inhabited regions of the Delta.

All appeared to see the hand of God in the events that led to their being banished from the land that had become their home, the desert. One day Daniel said to Ammoes, "Who can take God away from us? God is in the cell and also outside."[86] By constant vigilance over his heart, the monk always remained turned toward God.[87] "Wherever he goes," said another elder, "he remains forever in his cell,"[88] trying to maintain his observance without losing his peace.[89] He succeeded insofar as he retained the desire to find once again, as soon as possible, the solitude of the desert and the cell, like a fish out of water anxious to return to the sea.[90] The famous image offered by St Antony is enough to show that the desert cell is the privileged place, the natural and customary environment—but not the exclusive one—for the anchorite.

---

[86] A 187 (Ward, p. 52).
[87] A 711 (Ward, p. 186).
[88] N 435.
[89] A 879 (Ward, p. 228).
[90] A 10 (Ward, p. 3); VA 85.

THIRTEEN

The Community Weekend

The English weekend is generally considered to be an in-spired modern invention. Yet the Desert Fathers knew about it and practiced it in the fourth century. Absolute anchoritism in total solitude was always an exception, as we have said. Very quickly desert life became organized along semi-anchoritic lines according to a weekly rhythm. The monks stayed in their cells five days a week and got together on Saturday and Sunday. The set of documents at hand shows that this custom was prevalent in Scetis as well as in Nitria and the Cells.

Even if there are still many uncertainties about the begin-nings and evolution of this practice, and also on the manner in which the details came into being, there are enough sure facts to try to reconstruct the unfolding of this monastic weekend. It included several distinct acts of which the main ones were the Eucharistic liturgy and the community meal.

The Eucharist and Priesthood in the Desert

Participation in the Eucharist was certainly the foremost reason for the anchorites' weekly gathering. When the exodus to the great desert began, Antony and his emulators, Amoun and Macarius, did not seem to have had any scruples about leav-ing the community of the faithful and, by that very fact, being deprived of participating in the Eucharist. The monks who lived near villages and towns could easily continue to meet with the faithful in their churches on Sunday. For instance, at Terenuthis, brothers went to church on Sunday and received communion.[1] On the other hand, those who set out for the great desert were forced to spend months, even years, without communion. In Nitria, which was not far from populated areas, the anchorites could, from time to time, go to the village church for the Sunday liturgy. From early on, we know there was a church and priest there, while there was none in Scetis, nor even in the Cells, because, from Scetis, Macarius would sometimes go to Nitria, to Abba Pambo's Mass.[2] One day when he met St Antony, the same Macarius remarked to the Saint that there was no Mass in Scetis,[3] even though a number of Fathers already lived there. We do not know Antony's reply. Did Macarius perhaps begin the conversation with Antony in hopes that he could himself become a priest and celebrate the Eucharist?[4]

A Coptic biography of Macarius tells of his being ordained a priest while still pursuing an ascetic life near a village.[5] But the apothegms, an older and more reliable source, note only that people wanted him to join the clergy and because of this, Macarius fled elsewhere.[6] According to Palladius, Macarius was ordained a priest at the age of forty, or around the year 340, when he had been in the desert for ten years and would remain there for another fifty.[7] Following his death, his disciple John succeeded him as priest.[8]

Cassian says that at this time there were four churches in Scetis, each with its own priest. We know the names of Isidore and Paphnutius.[9] In the desert of Cellia, until the fourth century, there was only one church served by Macarius of Alexandria until his death in 394, then by Isaac.[10] When Palladius visited

---

[1] Arm 18, 88; SP, New Collection, p. 272 (II 434).
[2] A 455 (Ward, p. 125).
[3] A 479 (Ward, p. 133).
[4] Evelyn White, p. 69.
[5] *Annales du Musée Guimet*, XXI, p. 65.
[6] A 454 (Ward, p. 124).
[7] HL 17, 2.
[8] HL 17, 3.
[9] A 409 (Ward, p. 106); Cassian, Conf. 2, 5; 3, 1; 4, 1.
[10] HL 18, 1; A 372-373 (Ward, p. 99).

Nitria, there was one single church with eight priests, only one of whom exercised his priesthood.[11]

Many monks did everything they could to avoid ordination, not due to any scorn towards the priesthood but, on the contrary, because they were awed by its grandeur and felt themselves unworthy. When they wanted to ordain Isaac, he fled and hid in a field. Pursued, he was found thanks to a donkey that went to graze near him.[12] Even once ordained, some priests, deacons or bishops never wanted to exercise their ministry because of their humility.[13] An elder would be ordained to the priesthood when his virtues and saintliness were recognized. Not only did the priest carry out liturgical functions but often assumed the role of Superior, presiding over the Council of Elders and making important decisions.[14] He it was who decided which new recruits would be accepted and gave them the habit. It was also he who took it away from unworthy monks and expelled them.[15]

The Double Eucharist of Saturday and Sunday

As long as the desert monks had no churches, they participated as often as they could in the liturgy of the nearest church. After they built their own churches and began celebrating the Eucharist, we have every reason to believe they kept their general custom of a double weekly celebration on Saturday and Sunday. Actually, as the historian Socrates noted in his fifth-century *Ecclesiastical History*, "all churches in the world, except those in Rome and Alexandria, celebrated the Holy Mysteries every Saturday." He adds that even the Egyptians living near Alexandria, like those in the Thebaid, followed this custom but with one peculiarity — the Eucharist was celebrated in the evening after the regular meal.[16]

---

[11]HL 7, 5; A 772 (Ward, p. 197).
[12]A 372 (Ward, p. 99).
[13]A 292, A 521 (Ward, pp. 77, 144).
[14]A 496 (Ward, p. 138).
[15]A 585 (Ward, p. 168).
[16]Socrates, *Hist. Eccl.* V 22 (Migne, PG 67, 636 B).

The Pachomian documents give a very clear attestation of this custom of celebrating the Eucharist not only on Sunday but also on Saturday. In Tabennesi, Pachomius used to go with the brothers to the village church on Saturday and Sunday. Following the erection of a special church for the monks, the latter, not having a priest among them, attended a village church for the Saturday evening Eucharist, and the village clergy came to conduct the service at the monastery on Sunday mornings.[17]

For the monastic centers in Lower Egypt, there are numerous testimonies concerning the double Eucharistic celebrations of Saturday and Sunday at the end of the fourth century.[18] Strictly speaking, the two celebrations are not explicitly mentioned, but what is clearly stated is that the brothers got together on Saturday *and* Sunday. We do know that everywhere in Egypt, except for Alexandria, the Eucharist was celebrated on those two days. Sozomen, for example, says, "The first and last day of the week, the monks participated in the Holy Mysteries."[19]

Socrates made clear that in the region of Alexandria, the Saturday Eucharist was celebrated in the evening. Among the disciples of Abba Apollo, the daily Eucharist was at the ninth hour.[20] We cannot be sure about Scetis. According to Cassian, it was held on Saturday morning. In a Conference of Abba Piamoun, it is reported that the excommunicated Paphnutius would dash very early to the church Saturday and Sunday, not to receive communion, but to prostrate himself at the door.[21] The custom might have varied in the course of the fourth century but if the Eucharist took place on Saturday, following a community meal, it could only have been in the afternoon.

The anchorites, wearing their finest tunics,[22] gathered at the church for this meal, followed by the Eucharistic celebration. They sometimes had a long way to go. For the monks of Cellia,

---

[17]Veilleux, pp. 232, 237.
[18]A 805 (Ward, p. 213); Eth 13, 79; 14, 33; Cassian, Inst. 3, 2; 5, 26; Conf. 3, 1; HM 20, 7; HL 7, 5.
[19]Sozomen, *Hist. Eccl.* III, 14 (Migne, PG 67, 1072 C); VI, 31 (PG 1388B).
[20]HM 8, 51.
[21]Cassian, Conf. 18, 15.
[22]A 926 (Ward, p. 240).

Rufinus speaks of three or four miles,[23] but in Scetis, the cells of some hermits must have been much farther from the church. Paphnutius lived five miles away.[24] For Arsenius, an apothegm mentions thirty-two miles,[25] in which case it would certainly have been difficult to cover twice this distance, coming and going, in two days. When cells were not too far away, the monks could return to them at night and go back to the church Sunday morning.[26] But most would have to remain in prayer all night.

Eucharistic Liturgy and Communion

We have few details on the development of the Eucharistic liturgy. It was probably linked either to the morning or evening office. An account by Daniel about Scetis at the time of Arsenius says that during the celebration, the monks would stand on their bales of papyrus and had a good view of what was happening at the altar.[27] But concerning Arsenius himself, Daniel says that at church he would habitually stand behind a pillar "so that no one would see his face and that he himself couldn't see another."[28] Even today, this pillar is visible in the church at Deir-Baramus.

In the church of the Cells, Helladius was also noted for his contemplation. Never would he raise his eyes to see the ceiling.[29] After the breaking of the bread, the monks approached the altar to partake of the Body and Blood of Christ. Sometimes it might be granted to an elder to see angels intervening during distribution of communion, themselves giving the Blessed Sacrament to monks of eminent saintliness.[30] The priest Eulogius had the gift of being able to discern the state of soul of each communicant. When he noticed that one of them was in a bad mood, he would deprive him of communion.[31] Macarius greatly admired the

---

[23]HM Latin 22 (PL 21, 444); cf. HM 20, 8.
[24]Cassian, Conf. 3, 1.
[25]A 59 (Ward, p. 12).
[26]Eth 14, 33.
[27]A 189 (Ward, p. 53).
[28]A 80 (Ward, p. 19).
[29]A 225 (Ward, p. 62).
[30]HL 18, 25; Arm 18, 88; SP, New Collection, p. 272 (II 434).
[31]HM 16, 1-2.

fervor of the two young strangers he had received in the desert when they went to receive holy communion.[32]

A lovely apothegm by Poemen evokes the place held by the Eucharist in the lives of the Desert Fathers. Quoting a verse of the psalm, "As the deer yearns for running streams, so my soul is longing for You, O God," he applied it to the monk in the desert:

> One is burned by the venom of demons just like the stag is burned by the venom of the reptiles it swallows, so he longs for "Saturday and Sunday, to come to the source of the waters, that is, to the body and blood of the Lord, in order to be cleansed of the Evil One's bitterness."[33]

This text confirms that the desert monks received the Eucharist only on Saturday and Sunday. Cassian, however, mentions daily communion several times.[34] This was certainly the case in some parts of Egypt, such as among the disciples of Apollo in the Thebaid. One elder said, "Monks should communicate daily in the Mysteries of Christ. From then on as they continually commemorate the passion of Christ, it is useful for them to keep themselves ready each day and, so long as they're worthy, receive the celestial mysteries, because this is how we also gain the remission of sins."[35]

In the Cells and Scetis, it seems the most common custom was weekly communion. Cassian says that certain monks, judging themselves to be unworthy, received communion only once a year, but this practice was not recommended.[36] The recluses who never left their cells might receive the Eucharist brought to them by an angel—as happened daily to Anouph[37]—or from a priest who came by now and then. In this manner an Abba John received the holy sacrament every Sunday for three years and, like Anouph, lived off it since he took no other food.[38] We also

---

[32]A 486 (Ward, pp. 134ff).
[33]A 604 (Ward, p. 171).
[34]Cassian, Inst. 6, 8; Conf. 7, 30; 9, 21; 14, 8.
[35]HM 8, 56-57.
[36]Cassian, Conf. 23, 21.
[37]HM 11, 5.
[38]HM 13, 4.

learn of an Abba Mark the Egyptian who never left his cell for thirty years, with a priest coming in to celebrate the Eucharist.[39] It was therefore acceptable for some anchorites not to attend the weekly gatherings, without being censured for this practice. Among the latter was an elder from the Cells.[40] But we learn from Palladius of others whose conduct was condemned. Valens, for instance, claimed he didn't need communion because he had seen Christ. The Fathers put him in chains for a year.[41] The same happened to Heron and Ptolemy who also did not want to participate in the Holy Mysteries.[42] Motius advised a brother always to be like everyone else and not make himself conspicuous by saying, "I do not go to the *synaxis*; I do not eat at the *agape*."[43]

Legitimate or not, the exceptions confirm the rule. Contrary to what some historians have claimed, the Egyptian anchorites who withdrew from the local ecclesiastical communities did not, in any way, spurn the sacraments of the Church. It was in the course of the liturgy at his local village church that Antony first heard the calling to the perfect life,[44] and nothing leads to the conclusion that he never again participated in a Eucharistic celebration, even if his biographer, St Athanasius, doesn't mention it. Macarius in Scetis, like Antony on his mountain, no doubt went without communion for a long time, but it is interesting to note that at one of their meetings, they brought up the question of Mass.[45] We should also recall that Macarius didn't hesitate to walk almost thirty-five miles from Scetis to Nitria to attend the Mass celebrated by Pambo.[46] As soon as there were enough of them in Scetis, Nitria and the Cells, the anchorites had their own churches and priests. And in the desert churches, as in others, deprivation of communion was one of the penalties for serious faults.

---

[39] A 542 (Ward, p. 150); N 254.
[40] N 21.
[41] HL 25, 5.
[42] HL 26, 2; 27, 2.
[43] A 533 (Ward, p. 148).
[44] VA 2.
[45] A 479 (Ward, p. 133).
[46] A 455 (Ward, p. 125).

Meals Taken Together

The main purpose of the weekly gatherings was the Eucharistic celebration in which the desert monks manifested their fraternal communion among themselves and with the whole Church. This celebration was preceded on Saturday afternoon by a meal taken together which was also intended to express and maintain the links of charity which united all the anchorites in the vicinity. The name given to this meal—the *agape*—is exactly what the first Christians called the meal they took together and which culminated in the Eucharist.[47]

This meal was more carefully laid out than those taken individually in the cells during the week. The fast was broken on Saturday as well as Sunday.[48] The brothers were served cooked foods, vegetables and gruel, fruit and even wine. In principle, in those days the monks had to abandon their usual diet. One elder from Scetis, who usually abstained from bread and wine, was always the first to help himself to both at the community meal.[49] In the Cells, a brother one day declared in front of everyone, "I eat nothing cooked, only salt." One of the elders got up and told him, "It would have been better for you to have eaten some meat in your cell today instead of making such a declaration."[50]

The meal was taken in silence. Whenever brothers spoke, the priest or an elder reprimanded them.[51] One day someone began laughing and John Colobos wept over it.[52] Some, on the contrary, while eating and drinking like the others, were lost in prayer.[53] The service was usually conducted by young brothers but it did happen that a priest or an elder—such as Alonius[54]—also wanted to carry out this office. When goblets were being

---

[47]Cf. C. Donahue, "The Agapè of the Hermits of Scété," *Studia Monastica*, Vol. I, 1959, pp. 97-114. On many points we disagree with this author, though he did collect the documents on the subject.

[48]Cassian, Inst. 3, 11-12.

[49]Arm 17, 7; SP, New Collection, p. 269 (II 355).

[50]N 256.

[51]A 251 (Ward, p. 69).

[52]A 324 (Ward, p. 87).

[53]N 314.

[54]A 251 (Ward, p. 69); Bu II 117.

169

distributed, each had to say upon receiving one, "Pardon," the equivalent of our "Thank you."[55] One day when he was in Scetis, Theodore of Pherme was astonished at the brothers for not saying this and declared, "The monks have lost their nobility which is to say, 'Pardon.' "[56] Monks passing through could sometimes be astounded and scandalized by the voracity of the Scetiots, so the priest would explain to them that they would act in the same manner if their customary diet was as strict as that of the Scetis monks.[57]

In the early days, the *agape* was probably held in the church itself, then the only building apart from the cells. Later there was a refectory adjoining the church as well as other buildings used as storehouses. In fact, there had to be supplies in common for these meals which could attract several hundred monks.[58] A steward was put in charge of collecting and distributing them. Cassian knew an Abba John who took care of this job.[59]

Apart from the *agape* on Saturday evening preceding the Eucharist, there could be a second communal meal after the Sunday morning service, or at least a distribution of bread and wine. This explains better why some monks, having already partaken in the Saturday *agape* with the brothers, wanted to return to their cells as soon as possible after the Sunday Mass in order to maintain the fervor the Eucharist had given them. This is how Isaac put it to justify his departure right after Mass.[60] Sisoes the Theban and a brother from the Cells used to do the same.[61]

One might wonder if the Sunday meal had always been the normal practice. The brothers may have invited each other to eat in their cells.[62] One day in the Cells, the priest ordered the monks

---

[55]A 322 (Ward, p. 86).

[56]A 273 (Ward, p. 74).

[57]N 242.

[58]Cassian, Conf. 19, 1. But Cassian speaks here about a meal in a cenobitic monastery in the Diolcos regions.

[59]Cassian, Inst. 5, 40; Conf. 21, 9.

[60]A 423 (Ward, p. 110).

[61]A 840 (Ward, p. 219); N 160.

[62]A 591 (Ward, p. 169).

to cook their food before coming to church so as to return home right after Mass.[63] In Scetis, Paësius and Isaiah used to spend Saturday and Sunday together in Paësius' cell, but they attended the Eucharist celebration.[64] Did they eat together or with the brothers at the communal *agape*?

In one account of uncertain origin, we are told that seven brothers who each occupied a desert cell would meet on Saturday at the ninth hour, each bringing whatever food he could find — nuts, figs, dates, lettuce, cabbages. They would eat together, recite Holy Scripture, spend all night praising God and break up on Sunday afternoon.[65] The account makes no mention of the Eucharist.

Conferences and Discussions

"How good it is to sit down and prattle!" is the inscription celebrating the triumph of King Merneptah.[66] Egyptians always loved exchanging thoughts on the most diverse subjects during interminable discussions. Anchorites who spent almost the whole week in the silence of their cells liked to get together on Saturday and Sunday for spiritual discussions on interesting subjects — life in the desert, observances, the struggle against demons and thoughts — basically all the themes we find in the apothegms were bandied about on the weekends. Leaving the church after the liturgy or the *agape*, they would form a circle around an elder, and the brothers would question him on his opinions,[67] or an elder would pose a question, asking each one for his reaction.[68] Sometimes one or the other, through a sense of humility, said nothing or would simply reply, "I don't know."[69] The subject of the discussion might be words of Holy Writ. Or, like the Old Testament prophets, an elder would do something bizarre which intrigued the others and then he would

---

[63]VP VI 4, 31 in SP, New Collection, p. 207.
[64]Eth 13, 79.
[65]PA App 8.
[66]Quoted by Sister René-Joseph, *Le Nil et ses horizons*, Paris, 1958, p. 147.
[67]A 323 (Ward, p. 87).
[68]A 27 (Ward, p. 7); N 29.
[69]A 17 (Ward, p. 4).

explain the edifying meaning of the action.[70] Often a discussion would be about the superiority of the virtues and observances. For instance, Cassian reports that once the elders discussed with St Antony which virtue was most needed by a monk.[71] The Saint ended the debate by giving a solution which everyone found to be wise. But sometimes there were anti-establishment and proud types who dared openly attack a venerable elder, like Eucarpius who had the nerve one day to publicly hurl abuse at John Colobos, going so far as to call him a "prostitute who curries favors to get more admirers."[72]

Brothers might sometimes doze off and even fall asleep during a spiritual conference. Whenever this happened, all the elder had to do was tell a slightly frivolous story to wake the brothers up and get their attention.[73] It was Cassian who noted this fact, and also told about an elder named Machetes who, on the contrary, had received from God the grace to not fall asleep during a spiritual conference but who, on the other hand, would immediately drift off whenever spiteful talk about others began.[74] If a discussion ever got out of hand, an elder could always slip away so as not to lose his sense of peace and contemplation.[75]

Discussions could occasionally deal with abstract subjects but generally zeroed in on practical questions dealing directly with the spiritual life and monastic observance. Brothers might admit having had evil thoughts or to having committed faults. An elder gifted with the ability to read the heart might also point out and reveal the thoughts and sins of a certain brother,[76] or he might use a clever tactic to get a brother to admit his fault.

At times, when an important question surfaced or a serious scandal broke out, the elders would meet "in council" to judge and resolve the case. When the apothegms deal with this kind of extraordinary meeting, most often they recall the refusal of an

---

[70]N 621.
[71]Cassian, Conf. 2, 2-4.
[72]Regnault, p. 51.
[73]Cassian, Inst. 5, 31.1
[74]*Ibid.*, 5, 29.
[75]A 340 (Ward, p. 91).
[76]HM 12, 10-11.

elder to sit at this court because he knew himself to be a sinner. This is how Bessarion, Moses, Pior and no doubt many others acted.[77]

One day in Scetis, the elders gathered to discuss Melchizedek and forgot to summon Abba Copres.[78] The oversight might have been intentional, because they must have been aware of Copres' antipathy to biblical and theological discussions. Once, during this type of session in the Cells, Evagrius was put in his place in no uncertain terms by the presiding priest: "We know, Evagrius, that had you stayed in your own country, you'd be a bishop, but here you are nothing but a stranger!"[79]

It was at meetings like these that the elders decided on the penalties and penances for brothers who had seriously transgressed.[80] These were whipped, put in chains, excommunicated, locked up or banished from the desert. St Jerome tells about the elders of Nitria getting together to decide what to do with money found in the cell of a deceased monk. The money was buried with the corpse.[81]

These special meetings were held only now and then, unlike the liturgical gatherings each weekend. These provided the desert monks with a balance between solitary living and community living which is still followed today in Coptic monasteries, though under different forms. Since the disappearance of all the Pachomian convents, anchoritism remains the only type of monastic life in Egypt, though tempered always by regular and more or less frequent relations between the monks. This is called semi-anchoritism but, in this context, absolute eremitism still remains in the forefront. As noted, each monastery has its hermitages where one or another of the monks may live for a certain amount of time.

---

[77] A 162, A 497, A 779 (Ward, pp. 42, 139, 199).
[78] A 444 (Ward, p. 118).
[79] A 233 (Ward, p. 64).
[80] N 186; HL 18 and 25.
[81] St Jerome, *Letters*, 22, 33.

FOURTEEN

❧✙❧

Angels and Demons

With our modern mentality, imbued with scientism and positivism, we find it hard to imagine the conception the Desert Fathers had about the bonds between the visible and invisible worlds. To us, these are two absolutely distinct and different worlds. Only the visible world has consistency, the other being nothing but an unknown and unknowable world, filled with our fantasies and illusions. For the Egyptians of Antiquity it was, instead, the opposite. The visible was but an ephemeral and fleeting appearance where, more exactly, the two worlds were so closely mingled and somewhat interwoven one in the other that it was impossible to separate them. There was no border between the two, neither gulf nor gate. The links and exchanges were continuous, so much so that an anchorite in the desert was not very surprised to see appear before him an angel or a demon. Angels and demons were part of his universe and his horizon. The fact that they render themselves visible at certain moments changes nothing of the reality that they are always present in the world of the Desert Fathers.

More Angels Than Demons

The angels are assuredly more numerous than the demons, if one credits the story of a vision related in an apothegm by Abba Moses. One day when the former bandit was gripped by violent temptations, Isidore, trying to calm him, escorted him to the terrace roof and, gazing towards the Occident, they saw a vast crowd of demons thrashing about on all sides. Isidore then asked him to turn towards the East where there were many more multitudes of angels sent by the Lord to help people.[1] However, the good angels, one must admit, are not spoken of as much and, because of their humility, the Desert Fathers especially were more reluctant to talk about the apparition of angels than about the attacks of demons, the latter being neither a sign of perfection nor of honor as angelic visits could be.

We cannot imagine Antony without a few demons around him but was he often portrayed in the company of angels? It is true that his biographer goes on at some length about all the attacks upon him by the Devil while mentioning only one instance when an ecstatic Antony saw angels coming to help him against the demons.[2] But from the way in which the Saint describes the signs which enable us to recognize angelic apparitions, we see that he speaks from experience.[3] Certainly he was often visited by holy angels. The alphabetical collection of apothegms begins specifically with the story of an angel sent to comfort Antony, who was feeling helpless in his solitude.[4]

In all the apothegms one can find at least fifty cases of angelic interventions, at least twenty of which are found in the *History of the Monks* and the *Lausiac History*. They are worth pointing out since they allow us to counterbalance in a notable way all the emphasis generally given to the bad angels in the lives of the Desert Fathers

Angels and Monks Stand Up to the Demons

The good angels intervene first of all to thwart the action of demons. Macarius saw an angel chase away the demons which were settling likes flies on the eyes and lips of one of the two small strangers he had received in the desert.[5] Another elder, who had asked God to allow him to see the demons, saw them as

---

[1] A 495 (Ward, p. 138).
[2] VA 65.
[3] VA 35.
[4] A 1 (Ward, pp. 1-2).
[5] A 486 (Ward, pp. 134ff.).

bees around a man but he also saw angels chasing them away.[6]
Night and day the monk has beside him angels who are there to
dispel the demons.[7] All through his *Treatise on Prayer*, Evagrius
describes the presence of angels near a praying monk.[8] They encourage him, sustain him and pray with him, while the demons
do all they can to distract him from his praying.[9] In all his writings, Evagrius evokes the action of the good angels who fight for
us against the demons.[10]

But it is especially at the moment of death that the angels
intervene in favor of the souls they are charged with leading to
heaven—this is why they are called "psychopomps." They were
already part of ancient Egyptian mythology. These were traditional beliefs, but they were revitalized by the experience of the
great desert monks.

In this manner Antony saw the soul of Amoun taken to
heaven by angels and John Colobos saw that of Paësia, the sinner
who died the morning after her conversion.[11] Paphnutius had
also seen angels taking a soul and, later, some priests saw Paphnutius' own soul rising to heaven with an angelic escort.[12] But
many other cases, often anonymous, are reported in the apothegms. Sometimes the demons show up first to carry off the
soul of a monk who had not been too fervent, and the angels
snatch him away.[13] Most often the angels are the ones who take
the soul first and the demons try to steal it.[14] In some accounts,
angels come to warn a monk of his approaching death.[15] This
happened to Sisoes, who asked for a postponement in order to
do penance, but the Lord, anxious to greet the aged Saint who
had already reached perfection, told the angels, "Bring me the

---

[6]N 396.
[7]N 592/45.
[8]Evagrius, *Prayer*, 30, 74-75, 80-81, 96, 112, 145.
[9]*Ibid.*, 47, 69, 74, 90-92, 94-95, 98-99, 134, 138-140.
[10]Evagrius, *Praktikos*, 24 and 76.
[11]A 355 (Ward, pp. 93ff.); VA 60; HL 7, 6; 8, 6.
[12]HM 14, 17; 14, 23.
[13]N 88, N 367.
[14]N 622.
[15]N 340.

chosen vessel of the desert."[16] Usually the Fathers who are
in attendance near the dying one will see what's going on — as
with Anouph.[17] At other times it is an elder attending his dying
disciple and only the latter sees the angels.[18] Out of kindness,
they may even ask the one they've come to fetch if he wants to
go without delay or if they should return later. All don't react
like Sisoes and one answered the angels, "I want to go. Take my
soul."[19]

The angels are only carrying out their final duties toward
those they've been appointed to protect, accompany and help
throughout their earthly life. Most of the time their activities remain invisible to mortal eyes. One should not even wish to see
them. It is best to see only one's own sins.[20] The Desert Fathers
went so far as to say, "Even if an angel should really show itself
to you, don't receive it, but humble yourself saying, 'I am not
worthy to see an angel because I am living in sin.' "[21] In his
Treatise on Prayer, Evagrius tells of a monk walking in the desert,
engrossed in his prayer. Two angels appeared and started keeping pace with him, one on his right, the other on his left. But the
monk paid them no attention "so as not to lose what was better."[22] In the desert it was thought better to risk being impolite to
a real angel than to be duped by a demon disguised as an "angel
of light." Experienced anchorites like St Antony, nevertheless,
knew how to tell the good from the bad angels, and some among
them were not at all surprised to see angels intervening on their
behalf or on behalf of a brother in difficulty.

Angels Providing Food and Angels Bringing Succor

These interventions were extremely varied and could be
placed in several categories. First, there are "nutritive" angels,
those who bring to some anchorite either corporal or spiritual

[16]A 817 (Ward, p. 215).
[17]HM 11, 8.
[18]N 340.
[19]N 23.
[20]N 3332, N 745.
[21]N 311.
[22]Evagrius, *Prayer*, 112.

food. An elder in a vision saw angels giving Moses combs of honey.[23] It was undoubtedly a symbol, yet the *History of the Monks* tells about several Fathers—Or, Apollo, Anouph and Helle—who were actually fed by angels either occasionally or habitually for a certain period of time.[24] Palladius' companion on three occasions received freshly baked bread, wine, oil and wheat from an angel.[25] Lost and starving in the desert, Zeno was helped and fed by an angel.[26] In the Cells, an elder fell sick and an angel came to keep him company and serve him for a week. Then, when some brothers arrived, the angel disappeared and the elder died right after telling them about the miracle.[27]

Angels intervened perhaps more often than we think to physically feed some anchorites, yet their main task was to help those who were tempted and discouraged. We find them comforting monks who had decided to leave the desert and return to the world.[28] Most often they remained invisible and carried out their work discreetly without being noticed, but sometimes they hurriedly intervened in full view to save a monk in danger.[29] To overcome drowsiness, Sisoes would suspend himself above a precipice. An angel came and put an end to this perilous exercise.[30] It was also an angel who convinced a monk to give up his plan to move closer to a source of water. The angel stood beside him and counted his steps in order to reward him accordingly.[31] Another angel was content to assure a brother that his footsteps were counted and would earn him a great reward before God, but that it was not there to play the role of a taxi meter.[32]

These angels could be ranked with those spoken of by Evagrius and with others among the "companion" or "escort" angels. There are generally two who surround the anchorite

---

[23]A 76 (Ward, p. 18).
[24]HM 2, 9; 8, 6; 11, 5; 12, 3.
[25]HL 71, 3.
[26]A 239 (Ward, p. 66).
[27]N 212.
[28]N 34.
[29]N 169.
[30]A 836 (Ward, p. 219).
[31]N 199.
[32]N 441.

with dignity.[33] An elder who wanted to visit a dying saint in a town went there furtively by night so as not to be seen by anyone. God sent two angels to meet him, light the way and honor him.[34] Often angels came to the rescue of monks in distress in the desert, becoming their porters or carriers when needed.[35] This happened especially to Macarius and Amoun, when the latter was embarrassed to undress in order to cross a stream.[36]

Healing and Doctoring Angels

While their known interventions are rarer, one should especially mention the healing angels who become surgeons when needed. Abba John was healed instantly of purulent wounds on his feet by an angel.[37] The priest Piammonas, after having been roughly treated by a demon, was restored to perfect health by an angel.[38] An anchorite in Rhaithou suffered from hepatitis. An angel came, opened his stomach, removed his liver, cleaned it carefully, then put it back.[39]

Abba Serenus told Cassian that he had vehemently desired and asked God to free him from temptations of the flesh. In a nocturnal vision, an angel came, "opened his body, removed an inflamed tumor from his entrails, threw it away, then put all the viscera back in place as they were before."[40] For the same end, another monk, Elias, had a similar operation performed by angels. He looked after a monastery of 300 moniales and, as he was still young, he worried about his chastity. Three angels arrived, one grabbed his hands, another his feet and the third castrated him with a razor, not in reality but figuratively, notes Palladius.[41]

---

[33]N 19.
[34]A 353 (Ward, p. 93).
[35]N 132B; HM 21, 6.
[36]HL 8, 6.
[37]HM 13, 7.
[38]HM 25, 3.
[39]N 132 A.
[40]Cassian, Conf. 7, 2.
[41]HL 29, 3.

Angels on Special Missions

As can be seen, angelic actions sometimes take on unusual forms. One day an elder came to see John Colobos and found him asleep with an angel standing nearby fanning him.[42] The angels are full of gentleness toward the great ascetics but can be formidable when they have to give a lesson to some elder who is too stern. Isaac the Theban, who had condemned a brother, found an angel waiting for him at the door to his cell who told him, "God sent me to ask you where you want Him to put the guilty brother you condemned—in the Kingdom or in Hell?"[43] After such a rebuke, there was nothing left for the elder but to grieve and shed tears of penitence until the day he died. On the other hand, Paphnutius, who abstained even from judging people whom he had seen commit the basest acts, was congratulated by an angel.[44] Another elder who felt himself abandoned by God was told by a visiting angel that this had happened to him because he had judged a brother.[45]

If an anchorite is a little too pleased with himself and his asceticism, we've seen how God then sends an angel to inform him that many others match or even surpass him in virtue. Often the angels appearing to the Desert Fathers came to bring them a message or simply to relay to them the meaning of an event or give a commentary on a word from the Scriptures. One of the cherubim predicted to Macarius his future destiny and his innumerable spiritual descendants.[46] An angel also announced to Abba Or the influence and authority he would have on a large number of monks.[47] Another explained to an elder the interpretation of a biblical passage.[48] Others were sent either to reassure a monk on the fate of one of his friends in the hereafter,[49] or to

---

[42]A 348 (Ward, p. 92).
[43]A 422 (Ward, pp. 109-110); N 477.
[44]A 786 (Ward, p. 202).
[45]N 20.
[46]Am 118, 1.
[47]HM 2, 4.
[48]N 314.
[49]N 74.

explain the reasons for a particular surprising event.[50] Often the minor importance of the reason for the apparition leads us to the conclusion that the angels are really always besides the Desert Fathers, ready to seize the smallest opportunity to enlighten, help or comfort them. It is because they know what is at stake in the battle unfolding in the desert:

> Events happen like in a theater: on one hand God and his angels follow the struggle, encouraging the athletes of Christ. Facing them, the Devil and his demons arouse the passions. When a victory is scored, all the angels glorify God and cry, "The athlete has won an incomparable victory!"[51]

When we take note of the important place held by angels in the best references about the Desert Fathers, it is astonishing to see that later literature and popular imagery has almost completely left them out. It is only simple justice to recall their presence, without minimizing the presence and influence of the demons.

Demons in the Desert

The demons assuredly populate the desert as much as the monks. According to Abba Serenus, they are numberless, flitting about continually in the air, taking on multiple forms.[52] Happily, divine providence usually prevents people seeing them, otherwise they would live in dreadful terror.

In Christian Antiquity, the existence of demons was not a widespread belief among simple and uneducated people.[53] And the greatest minds of the period — Tertullian, Origen,[54] Evagrius, Athanasius and Cassian — couldn't be bothered with such "childish credulity." Yet demons are, nevertheless, visible enough in the Gospel that it isn't necessary to quote other sources to prove their presence in the Egyptian deserts of the fourth century.

[50]N 368, N 461, N 521.
[51]N 454.
[52]Cassian, Conf. 8., 12.
[53]A. J. Festugière, Les Moines d'Orient, I, p. 24.
[54]Cf. J. Daniélou, Dictionnaire de spiritualité, Vol. 3, col. 174-189.

What the monks say about them doesn't come from wild Gnostic or Manichean imaginings but from their own experience. Antony mentions it several times in his great discourse on the demons. He wants to communicate to his disciples the fruits of this experience, so that they in turn can fight the evil spirits fearlessly.[55] As Louis Bouyer notes, "This doesn't mean that we don't find in the *Life* and related texts many undeniably folkloric elements. But these inform us of them, giving to their presence in our texts, a deeply Christian meaning."[56]

In the Gospel, we find the demons who have been chased away by Jesus hiding out in arid and desert places.[57] And Jesus himself had been led by the Spirit to the desert to be tempted by the Devil.[58] When Antony got there, the demons tried to scare him away: "Get out of our territory!" they yelled. "What have you come to do in the desert?"[59] In some way, the desert became the domain of the demons because, as paganism gave way to Christianity, Satan had to retreat. He laments to Antony that there is no longer a place or town for him: "Now there are Christians everywhere and, to top it all off, the very desert is filling up with monks."[60] This is the reason why the Devil tried to ban Antony from the desert, "fearing that, in no time, the desert would be taken over by asceticism."[61]

At that time, Antony settled in a tomb but, like the ruins of pagan temples, the tombs were also places of refuge for the demons. An anchorite lived in an old temple and the demons came to tell him the same as they had to Antony, "Get out of our place!"[62] When Macarius wanted to enter the garden tomb of Jannes and Jambres, which had belonged to some magicians, seventy demons immediately came to meet him and, beating their wings like ravens against his face, asked him, "What do

---

[55]VA 16, 22, 28, 29.
[56]L. Bouyer, *La Vie de saint Antoine*, p. 73.
[57]Mt 12:43; Lk 11:24-26, Lk 8:29.
[58]Mt 4:14.
[59]VA 13.
[60]VA 41.
[61]VA 8.
[62]A 265 (Ward, p. 71).

you want, Macarius? Why do you come to our place? You can't stay here." Unperturbed, he told them, "I'm just going in to look around and then I'll leave."[63]

Violent Assaults on Anchorites

What follows explains why the Desert Fathers—especially the greatest among them—had so many dealings with demons. The latter were evidently keen on attacking the most advanced monks, those who were greater threats and did them the most harm. Of all the demons who came to drag someone into sin, the champion who won the palm was the one who succeeded in making a monk give in to lust—with a moniale!—after besieging him for fifteen or even forty years.[64] The Devil took it out more on monks than lay people[65] and, among the monks, he picked on the most fervent, usually leaving the half-hearted and negligent ones alone.[66] A great anchorite asked, "Why, Satan, do you fight me like this?" He heard the Devil reply, "You're the one who's fighting me ferociously."[67]

To these, Satan often appeared openly, without disguise and without an intermediary, that is, explains Evagrius, without anyone taking his place.[68] We know that Moses, Arsenius, Cronius and others were subjected to terrible assaults in this fashion.[69] But no doubt it was Antony who had the worst time with the demons, as his biography attests. It seems that the Devil threw in all his troops, let loose with all his ammunition and deployed all his arms against the one who was the first and greatest of the Desert Fathers. Against each of those who came after him, the demons used but a small number of their ruses and tricks, and their attacks were not as bad. At the end of the fourth century, Serenus declared that the demons no longer showed the same strength and violence as in the days of the first

[63]HL 18, 7.
[64]Cassian, Conf. 8, 16; N 191.
[65]N 550.
[66]N 401-402.
[67]N 35.
[68]Evagrius, *Praktikos* 5.
[69]A 41, A 495 (Ward, pp. 9, 138); Eth 14, 53; HL 19, 9; HM 1, 40-44.

anchorites.[70] But a little earlier, Sisoes said that Satan "hounds the monks more at present, because his time is coming and he's becoming agitated."[71]

Evidently this assessment is relative and depends on the experience of each anchorite. What is certain is that the Devil is still present in the desert, and he's there to fight:

> One of the elders related that one night he had begun to pray in the inner desert, when he heard the very loud sound of a horn, like a call to battle. He was astonished, telling himself the desert was empty and no one was there. So where did the sound of a horn come from in such a desert? Would there be a war? Then the demon came face-to-face with him and said in a loud voice, "Yes, monk, it's war. If you want, fight; if not, surrender to your enemies."[72]

The Devil, recognizing in the anchorites his greatest adversaries, did everything he could to sidetrack them from their plan of living in the desert and, once they arrived, he would try to force them to return to the world. It was enough of a victory for him to get a hermit out of his cell and to do so, as we've seen, he would use every tactic and all the violence possible. He even went so far as to grab a monk's hand and drag him outside.[73] Sometimes the demons would simulate a hurricane and create an infernal din, shaking the cell walls until it looked like they would collapse.[74] One day they set fire to Macarius' cell and the mat under him was consumed.[75]

They wanted to terrify the monk any way they could to make him leave the area. For this, they would transform themselves into all kinds of animals: dogs, lions, bears, leopards, bulls, wolves, horses, wild asses, serpents. asps and scorpions.[76]

---

[70]Cassian, Conf. 7, 23.
[71]A 814 (Ward, p. 214).
[72]Unpublished apothegm translated from Arabic.
[73]A 265 (Ward, p. 71).
[74]VA 39; HL 16, 6.
[75]HL 18, 18.
[76]VA 9 and 39; HL 16, 6.

The demoniac bestiary in the *Life of Antony* is especially rich and varied. Jerome takes it up again in the *Life of Hilarion* but, for good measure, he adds foxes and sheep.[77] Serenus' list, reported by Cassian, is even longer: onocentaurs (monsters that were half-men, half-donkey), satyrs, mermaids, owls, ostriches, llamas, hedgehogs, basilisks, lions, dragons and, according to Serenus, there is a link between the demons and each of these animals.[78]

In his *Chapters on Prayer*, Evagrius recounts that one monk, as soon as he extended his arms to pray, saw the Devil assaulting him in the shape of a lion who "stood straight up on its front paws and sank its claws into the athlete's two cheeks, without letting go its grip as long as he didn't drop his arms."[79] He also tells of the demon who attacked John the Dwarf "in the form of a dragon wrapping itself around his body, pummeling his flesh and belching in his face."[80] Another anchorite "was assailed by demons and, for two weeks, they played with him as if he were a balloon, tossing him into the air and catching him with a mat."[81]

The elders who were handled roughly like this didn't budge and continued praying, but they didn't always emerge from the battle unharmed. Antony was often beaten black and blue by the Devil. One morning he was found unconscious in the tomb which would become his cell; only the next evening did he regain consciousness, when his disciples had begun preparing for his burial.[82] As for Moses, while drawing water from a well, he received such a terrible blow to the small of his back that he was infirm for a year.[83] A statement by John of Lycopolis confirms that one monk was so badly tortured that after three years, he was nearly dead,[84] while another was almost strangled to death by the demons.[85]

---

[77]*Life of Hilarion*, 6-7.
[78]Cassian, Conf. 7, 32.
[79]Evagrius, *Prayer*, 106.
[80]*Ibid.*, 107.
[81]*Ibid.*, 111.
[82]VA 8 and 40.
[83]HL 19, 9.
[84]HM 1, 40-43.
[85]HM 12, 13.

Such cases of violence are without doubt exceptional and the apothegms do not make too much of them. But the demons, according to Evagrius, can also do things to the anchorite's body which are less cruel but, nevertheless, very unpleasant.[86] They would touch his limbs and side, scratch his ears and tickle his nostrils, chill the stomach muscles or, on the other hand, burn him like a cupping-glass. And, getting into his mouth, they would make him yawn; by shutting his eyelids, they would force him to sleep. These types of treatment, though, appear to have been reserved for the great elders.

Thoughts and Images Suggested by Demons

For ordinary monks, the Devil prefers not to act directly. He most often attacks via thoughts which arouse one's tendency to do evil. Evagrius has classified these diverse "evil thoughts" which match the eight principal vices and as many demons: greed, lust, avarice, sadness, anger, boredom ("acedia"), vainglory and pride. This is the origin of our seven "deadly sins," "acedia" having been dropped as distinctive for hermits or linked to sadness.[87]

In Evagrius' teachings, the demons cannot act directly on the intellect. They arouse evil thoughts by working on the memory and imagination. They remind the anchorite of the relatives, friends, goods and riches he gave up or they make him see images which excite the passions. For this, they usually resort to sensory illusions and hallucinations. They often take the form of a beautiful and desirable woman,[88] but can also look like a priest bringing the Eucharist,[89] even disguised in episcopal garb. A brother thus received a so-called bishop who wanted to become a monk, and set him up in a grotto near his cell.[90] But they are not always illusions. The Devil can take advantage of a visit by

---

[86]A. and C. Guillaumont, *Dictionnaire de spiritualité*, Vol. 3, col. 203.

[87]A. and C. Guillaumont, SC 170, pp. 63-93.

[88]VA 5 and 23; HL 23, 5; HM 1, 33-35; 13, 2.

[89]HM 13, 5.

[90]Arm 19, 53; SP, New Collection, p. 273 (II 498).1

bishops or women of real flesh and bone to tempt the anchorite.[91] The form he appears to like best is that of an Ethiopian man or woman whose dark skin evokes the black tint of malice. When going to bed, one monk found an Ethiopian on his mat.[92] Pachon saw a young Ethiopian girl sitting on his knees.[93] Another demon tempted a very young monk who came to Scetis with his father.[94]

The Ethiopian girl is usually the personification of lust.[95] Apollo saw the demon of pride in the form of a young Ethiopian sitting on his neck.[96] The Devil appeared to Antony looking like a picaninny and the Saint told him, "You're really very despicable because spiritually you're black, and weak as a child."[97] One day during the psalmody, Macarius saw a number of small Ethiopians running from left to right around the praying brothers, placing their fingers on the eyes or mouth of one or the other, doing a thousand tomfooleries to distract and disturb them.[98] In Cassian's *Conferences*, we also find the demon appearing several times in the form of a "hideous Ethiopian."[99]

The Devil doesn't always show up looking repulsive. He also knows how to take on appealing and seductive forms, not only feminine but angelic ones too. They are apparently personages of radiant light who come to awaken a brother for the Office,[100] or offer a brother sound advice, only to finally lead him into the crime of killing his father with an ax.[101] The demons used to come and talk with Valens, who mistook them for angels. One day the Devil appeared to him as Christ, surrounded by a multitude of angels, and the poor proud fellow believed it.[102] On the contrary, experienced monks did not allow

[91]HL 16, 3-4; A 66; N 176; Bu II 420.
[92]A 267 (Ward, p. 72).
[93]HL 23, 5.
[94]N 173.
[95]Eth 14, 27.
[96]HM 8, 3.
[97]VA 6.
[98]R 43 in SP, New Collection, pp. 202-204.
[99]Cassian, Conf. 1, 21; 2, 13; 9, 6.
[100]N 224.
[101]N 480.
[102]HL 25, 1-5.

themselves to be deluded. To the demon showing up as the archangel Gabriel, a monk replied, "Go see if you haven't been sent to someone else because I'm not worthy of this."[103] Before the Devil pretending to be Christ, another elder closed his eyes, saying, "I don't want to see Christ down here."[104] Guessing the same ruse, yet another elder declared, "I believe in my Christ Who said, 'If someone says to you, here is Christ, there is Christ, don't believe him.' "[105] Abba Or was visited by a king sitting on a chariot of fire accompanied by a whole cortege of angels, who told him, "You've done well with all the virtues, my friend. Now adore me and I'll carry you to heaven like Elias." The anchorite simply replied, "My King is Christ Whom I adore without ceasing. You, you're not my king."[106] Then in this case as in all the other similar ones, the demon promptly disappeared.

An even more subtle ruse is for the demon to appear bearing the features of another monk, of a venerable elder coming to give a brother useful advice. A monk brought some loaves of bread to Antony one day and said, "Eat and stop your great works; you're a man, too, and you'll weaken yourself."[107] It was a demon and the Saint scared him away by praying. On the contrary, at other times the demons invited the monks to stop eating altogether; at night, they kept waking them up for prayer, so much so that, lacking food and sleep, their victims ended up finding monastic life unbearable.[108] Or else, stricken with boredom and discouragement, the monks convinced themselves that they were ill and incapable of fasting.[109] The demons never ran out of resources and always found new stratagems to fool the anchorites. When necessary, they quoted Holy Writ but only the Old Testament.[110] They cheerfully made predictions.[111] They

---

[103]N 310.
[104]N 312.
[105]N 313.
[106]HM 2, 9-10.
[107]VA 40.
[108]VA 25.
[109]A 311 (Ward, p. 83).
[110]N 632.
[111]VA 35, 39.

went so far as to speak truthful and wholly reasonable things in order to make it easier to follow up with their lies and fictions.[112]

Weakness of the Demons

When we collect all the accounts in which the Desert Fathers related such experiences, we find ourselves in the presence of an impressive number, enough to frighten us, and are tempted to ask if they were right to reveal the artifices and ruses used by the Devil to attack and destroy the monks. But in reality, if we look more closely, everything about this diabolical strategy transmitted to us serves, on the other hand, to encourage the monks and sustain them in their battles with the demons. For one thing, we find that they don't intervene as often as we might think. For instance, Antony explains that carnal movements sometimes can very well be provoked by demons, but may also be caused by nature or too much food or drink.[113] Dioscorus, speaking of seminal losses produced at night, doesn't even mention demons.[114] They don't have to go after those monks who follow their own will.[115]

It should be recognized that most of the anecdotes related end in the defeat of the Devil, and are intended to show that, in the end, he isn't so formidable. The *Life of Antony* especially always casts the Devil as a weak and contemptible being.[116] If he makes so much noise, if he uses so many artifices and stratagems, it is because he is powerless by himself. Christ overcame and chained him. He has no power over us except as we connive with him.[117] He is compared to the iron head of an ax which can't serve to cut down a tree unless it has a handle; the handle is our will.[118] As long as the monk prays and meditates, the Devil has no power over him,[119] but if he slips into negligence, covet-

---

[112]VA 26.
[113]A 22 (Ward, p. 6).
[114]HM 20, 2.
[115]A 641 (Ward, p. 176).
[116]VA 28.
[117]VA 24.
[118]Sy 10, 131.
[119]A 685 (Ward, p. 183); N 241, N 268, N 366.

ousness, anger, disobedience or some other passion, only then does he become vulnerable.[120]

Farcical and Ridiculous Demons

Again, Antony says demons are like actors playing on a stage. They disguise themselves, change masks and clothes, but remain the harmful beings they've become through their rebellion against God.[121] They willingly become imps and buffoons, bursting with laughter, whistling and dancing.[122] According to Cassian, some even specialize in this buffoonery, getting more fun out of laughing and amusing themselves than others.[123]

One day, in front of Pambo, they were having so much fun with a piece of wood and a feather that they made the strict ascetic laugh. Then they guffawed, "Ha! Ha! Pambo laughed!"

"Yes," he said, "I laughed at your weakness, imbeciles."[124]

One evening, taking advantage of a distraction which came upon Hilarion during his prayer, the Devil jumped on his back and straddled him, spurring him in the sides, striking the nape of his neck with a whip and shouting, "Come on! Why are you falling asleep?" Bursting out laughing, he asked him if he felt faint and needed a handful of barley.[125] After tormenting John of Lycopolis all night long, the demons threw themselves at his feet to mock him, saying, "Forgive us, Abba, for causing you trouble all night long."[126]

Despite this sort of thing, the Desert Fathers were not outdone by the demons. Some, wanting to entice Hierax, who was already a nonagenarian, into giving up his asceticism at the prospect of living much longer, came to tell him, "Old man, what will you do—you still have another fifty years to live?"

---

[120]A 20, 265, 267, 456, 805 (Ward, pp. 5, 71, 72, 126-127, 213); N 401, N 574.
[121]VA 28.
[122]VA 26, 39.
[123]Cassian, Conf. 7, 32.
[124]A 774 (Ward, p. 197).
[125]*Life of Hilarion*, 8.
[126]HM 1, 61.

He retorted, "You're upsetting me greatly because I was prepared to live 200 years."[127]

In Scetis, an elder took on the very demon he had banished from a possessed person. Finally, after twelve years, seeing the demon depart, he said to him, "Why are you running away? Stay a bit longer."[128]

When Macarius found shelter for the night in an old temple, he used a mummy as a pillow. To scare him, the demons spoke as if to a woman, "So and so, come for a swim with us." Then, taking on a feminine voice, one replied, "I have a stranger on me and can't come." So the elder bravely slapped the mummy and said, "Get up and go, if you can."[129] Obviously, Macarius was no more afraid of the demons than he was of women. One day, another elder set out to sell his baskets. The Devil made them disappear. The elder gave thanks to God and the Devil, frustrated, cried out, "Here are your baskets, you rotten old man!"[130]

In the apothegms, above all, the demons often appear to be ridiculous. Theodore saw one come to his place followed by a second. He tied both to his cell door. A third arrived and asked them, "Why are you staying outside?" Thinking himself stronger than the other two, he tried to enter and the elder tied him up in turn. All three pleaded with him to let them go and left, full of shame.[131]

Joseph of Panephysis, when dying, noticed the Devil sitting near the door. He asked his disciple to bring him his staff. Then the elders who were gathered around him saw the Devil flee like a dog.[132] At the approach of death, the anchorites would joyfully retaliate against the demons who, until the very end, hoped to succeed in abusing them.[133]

---

[127]N 33.
[128]N 12.
[129]A 466 (Ward, p. 130).
[130]N 45.
[131]A 294 (Ward, p. 78).
[132]A 394 (Ward, p. 104).
[133]HL 18, 26; N 546.

Demons Driven Out by Anchorites

Having beaten and mastered the Devil at home, the Desert Fathers could easily expel him from possessed people who came to them for help. There is enough material on the subject for a whole chapter because, like the Gospel, ancient monastic literature is filled with accounts about this type of healing.[134] Here, more than anywhere else, is seen the weakness of the demons who cannot resist the injunctions of the Fathers.

One obstinate demon, whom the clerics could not subdue, was expelled by Bessarion, without the elder's being aware of it.[135] Those seeking the cure often didn't want to risk the anchorite's shying away from the task due to humility; therefore subterfuges might have to be employed. For instance, an anchorite was taken to a house where a possessed woman was supposed to pay him for the baskets she purchased. Upon his arrival, the possessed woman slapped him in the face and he turned the other cheek, following the commandment of Christ in the Gospel. The demon cried out, "Oh, Violence, the commandment of Jesus chases me away," and immediately the woman was cured.[136]

Sometimes, again because of humility, an elder would refer a possessed person to another elder. Longinus thus referred one to Zeno, but the demon made a point of admitting that, if he left, it wasn't due to Zeno's injunction but to Longinus' prayers.[137] If necessary, someone might even steal an elder's cloak by the grace of which the possessed person was cured.[138] Some Fathers were known especially for their power to expel demons. Antony recognized this power in his disciple Paul. And the latter did, in fact, order the Devil to depart in the name of Antony until finally he would leave, shouting, "Oh, Violence! Paul's simplicity chases

---

[134]Cf. *Dictionnaire de spiritualité*, Vol. 3, col. 195-196.
[135]A 160 (Ward, p. 41).
[136]A 185 (Ward, pp. 51-52); N 298.
[137]A 452 (Ward, p. 123).
[138]Sy 19, 9.

me away."[139] Antony also was known to have expelled many demons in the name of Christ.[140]

Expelling demons is said to have been done by many other elders as well: Or, Macarius the Egyptian, Pityrion, Copres,[141] Xanthias. The latter was sipping wine when they brought him someone who was possessed. The demon began to revile him, "You've brought me to this wine-bibber!" But before the elder had emptied his glass, the demon was forced to depart.[142] As for Macarius of Alexandria, "he cured so many possessed people that it is impossible to count the numbers."[143]

We often see that humility forces the departure of the demon, which even he admits.[144] One day, an elder ordered the Devil to depart from a possessed person. But first the clever demon posed a question, "Tell me, who are the goats and who are the sheep?" Answered the elder, "The goats are me but the sheep, God knows them." Hearing this, the demon shrieked, "Because of your humility, I have to go!" And so he left.[145] In the offensive and defensive battle against the demons, humility is always—along with prayer, the invocation of Jesus' name and the Sign of the Cross—the all-powerful and supremely efficacious weapon.[146] Against it the demons can do nothing; it is like a suit of armor of which they are completely deprived.

---

[139]HL 22, 9-12; HM 24, 10.
[140]VA 61-64, 71.
[141]HM 2, 6; 10, 1; 15, 1; HL 17, 11.
[142]A 569 (Ward, p. 159).
[143]HL 18, 11.
[144]A 314 (Ward, p. 84).
[145]N 307.
[146]VA 23, 41; A 7, A 185, A 298, A 307, A 488 (Ward, pp. 2, 51, 79, 81, 136).

FIFTEEN

✦✝✦

The Desert Bestiary

In this world, both the visible and the invisible, which the Desert Fathers inhabited, angels and demons were not their only companions. Animals were also very close. Though they are rare in the desert today, they were numerous in the days of the first anchorites.

Egyptians had animals living with them from the very beginning. Even today, in the villages of Upper Egypt, the fellah with his family not only live under the same roof, but in the same room as their livestock — buffaloes, donkeys, camels — and their poultry. In the ancient temples and tombs, sculptures and paintings attest to the peaceful and familiar relations between people and their animals, here below as well as in the other world. It is not only the representations of the divinity by creatures that are half-men, half-beasts that suggest the close link between humans and animals. The sphinx of Giza, with its head of a man and body of a lion, is the best known figure.

The Devil, who knew all this imagery well, came one day to pull on the cord Antony was twisting, appearing with the features of an onocentaur, that is, a beast that is half-man, half-donkey. Antony recognized him immediately and chased him away.[1] In his *Life of Paul*, St Jerome, to alter his model, made him a hippocentaur, half-man, half-horse, which showed Antony the road to take to reach Paul.[2] Suddenly he was no longer an intervention of the Devil but an instrument of divine providence.

---

[1] VA 53.
[2] *Life of Paul*, 7.

194

Jerome's imagination introduces here a false note in the harmonious concert of relations between animals and anchorites. Contrary to what one might think, these relationships are ruled by rigorous and constant laws. God doesn't amuse himself — if we can put it that way — by creating monsters to distract or help the Desert Fathers, and the demons don't have the power to do so. They can't even make existing animals serve their evil purposes. (They required the permission of Christ to enter the pigs and throw them into the sea.) They can only project phony, terrifying beasts and at the same time produce the cries, occurrences and gestures to impress or give the monks a rough time. They really are nothing but fictions and hallucinations. Real animals serve only God and humans, and if they sometimes appear to harm mortals, it is because the people deserve it because of their sins.

In the sources at our disposal, there is no scarcity of beautiful stories to illustrate this truth. There's no need to invent any, as do modern novelists from Gustave Flaubert to Anatole France. I wouldn't dare assert that collectors of fifth- and sixth-century apothegms never allowed themselves to make a few things up but, if they sometimes did, it was always in the spirit of the Desert Fathers.

We won't return to the bestial forms taken by the demons except to note that, regardless of their appearance, the experienced anchorite recognized the diabolical presence. One day when Palladius went to draw water from a well, he noticed an asp there. Terrified, he immediately went to his elder and told him, "We're dead, Abba. I saw an asp at the bottom of the well!" The elder smiled, gave his disciple a grave look, then told him while shaking his head, "And if the Devil felt like changing himself into a serpent or a turtle in every well and put himself in every source of water, you wouldn't drink any more, then?" He went out to draw some himself and took the first drink, saying, "Where there's the mark of the Cross, there can be no evil."[3]

---

[3]HL 2, 4.

Comparisons and Lessons from the Animal World

Before reporting the marvelous or simply astonishing facts which testify to the generally cordial relations between monks and beasts in the desert, the great number of comparisons taken from the animal world by the Fathers to illustrate their remarks must be mentioned. Some of these comparisons are from the Bible; for instance, when it is said we must be wise as serpents and gentle as doves,[4] or when we are reminded that we've been given the power to trample serpents and scorpions underfoot.[5]

Like all other harmful or dangerous animals, these are figures of the demons. But some are versatile. The Devil may be like a roaring lion[6] but the monk must be as dreadful to the demons as the lion is to the wild asses.[7] Also the latter, along with the camels, are models of patience and endurance.[8] The same applies to the dog, the most detestable animal for the Egyptians, who represents either the demon because of its voracity,[9] or the docile monk who comes and goes according to orders given him,[10] or the monk relentlessly sticking to his objective.[11] The demons set upon the monks like bees[12] but these are also good examples of ardor and steadfastness at work.[13] Birds can represent, at the same time, demons throwing themselves upon the monk like prey,[14] and the monk rising above the earth and earthly things.[15]

Bad thoughts which constantly pester the monks are like mice,[16] lizards, scorpions or foxes, flies or midges.[17] Passions that ravage the soul are like worms infesting a field or the body of an

---

[4] A 909 (Ward, p. 234); Bu II 167.
[5] N 383.
[6] A 409 (Ward, p. 106), A 752.
[7] A 689 (Ward, p. 184).
[8] A 562 (Ward, p. 155); N 436.
[9] A 20 (Ward, p. 5).
[10] N 306, N 573.
[11] N 203.
[12] N 369.
[13] A 631 (Ward, p. 174); N 399; Am 146, 10.
[14] A 20 (Ward, p. 5); N 277; Sy 8, 30; Eth 14, 13.
[15] A 167 (Ward, p. 42); N 565; Am 145, 13; 146, 4.
[16] N 535.
[17] A 595 (Ward, p. 170); N 383; Am 174, 9; Eth 13, 84; 14, 13.

animal.[18] Anger is particularly symbolized by the lion, lust by the bear.[19] The monk must maintain a respect for his body by fasting, the same as one keeps a donkey on the right road by using the stick.[20] The hermit's thoughts in his cell are like the little donkey who gets lost here and there and always ends up finding the way back to its mother.[21] The monk must not keep his mouth open like the sardine nor accumulate things like the ant.[22]

The above are only a few samples gleaned from all the collections of apothegms but they attest, by their number and variety, to the familiarity of the Desert Fathers with animals of all kinds—wild or domesticated, from the greatest to the tiniest, from the camel to the ant or midge. Most of these beasts or tiny creatures lived in the desert and the anchorites could see them from near or far, often or rarely. With their minds constantly turned to spiritual things, they found them to be good examples to follow or avoid and cheerfully drew from them useful and healthful lessons. "Nothing is more repugnant than a sinful man —not even the dog, pig or hyena—because these are beasts and respect their condition, while man is created in the image of God and doesn't guard his own condition," said an elder.[23] This is why Abba Xanthias said, "The dog is better than I, because he loves his master and will not be judged."[24]

Encounters Between Beasts and Anchorites

Apart from diabolical interventions, relations between the Desert Fathers and animals may be classified in three categories or degrees: occasional encounters, mutual good services, and peaceful or conciliatory cohabitation. First of all, a more or less ferocious beast might find itself in the way of an anchorite. Either the monk would flee, as did Nisterus one day to avoid vain-

---

[18]A 750 (Ward, p. 191); Am 155, 1; Eth 14, 36.
[19]A 689 (Ward, p. 184).
[20]N 431.
[21]N 198.
[22]Am 147, 6.
[23]Eth 416.
[24]A 570 (Ward, p. 159).

glory,[25] or the animal would steal away. An ostrich with its young ones ran away from Antony.[26]

If necessary, the monk might order the beast to leave. When Pachomius and his brother John were soaking reeds near the Nile, a crocodile emerged from the water. John was terrified. Pachomius reassured him, then threw some water on the reptile's head, while saying, "May the Lord order you never to come back here!"[27]

One day John, Paul's disciple, on orders from his Abba, went to gather dung near a hyena's lair. He asked the elder what he should do with the hyena. Paul replied, joking, "If it comes to you, tie it up and bring it here." John met the hyena who ran away. Pursuing it, he shouted, "My Abba told me to tie you up!" Suddenly the hyena let itself be taken and the elder, who had nervously been waiting for him, saw his disciple arriving with his prey on a leash like a dog.[28]

But an animal didn't always escape unharmed from such an encounter. Going one day to a pond to draw water, Ammonas saw an asp. He threw himself upon the ground, crying, "Lord, I die, or it does!" And immediately, "by the power of Christ, the asp expired."[29] A similar story is attributed to Amoun. It concerns a great serpent ravaging the land. Amoun condemned it and the creature died on the spot.[30]

Normally the Desert Fathers didn't exterminate harmful animals. They chastised them, telling them not to return. A hippopotamus was wreaking havoc in the area where Abba Bes lived. After the peasants asked him, he went there and, spotting the beast which was enormous, he commanded it in a mild voice, "In the name of Jesus Christ, I order you to devastate the country no longer." The animal, as if expelled by an angel, was seen no

---

[25]A 556 (Ward, p. 154).
[26]Am 24, 7.
[27]Veilleux, p. 43.
[28]A 421 (Ward, p. 109).
[29]A 114 (Ward, p. 26).
[30]HM 9, 8-11.

more in the region. Another time, he did the same and expelled a crocodile.[31]

It could happen that an anchorite might suffer some misfortune caused by wild desert beasts. Antony lost a small garden where he cultivated vegetables, near a spring at the bottom of his mountain. At first, the neighboring beasts, coming to drink, often ruined his seeds and plants. He gently captured one of the beasts and told them all, "Why are you harming me? I do no harm to any of you. Go away and in the name of the Lord, don't come near here again!" From then on, as if respecting his command, they came there no more.[32]

A mosquito bit Macarius' foot; he crushed it, then, full of remorse, went and exposed himself, naked, to the large mosquitoes in the Scetis marshes for six months.[33] Yet another time, without any scruple, he killed an asp that had bitten him.[34] On the other hand, another asp refused to bite Pachon, who had laid him on his genitals as a penance.[35]

Mutual Services

Not only could the animals and the Desert Fathers live together without harming each other but they might even render mutual services, according to their respective capacities. For example, an anchorite might happen to assist some beast whose suffering touches his compassionate heart. While praying, Macarius had a hyena come up, nip his tunic and draw him to a neighboring grotto where its little ones had been born blind. Macarius prayed and the babies were able to see. To thank him, the hyena brought him a ram's skin. "Macarius," says the text, "smiled at it as if it were a person filled with gentleness and sensitivity, then he took the skin and made himself a carpet. This skin, even now, is still kept by one of the brothers."[36] We know

[31]HM 4, 3.
[32]VA 50.
[33]HL 18, 4.
[34]HL 18, 10.
[35]HL 23, 5.
[36]HL 18, 27-28; HM 21, 15. [Ed. note: The *Lausiac History* attributes this incident to Macarius of Alexandria; the *History of the Monks* to Macarius of Egypt.]

from Palladius that Macarius had offered the skin in question to Melania,[37] but she in turn might have given it to a monk. In the story Palladius says he heard from Paphnutius, there was only one little blind one and it is said that after seeing it cured, the hyena suckled it. And again, according to Palladius, Macarius himself was suckled by an antelope.[38] In the *Dialogue* of Sulpicius Severus, it wasn't a hyena but a lioness, and Macarius was not named.[39] In the Coptic tradition, it was a gazelle whose little ones were born deformed, with chins in their backs. Macarius cured them on the spot.[40] The same tradition tells us Macarius also removed a straw from a dragon's eye, after which the grateful beast bowed three times and kissed the Saint's feet before departing.[41]

It is more frequent and normal for the beasts to be of service to the Desert Fathers. An elder, for instance, almost died after eating poisonous herbs. He was visited by an ibex, a wild goat, which showed him the plants he could eat and those he could not.[42]

Were some elders tired out from a long trek in the desert? They were helped by some wild asses who asked nothing more than to carry the anchorites.[43] As for Helle, he got a she-ass to carry his baggage, and when he had to cross the Nile, he didn't hesitate to requisition a crocodile who "had already devoured many people." After crossing the river again by the same means, having invited a priest (who declined) to get onboard with him, Helle led the beast to the river bank and, by prayer, caused it to die, "deciding it deserved this punishment for all the people it had devoured."[44]

Animals could render a multitude of services to the monks. Amoun got two big serpents to guard his door because bandits

---

[37]HL 18, 27-28.
[38]HL 18, 9.
[39]Suplicius Severus, *Dial.* I, 15.
[40]Am 134, 8.
[41]Am 194, 4.
[42]Sulpicius Severus, *Dial.* I, 16.
[43]A 14 (Ward, p. 4).
[44]HM 12, 5-9.

often came to steal his supplies. When the rogues came back, they were terrified upon seeing the serpents and the elder found them half-dead from shock. He chastised the men, then offered them a bite to eat. Suddenly the thieves converted and "became better than most." Soon afterwards, they, too, began performing miracles.[45]

Though always ready to cooperate with the anchorites, the animals, on the other hand, refused to do so with people intent on harming the monks. Thus the camel on which a thief had loaded Macarius' furniture refused to leave before the load was taken off.[46] Another thief, carrying things stolen from a monk, was almost eaten alive by a crocodile and was saved only by the intervention of a monk.[47]

In the *Life of Paul*, St Jerome carefully introduces animals as "servants of the servants of God." Antony, while searching for Paul, began to become discouraged when a she-wolf escorted him directly to the old man's grotto.[48] Later, while talking about heavenly matters, the two elders saw a raven fly in with a loaf of bread. Usually it only brought Paul a half-loaf. This time, inspired by God, it had doubled the ration.[49] Later, when Paul died and Antony was in a predicament about burying him, not having a tool to dig out the earth, two lions bounded in from the depths of the desert with manes flying. At first sight, Antony trembled, then, lifting his soul to God, he remained as quiet as if he had seen doves. Digging out the soil with their claws, the lions soon had a hole large enough for Paul's body. They then approached Antony, twitching their ears and lowering their heads, and licked his hands and feet. The old man understood they were waiting for his blessing.[50]

Another lion story shows how the desert beasts respond to God's commands and the prayers of his servants. Three monks lived in solitude while a fourth brought them what they needed.

[45]HM 9, 6-7.
[46]A 493 (Ward, pp. 137-138).
[47]N 610.
[48]*Life of Paul*, 9.
[49]*Ibid.*, 10.
[50]*Ibid.*, 16.

Two died, and the fourth continued to look after the third but he fell into fornication. Seeing this from above, the two deceased ones asked God to have him eaten by a lion so that, through this cruel death, he would be cleansed of his sin. As if by chance, a lion came across him. But the other hermit who lived there had a vision of what was happening and immediately prayed for him. The lion was immobilized on the spot and remained perplexed, because in heaven the two deceased were praying for it to eat the brother while on earth the elder was asking for the opposite. God decided it was better to grant the latter's prayer and immediately the lion left without having devoured the monk.[51]

When an animal devours an anchorite, it is generally for the anchorite's own good. A pious layman, taking bread to an elder in the desert, found that he had been eaten by a hyena, and it was revealed to him that this had happened through divine mercy so that the monk should be purified of his little misdeeds.[52] Another monk, the disciple of a great old man, was nipped in the belly by a wolf as punishment for a bad thing he had done. Cured by the elder, he nevertheless still had the scars of the wound on his belly and, whenever tempted by the demon, would place his hand there and say to himself, "Oh, my soul, these bites were caused by this sin, so watch out that something worse doesn't happen to you."[53]

Crocodiles didn't usually eat the good monks; instead, they only went so far as to lick their bodies.[54] Antony and his companions had no trouble quietly crossing the Canal of Arsinoe among a large number of crocodiles.[55] When the water was too deep, the crocodiles offered their backs to the monks and transported them from one bank to the other.[56] It could happen that a crocodile might eat a monk by mistake, taking him for a layman. We've already mentioned the Scetis brother who, walking by the

---

[51]N 597.

[52]N 368.

[53]Document translated from Arabic by J. M. Sauget in *Corpus Scriptorum Christianorum Orientalium*, vol. 495, Louvain, 1987, pp. 195-196.

[54]N 294.

[55]VA 15.

[56]N 46; Am 191, 3.

Nile in the heat of day, took off his clothes for a dip in the river. A crocodile grabbed him. Seeing this, an elder passing by cried out, "Why are you eating the Abba?" The beast replied, "I'm not eating an Abba. I found a layman and I'm eating him. There's no monk here."[57]

Peaceful Coexistence

As can be seen, the anchorites often had no trouble understanding the language of the animals and this was mutual. Antony, when he chased away an ostrich with its little ones, heard it say to them, "Throw up some stones so you don't get caught."[58] Macarius heard a starving wolf howling to heaven for its food. He was astounded—and so was the wolf—that the brothers around him didn't hear what it was saying.[59] As for the elders, they got along just fine with the animals. Some coexisted in perfect harmony with them. Agathon found a grotto and decided to move in. A large serpent living there immediately decided to give up its spot but the elder pleaded with it not to do so. "If you go, then I won't stay either." So they both stayed and the two of them would go to feed on the sap of a sycamore tree in the region.[60]

Other anchorites lived among the buffalo.[61] Theon kept company with antelope, wild asses, gazelles and bands of many other animals "and never ceased to find them delightful."[62] Postumianus, the traveler whose recollections of a trip to Egypt are reported by Sulpicius Severus, met anchorites who habitually fed a lion or a she-wolf with fruit! A she-wolf came regularly to eat with a monk in his cell, at the sixth hour, the ninth, or at night, depending on the rules of fasting. She never got it wrong. Unfortunately, one day when the monk was absent, she stole a loaf of bread and didn't dare return for several days. Having

---

[57]Sy 18, 53.
[58]Am 24, 7.
[59]Am 153, 10.
[60]Ch 235.
[61]N 62, N 132A, N 516.
[62]HM 6, 4.

shown her regret, she was forgiven for her fault and again took up the habit of coming each day to eat with the anchorite at the appointed hour.[63]

The most astonishing anecdote is told by an Abba James. An elder had told him that, when living in the desert, his neighbor was a child living all alone. One day he saw him praying and heard him ask God to be able to live in peace with the wild beasts. After prayer, a hyena was there suckling its little ones, so the boy slipped underneath the mother and began sucking with them. Another time he saw him praying in the midst of flames.[64]

As in Paradise

A certain Abba Paul, originally from Lower Egypt but living in the Thebaid, used to pick up horned vipers, scorpions and snakes with impunity. Asked by some brothers where he had obtained this power, he replied, "If someone has acquired purity, all things submit to him as with Adam, when he was in paradise before breaking the commandment."[65] This is what the Fathers usually thought about relations with animals and explains the marvelous facts which have been reported. Cassian said, "If we succeeded in amending our faults, we would find it very easy to live — not necessarily with people — but certainly with animals and wild beasts."[66] Poemen even said that it was easier to get along with the beasts than with a brother who lives with you: "If a man can put up with the company of a brother living with him, he can live just as easily with the beasts."[67]

St Antony used to say, "Obedience, along with temperance, gives men power to tame wild beasts."[68] It does more than tame them; it often makes them docile. A monk living near the Jordan cheerfully slept in the dens of lions. One day he found two lion cubs in a grotto and took them to church, hiding them under his

---

[63]Suplicius Severus, *Dial*, I, 14.
[64]A 963-964.
[65]A 791 (Ward, p. 204).
[66]Cassian, Inst. 9, 8.
[67]Eth 14, 2.
[68]A 36 (Ward, p. 8).

coat and, showing them to the brothers, who were not too reassured, said, "If we kept the precepts of our Lord Jesus Christ, these animals would fear us. But through our faults we have become slaves and so it is rather we who fear them."[69]

The monks in Palestine proved to be worthy emulators of their brothers in Egypt. They even appear to have surpassed them in their cordial relations with animals.[70] We know the famous story about the grateful lion, wonderfully told by Paul Cazin in his *Bestiaire des deux Testaments*, attributing it to Saint Jerome.[71] In reality, it happened to the holy Abba Gerasimus. Something would be missing from our bestiary if we did not conclude with this story, as touching as it is surprising.

The saintly Abba Gerasimus, going one day to the edge of the Jordan, found a lion moaning because of a splinter buried in its paw. The compassionate monk pulled out the splinter and put a dressing on the wound. Thus cured, the lion wouldn't leave Gerasimus but, "like a true disciple, followed him everywhere he went, so much so that the elder was filled with wonder at the beast's gratitude. From then on he fed it bread and soaked beans." He trusted it to such an extent that he put it in charge of the donkey that went to the bank of the Jordan, carrying back water drawn from the river for the monk's needs. One day the donkey got lost and was taken by camel-drivers who were passing through and the lion returned alone, full of sadness, to its Abba. The latter assumed it had eaten the donkey and imposed on it as penance the donkey's work. Some time later, the camel-drivers returned to the region. The donkey spotted the lion, who recognized the donkey and both ran off to the monastery. Gerasimus understood that he had slandered the lion. He gave it the name Jordan and the animal again took its place next to him. When the saintly Abba died, the lion refused to eat and died of grief on the tomb of its friend.[72]

[69]J. Moschus, *Pratum spirituale*, 18.
[70]Cr. A. J. Festugière, *Les Moines d'Orient* I, pp. 53-57.
[71]P. Cazin, *Le Bestiaire des deux Testaments*, Paris, 1928, pp. 134-141.
[72]J. Moschus, *op. cit.*, 107.

Certainly in this bestiary, one must grant a bit of leeway to imagination and exaggeration. The anchorites who lived continually in peace with the desert beasts must have been rare and indeed this is why they were so much admired. On this subject, we can quote a testimony from the *History of the Monks*:

> We saw there (in Nitria) a man by the name of Didymus, old in years with a pleasant appearance, who crushed with his feet scorpions, horned vipers and asps, which no one else dared do; or rather, many others, thinking they could succeed, were killed by the beasts when they only touched them.[73]

Whatever the reality may be, the guiding thought of all the Desert Fathers is, nevertheless, that the saints, through their submission to God and their humility, share the privilege of Adam in the Garden of Eden before the fall. But if they end up emulating Adam's pride and rebellion, they lose the immunity and invulnerability they enjoyed. From that point on, they are at the mercy of the first lion or asp which might show up.

Henri Brémond concludes nicely:

> And besides, the desert is not a menagerie, not even a garden of plants. Instead it must resemble the surroundings of the earthly paradise, during the weeks immediately following the first sin when, on either side, they had not yet forgotten how to live in happy friendship.[74]

---

[73]HM 20, 12.
[74]H. Brémond, *Les Pères du désert*, Paris, 1927, I, pp. XXXI-XXXII.

SIXTEEN

❧✝❧

The Wonders of God

One day Arsenius said frankly, "If we search for God, we'll see him; and if we hold onto him, he'll stay with us."[1] Neither wild beasts nor demons, nor even the angels could have kept the anchorites in the desert for long, and their spiritual descendants would no longer be there today if God had not been more present to them there than anywhere else.

The collection of apothegms could mislead us on this point. They don't often mention God, or Christ, or the Virgin Mary, but we don't generally speak of realities that are most familiar and intimate to us. The Fathers especially did not talk about these things when their words might lead others to think they had been favored with extraordinary graces, visions and apparitions. However, the little confidences that slipped out now and then, despite their humility (like that of Arsenius quoted above), are enough to convince us that they were, for the most part, great contemplatives. The evidence we find for this in the ancient documents should be collected and examined with care.

Predictions and Revelations

When the apothegms mention apparitions or visions, they mostly deal with revelations of terrestrial events which have not yet occurred, or will only be realized in some distant time or place. Antony, filled with the Spirit, knew what was happening in the world and what must come to pass, but rarely spoke about

---

[1] A 48 (Ward, p. 10).

it.[2] However, one day he admitted seeing the death of a donkey some distance away.[3] The *Life* of the Saint reports several visions or revelations of this kind. Once he saw, in his mind, two brothers dying of thirst in the desert[4]; another time he announced the early arrival of visitors.[5] He also predicted the violence that would be spread by the Arians.[6] Bessarion foretold the destruction of the pagan temples;[7] another elder, the devastation of Scetis.[8] John of Lycopolis, Pambo and Macarius, like Antony, regularly predicted the future.[9]

These are, evidently, expressions of extraordinary gifts of God to anchorites of exceptional holiness, but Antony seemed to find this normal. "I believe," he said, "that a totally purified soul can become more clear-sighted, may see more things and greater ones than can the demons because he has the Lord to reveal them to him."[10]

The "greater things" the demons are unable to see include, above all, supernatural ones and celestial visions. Several heroes in the *History of the Monks* and the *Lausiac History* had, for instance, the gift of reading hearts and perceiving secret thoughts: John of Lycopolis, Eulogius and Helle,[11] for example. Others saw miraculous occurrences happening to brothers or around them. Moses saw the Holy Spirit descending upon Zacharias in the form of a dove.[12] A brother doing penance for a grave sin he committed noticed a dove coming to him and entering his mouth as a sign of divine pardon.[13] Of another monk, it is said that he saw "the grace of God descending on his brother" and con-

---

2A 30 (Ward, p. 14).
3A 12 (Ward, p. 3).
4VA 59.
5VA 62.
6VA 82.
7A 159 (Ward, p. 41).
8N 361.
9HM 1, 1-11; HL 10, 1; 17, 2.
10VA 34.
11HL 35, 7-9; HM 12, 10-11; 16, 1-8.
12A 244-245 (Ward, p. 68).
13N 190.

cluded from it that he was forgiven.[14] Another elder saw crowns above a brother who had resisted temptations.[15] During a devastation of Scetis, a brother saw crowns descending upon the heads of seven monks massacred by the barbarians.[16]

One monk, coming to see Arsenius, saw through the cell window the elder all on fire.[17] Mark the Egyptian saw the priest who came to celebrate Mass at his place as a pillar of fire.[18] It was also a pillar of fire seen by Theodore that made him decide not to exercise his office of deacon.[19] Joseph extended his hands towards heaven and his fingers became like flames. He then told Lot, "If you will, you can become wholly like fire."[20] One day during a meal, an elder saw the same foods changing into honey, bread or garbage according to the disposition of each one's soul.[21] Another elder, in Nitria, saw two brothers whose sins appeared inscribed on parchment and were erased little by little by their tears.[22] In Scetis, an elder saw Moses and Arsenius on two small boats with the Spirit of God or angels.[23] According to Sisoes, a brother saw "the virtue of God walking with Abba Macarius."[24]

Visions of the Hereafter

The greatest number of visions, told with more or less detail, concern the hereafter, judgment, hell or heaven. An anchorite saw himself transported to hell and, having seen the torment of the damned, couldn't console himself.[25] Another saw his mother there.[26] An elder was favored with a vision of the patriarchs from

---

[14] N 255.
[15] N 211, N 454.
[16] A 504 (Ward, p. 140).
[17] A 65 (Ward, p. 13).
[18] A 542 (Ward, p. 151).
[19] A 292 (Ward, p. 77).
[20] A 390 (Ward, p. 103).
[21] N 85.
[22] N 521.
[23] A 76 (Ward, p. 18).
[24] Am 221, 3.
[25] Sy 3, 48; N 141.
[26] N 135.

Adam to Melchizedek,[27] while another had a vision of the Fathers, the first anchorites.[28] In ecstasy, Silvanus was taken to the judgment and saw many monks being sent to hell while a great number of lay people entered the Kingdom.[29] Another time he was taken to heaven where he saw the glory of God.[30] In both cases, Silvanus spoke only after being constrained by his disciples and he told only the minimum.

If an elder decided that his vision would edify his brethren, he might tell it in more detail but then attribute it to an older anchorite, a subterfuge which fooled no one. This is what John Colobos did when he had a vision of three winged monks, one of whom could not cross a river because his wings were too feeble.[31] An account attributed to Paul the Simple tells of a vision he had of his deceased disciple in a state of sin and condemned to punishment, but who was finally saved by the intercession of the Virgin Mary.[32] This story is mentioned nowhere in the ancient traditions and certainly doesn't go back to the fourth century. As Guillaumont noted, we have every reason to question this type of story, drawn largely from various apocalyptic literature, pious Hellenistic themes or Egyptian folklore.[33]

Discretion of the Fathers About Their Ecstasies and Visions

Apothegms of the best type are distinguished by their great restraint. Zacharias, for example, had at least two of the most authentic visions, because they are substantiated by the authority of his elders, Poemen and Moses,[34] but they said nothing about them and knew no details. One old father saw "great things."[35]

---

[27]A 190 (Ward, p. 54).

[28]A 28 (Ward, p. 7).

[29]A 858 (Ward, p. 222).

[30]A 859 (Ward, p. 222).

[31]A 329 (Ward, p. 88).

[32]N 599.

[33]Guillaumont, p. 142.

[34]A 246-247 (Ward, p. 68); Eth 14, 35.

[35]Arm 6, 16; SP, New Collection, p. 258 (I 713).

Another saw "everything there is in heaven and everything held in the depths of hell."[36]

These are almost always phrases which only arouse our curiosity and leave it totally unsatisfied. Antony, John Colobos, Sisoes and Silvanus had ecstasies we're told, but we don't know what they saw, heard or experienced at the time. Antony on his mountain "rejoiced to contemplate divine things." Often during a discussion with visitors he would suddenly stop talking and remain silent for a long time, his companions then realizing that he was having a vision.[37] But he would seldom talk about it later. John Colobos, absorbed in his work, was transported out of himself and did not notice he was making a single basket with cord set aside for two[38] and, when the camel-driver came to take the baskets away, he had scarcely greeted him when he forgot the reason for the man's coming.[39] Silvanus used to have ecstasies lasting for several hours.[40] While praying, all Sisoes had to do was lift his arms and he would be carried away immediately so that, when in the presence of the brothers, he took care to keep them lowered.[41] Cassian also speaks about an Abba John who was sometimes so wrapped up in contemplation that at night, he didn't know if he had eaten or in the morning, if he had fasted the day before.[42]

More of the same appear in the *Lausiac History* and the *History of the Monks*. In general, accounts of visions are still rather vague. Isidore often had ecstasies, even during meals. Pressed to reveal what he had seen, he was content to reply, "My thought is gone, taken away by some contemplation."[43] Patermuthius said he was "taken to the heavens in a vision and saw all the good things awaiting the true monks, which no discourse can convey." He also says he "was physically transported to paradise and saw

---

[36]N 371.
[37]VA 82, 84.
[38]A 326 (Ward, p. 87).
[39]A 346-347 (Ward, p. 92).
[40]A 858 (Ward, p. 222).
[41]A 910 (Ward, p. 234).
[42]Cassian, Conf. 19, 4.
[43]HL 1, 3.

there a throng of saints."[44] Piammonas was "constantly delighted to receive visions."[45] Apollo, too, had visions or revelations. For example, "he saw his elder brother who had died in the desert, sitting on a throne next to the apostles and interceding for him."[46] Before dying, Anouph said,

> God has hidden nothing concerning earthly things which he hasn't revealed to me.... I often saw myriads of angels helping God; I saw the choirs of the just; I saw the dense throng of martyrs; I saw the congregations of monks; I saw the office of all those who sing the praises of God. I saw Satan delivered to the fire, I saw his angels being punished; I saw the just enjoying eternal bliss.[47]

Unfortunately, as can be seen, the list keeps to generalities and doesn't teach us very much.

On this subject, the Desert Fathers were artful in eluding indiscreet questions. In the Cells one day, Olympius received a pagan priest who admired the monks' asceticism and was astonished that, with all the afflictions to which they subjected themselves, they received no visions of their God. "Surely," he said, "if you have no visions, it is because you have bad thoughts in the heart which separate you from your God and this is why he won't show you his mysteries." This pagan priest's conclusion was fully endorsed by the elders: "Yes, this is truly how it is. Impure thoughts separate God from people."[48] As Guillaumont remarks, "It is not a negation of all possible contemplation of the mysteries of God," it is, first of all, an invitation to fight against the bad thoughts which radically prevent man from arriving at contemplation.[49] One of the Fathers said, "Just as it is impossible for someone to see his face in troubled water, so is it impossible

[44]HM 10, 20-21.
[45]HM 25, 2.
[46]HM 8, 16-17.
[47]HM 11, 6-7.
[48]A 571 (Ward, p. 160).
[49]Guillaumont, p. 137.

to contemplate God in prayer if it [the prayer] isn't purged of irrelevant thoughts."[50]

Visions of Christ

Poemen, who never wished to talk about "celestial matters,"[51] nevertheless gave an account one day of his marvelous vision of Mary weeping near the cross of Jesus.[52] Only Isaac, who witnessed the ecstasy and was very close to Poemen, was able to insist on extracting the secret. But did Christ, for whom the Desert Fathers had given up everything, ever reveal himself to them? As we've said, they dreaded seeing the demon come to them in the guise of the Lord, but this could not have prevented Jesus from manifesting his presence, and he no doubt did so, much more frequently than the texts say or lead us to believe. In the *Life of Pachomius*, it is recounted that the demon appeared to him one day "in the form in which the Lord usually appeared to him."[53] Again for Pachomius, it must be admitted that the biographies have more to say about apparitions of angels or demons than visions of Christ himself. And Pachomius shied away when a brother asked him, "Tell us about the vision you had."

"As far as visions are concerned," replied Pachomius,

> I, a sinner, don't ask God for any. ...However, consider what constitutes a great vision: when you see a pure and humble man, that's a great vision. In fact, what is greater than to see the invisible God in a visible man, who is His temple? This is the visionary faculty which the saints have at all times of seeing the Lord.[54]

Such side-stepping is more than an acknowledgment. Very often, when reading the accounts which we have, we get the impression that the Desert Fathers do not want to state categorically that they have seen Christ; they only want to hide the fact

---

[50]N 379.
[51]A 582 (Ward, p. 167).
[52]A 718 (Ward, p. 187).
[53]Veilleux, p. 161.
[54]Guillaumont, pp. 143-144.

that they have really seen him. For instance, we wouldn't doubt that Antony saw the Lord arriving to comfort him, though the *Life* doesn't say so explicitly:

> The Lord did not forget Antony's battle but came to his aid. Lifting his eyes, Antony saw the roof as if open and a ray of light reaching down to him...Antony called out to the vision, "Where were you? Why didn't you appear at the start to put an end to my suffering?" He heard a voice say, "I was there, Antony."[55]

In two other similar accounts given in apothegms, nothing more explicit is said about an elder seeing Christ with whom he conversed.[56] Abba Cronius doesn't even name Christ but says only, "Someone is coming to me." And when the elder asked, "Where were you until now?" he received the reply, "I was here and left you to see whether or not you would be patient."[57]

One can truthfully state that the Desert Fathers did not, under any circumstances, want to declare they had seen Christ, this striking them as an unthinkable mark of arrogant pretension. One would have to be crazy to come, as did Valens, to tell a full congregation, "Today, I saw Christ,"[58] so much so that one is tempted to question the authenticity of a scene where an elder tells Macarius, "While sound asleep, I was taken away and saw a vision of Christ, the King...."[59] We readily give more credence to the more vague statements found in the Ethiopian tradition: "I was seeing a vision of the Lord."[60] John said, "If Moses had not entered the darkness, he would not have seen the Lord."[61] And Abraham: "If man perseveres in his mortifications, he will be victorious and see the power and marvels of the Lord."[62]

---

[55]VA 10.
[56]A 265 (Ward, pp. 71-72).
[57]Eth 14, 53.
[58]HL 25, 5.
[59]Am 163, 7.
[60]Eth 14, 4.
[61]Eth 14, 16.
[62]Eth 14, 8.

Evagrius and Cassian tried their best to give a few descriptions and clarifications about these mystical experiences of the Desert Fathers. According to them, they were normal among the great anchorites who were completely detached from the world and totally purified. But they also agree with their Egyptian masters and condemn any presumption and any pretension of being able to reach these sublime heights by oneself. "It is an eminent gift of divine grace," and those so favored feel incapable of talking about it because of humility and, at the same time, because it is too great to be described in words.[63]

Miracles of the Monks in Egypt

The marvels of the Lord are not only those which were seen but also those performed by the Egyptian anchorites. By simply reading the *History of the Monks*, one would suppose that all the Desert Fathers worked numerous miracles. Beginning with the Prologue, the reader learns that "many among them halted the flow of rivers, crossed the Nile on foot, killed ferocious beasts, performed healings — as many wonders and miracles as the holy prophets and apostles."[64] In each chapter, the expression returns like a refrain: "He did many wonders," or "He never stopped performing cures."[65] Theon "worked a great number of miracles."[66] Elias "each day performed many miracles and never stopped healing the sick."[67] Apollo had to his credit great works: "the Lord used him to perform many miracles, all kinds of wonders were accomplished by him."[68] Another "by the name of Amoun performed a number of miracles in this region."[69] In the same area, "Copres also worked many miracles, treating the sick, healing, chasing out demons and accomplishing many won-

---

[63]Cf. J. Kirchmeyer, *Dictionnaire de spiritualité*, Art. "Extase," Vol. 4, col. 2099-2101 and 2109-2110.
[64]HM Pr. 9.
[65]HM 2, 6.
[66]HM 6, 1.
[67]HM 7, 2.
[68]HM 8, 2.
[69]HM 9, 5.

ders,"[70] but Copres was careful to point out that all he did was nothing compared to what his master Patermuthius had done. In fact, the latter regularly walked on water, flew in the air wherever he wanted to go (and deserves to be counted among the patron saints of aviators) and Copres ends by saying, "Why should it astonish, then, if we, the little ones, accomplish these small exploits, curing the lame and blind, all things which, by their artistry, doctors also carry out."[71]

But we must remember that all these miracle-worker monks lived in the Nile Valley or nearby and so had a large number of clients who depended on their good offices. For instance, it is said that Apollo resided "in the desert near a populated country, living in the power of the Spirit, accomplishing miracles and marvelous healings, which we could not describe because they surpass admiration."[72]

Most of the miracles detailed in the *Life of Antony* are carried out not in his "interior mountain," but near populated regions. They include the curing of lay people who came to see him to recover their own health or to seek the healing of one of their loved ones.[73] An important person named Fronto was cured of a terrible illness. "He was ripping his tongue with his teeth and could have died." Antony promised he would be cured as soon as they left the desert.[74] That was a clever way to avoid the thanks and praises which the cured ones usually wanted to give to the miracle-worker, or thaumaturgist, as they were called.

A young girl from Busiris in Tripolitana had a horrible and repugnant disorder. "Her tears, mucus and secretions from the nose and ears turned immediately into worms, she was paralyzed and had deformed eyes." The parents of the invalid went to see Antony, who refused to let the young girl come right up to him, "Go back. If she isn't dead, you'll find her cured. I don't have the power to heal, that she should come to me, poor wretch

---

[70]HM 10, 1.
[71]HM 10, 20; 10, 24.
[72]HM 8, 7.
[73]VA 14, 57, 58, 61, 62.
[74]VA 57.

that I am. Healing is the work of the Lord." The girl was cured within the hour.[75]

It was also from a distance that Antony cured Polycratia, a virgin of Laodicea, "who suffered terribly from pain in her stomach and sides, having followed too strict a discipline."[76] Antony shared in the prayers of all those who came to him, but the sick were not always healed. At any rate, the Saint consoled them, telling them not to despair and "reminding them that healing comes neither from him nor from anyone else; that it belongs to God, who accomplishes it when he wants and for whom he wants."[77]

Miracles in the Desert

Anchorites living deeper in the desert no doubt had fewer occasions to perform miracles. It is remarkable that the apothegms, like those found in the *Lausiac History* and the works of Cassian, mention far fewer marvelous events than the *History of the Monks*. In his Prologue, Palladius says of his heroes, "The wonders they did are numberless; I relate only the main ones."[78] In fact, apart from the expulsion of demons and the astonishing familiarity with animals, his work presents very few accounts of miracles. He speaks of two elders, Benjamin and Pior, who had "the gift of healing," but gives no details.[79] The only two miracle-workers about whom he speaks to any great extent are the two Macarii.

The Egyptian Macarius had gained such a reputation that he always had with him a disciple to greet his "clients," "because of the large numbers of those coming for healing." When too many people bothered him, he would steal off to his grotto by the underground tunnel he had dug.[80] His most spectacular healing was that of a woman who had been metamorphosed into

---

[75]VA 58.
[76]VA 61.
[77]VA 56.
[78]HL Pr. 4.
[79]HL 12, 1; 39, 4.
[80]HL 17, 3; 17, 10.

a mare by a magician. One can imagine the shock of the brave husband coming home to find a mare in his bed. "He cried, became upset and tried to speak to the animal, all to no avail." Since the village priests didn't know what to do, the husband "put a halter on her like one does on a horse and led her like this through the desert" right to Macarius' cell. The elder prayed and poured holy water on the head of the animal, who instantly "regained the appearance of a woman before everyone's eyes."[81]

In the Cells, Macarius of Alexandria had similar abilities and the reputation of a healer. A village priest with cancer in his head came to plead with him. "Macarius laid his hands on him; the man was healed in a few days, grew new hair and returned home in good health."[82] In light of the elder's success, the demon suggested that Macarius would do better to leave the desert and go to Rome where he could put the gift he had received from God to wider use. Macarius managed to overcome the diabolical temptation, though not without pain, said Palladius.[83]

Like Palladius, Cassian also avoids making a show of the marvelous works accomplished by the Desert Fathers. At the beginning of his *Institutes,* he announces that he won't try at all "to create an account of the marvels of God and the miracles," even though he had heard talk of many and even "seen with his own eyes a large number, and some incredible ones."[84] In a similar vein, in one of his *Conferences,* Cassian said he thought it best to keep silent about the miracles and wonders done by Piamoun, which he witnessed, so as to concentrate on salutary teachings and "not feed his readers' vain curiosity."[85]

He speaks often about some extraordinary cures by two elders. One, Abba Paul, is the monk whose misadventure we encountered earlier. Having fled at the sight of a woman he met on his way, he had become paralyzed. Yet his power was so great "that the oil which had touched his body immediately

---

[81]HL 17, 6-9.
[82]HL 18, 19-21.
[83]HL 18, 23.
[84]Cassian, Inst. Pr.
[85]Cassian, Conf. 18, 1.

healed the sick on whom it was used as unction, regardless of their illness."[86]

Another Abba, Abraham, left the desert to do harvesting. A woman, cradling in her arms a child who was languishing and half-dead for lack of milk, came to beseech him with her prayers and tears. Finally, he gave her a glass of water upon which he had made the Sign of the Cross. No sooner had she gulped it down than her dried-up breasts were marvelously filled and the surplus of milk began seeping out.[87] Another time, passing through a market town, Abraham cured a man who could no longer walk.[88]

Among the miracles mentioned in the apothegms we find, first of all, a few extraordinary events attesting to the mastery the anchorites sometimes exercised over the elements of nature: water, fire, sun, rain.[89] In this sphere, Bessarion seems to have been the most favored and rivaled Patermuthius. Like the latter, he walked on water and stopped the sun.[90] One day he made sea water drinkable to quench his disciple's thirst. As for Antony, he made water gush forth right in the desert.[91] Through their prayers, Xoius and another elder made it rain.[92] A disciple's obedience made water rise in a well so he could fill his jug.[93] It was also obedience that gave new life to a piece of dry wood stuck in the sand,[94] while another stick flowered and bore fruit to prove the purity of an elder who had cohabited with a virgin.[95] Ordered to do so by his elder, Elias put his hand in fire with impunity.[96] But this is nothing compared to the exploit of Copres who remained in a blazing inferno for a half-hour,[97] or that of

---

[86]Ibid., 7, 26.
[87]Ibid., 14, 4.
[88]Ibid., 15, 5.
[89]A 157-158, A 260 (Ward, pp. 40-41, 71); HM 9, 13 and 20.
[90]A 156 (Ward, p. 40).
[91]VA 54.
[92]A 567 (Ward, p. 158); N 626.
[93]N 27.
[94]A 316 (Ward, p. 85).
[95]A 428 (Ward, p. 113).
[96]Ch 270.
[97]HM 10, 30.

Helle who "in the folds of his tunic often carried fire to brothers in his neighborhood,"[98] or again that of Apelles who, working as a blacksmith, "handled the red-hot iron in his hands without suffering any injuries."[99]

As for cures, the apothegms mention only five, including two by Longinus in the area of Alexandria for a woman suffering from breast cancer and another with an incurable wound on the hand.[100] In both cases, healing took place more or less without the elder's specific agreement to pray for it. Macarius unconsciously cured a paralyzed infant left on the doorstep of his cell by the father.[101] Isidore made a blind man see,[102] but we do not know how the miracle occurred. Finally, a young cousin or nephew of Poemen "whose face, by an evil spell, was turned backwards" was taken by his father to the elder, who was then in the company of other elders. So that Poemen couldn't shirk his obligation, each of the elders was asked to make the Sign of the Cross on the little one. The child was cured at the moment Poemen made his.[103]

The Dead are Raised

The miracles which best prove the divine power working in the Desert Fathers must surely be resurrections of the dead. The apothegms tell of several that are extraordinary enough. In certain cases, it is only a short return to life — giving the deceased enough time to reveal something useful, for example, the identity of his assassin or the spot where money is hidden.[104]

Other resurrections last longer. To confound a monk fallen into heresy, Macarius, through prayer, "brought back to life a man, not a recently-buried corpse, but one of the most ancient who had lived well before Christ."[105] After baptizing him,

---

[98]HM 12, 1.
[99]HM 13, 2.
[100]A 451 (Ward, p. 123); Sy 19, 7.
[101]A 468 (Ward, p. 130).
[102]Eth 14, 38.
[103]A 581 (Ward, p. 166).
[104]A 531 (Ward, p. 147); Ch 227.
[105]N 490B; HL 17, 11; Cassian, Conf. 15, 3.

Macarius took him to the desert where "he kept him around for three years, after which he really died for good," says the narrator.[106] It was also three extra years of life that Patermuthius obtained for a dying man who should have been damned for his faults.[107]

Several accounts show the prodigious power of certain monks — or moniales — over life and death. An anchorite brought back to life a shameless woman who had come to seduce him and fell down, stone dead.[108] An elder obtained the resurrection of his disciple, threatened with death as a chastisement for a fault committed and who was truly dead.[109] In the same way, a layman who had mocked Amma Sara when he saw her crossing a brook, was killed by a single word pronounced unconsciously by the moniale. But a simple prayer immediately obtained the return to life of the disrespectful man: "My Jesus, bring him back to life, and from now on I won't ever utter such words again."[110] The narrator says that Sara "was not aware of the grace of God residing in her."

This was also true of Sisoes. One day a layman came with his son to visit the elder. The son died on the way there. The father, unperturbed, brought the corpse and laid it at the feet of Sisoes. Now the latter, not noticing that the child was dead and thinking he had prostrated himself before him, just said, "Get up. Go outside." And immediately the child rose and rejoined his father, who then told the elder about it. Sisoes, "when he heard, was upset because he didn't intend this to happen."[111]

We can understand how the humility of these anchorites was sorely tested by such miracles. But they knew they were incapable of doing these things by themselves and acknowledged the work of the Lord, as Antony delighted in saying.[112] The *History of the Monks* underlines this also: "To this day, these

---

[106]N 490B.
[107]HM 10, 17-19.
[108]N 189.
[109]PA 80, 1.
[110]PA 80, 2.
[111]A 821 (Ward, p. 216).
[112]VA 38; VA 83-84.

people raise the dead...and everything the Lord accomplished through the saints, He accomplishes now through them."[113]

All of them knew well that such power doesn't constitute holiness.[114] As Agathon put it, "The quick-tempered, even if he resurrects a dead person, is not pleasing to God."[115] And Abba Nesteros said to Cassian: "The sum of perfection and of beatitude doesn't consist in doing wonders, but in the purity of charity."[116] However, we are led to believe that these miracle-workers of the desert were really great friends of God.

---

[113]HM Epilogue 1.
[114]N 547, N 745.
[115]A 101 (Ward, p. 23).
[116]Cassian, Conf. 15, 2.

SEVENTEEN

From the Desert to the Promised Land

Longevity of the Anchorites

When we read the beautiful description of Antony's state of health at the end of his life, at the age of 105, we ask ourselves how he may have died: "The old man had remained absolutely unharmed; his eyes were not dimmed and he saw clearly. He had not lost a single tooth...his feet and hands were perfectly healthy; he appeared in better health and stronger than those who use different foods, baths and assorted clothes...."[1] At the monastery of a certain Isidore in the Thebaid, "the monks were so saintly, they could all accomplish miracles, and none had ever taken sick before dying. When there came, for each of them, the hour of transition, they announced it in advance to all, then, lying down, fell asleep."[2]

We know of a certain number of anchorites who passed in this manner from life to death all at once, without a hint of bad health, simply by extinction of strength, at a more or less advanced age. For example, Pambo died in Nitria at 69 years of age, without fever, without illness, while weaving a small basket.[3] But in these cases, as for St Antony, the narrator or biographer seems to have a scarcely-hidden agenda showing desert life to be not only good for the soul but also beneficial for the

---

[1]VA 93.
[2]HM 17, 3.
[3]HL 10, 5.

223

body, healthier than life in towns and villages. This might have been true for the original Egyptians, but for strangers coming to live in the desert, the change of climate, living conditions and diet were undoubtedly not favorable to good health, even if they did not go for excessive austerities.

It is remarkable that most of those we have come to know were often sick and did not live to a ripe old age, except Arsenius, who made it to the age of 95,[4] though he had a fragile constitution and was ill many times in Scetis, Alexandria and Petra of Troë.[5] Evagrius, coming from Asia Minor with a delicate and opulent background, had a hard time on a diet of bread, salt and oil, suffered from a stomach ailment and died prematurely at the age of 54.[6] His companion and friend, Palladius, also suffered from the strict discipline of the Egyptian anchorites. He couldn't stay for long with the great ascetic Dorotheus.[7] He took sick on a trip to the Thebaid, then endured spleen and stomach troubles. Finally, dropsy forced him to seek treatment in Alexandria; there the doctors advised him to move to Palestine, where the climate would suit him better.[8] The two young strangers received by Macarius in Scetis didn't develop any "old bones" because they died three years after their arrival. They too "were delicate and came from a well-to-do background."[9]

It is notable that the ages of the old ones are rarely mentioned in the apothegms, while they appear to interest Palladius. We learn from him that Macarius the Egyptian was 90 years of age,[10] Isidore died at 85,[11] Amoun of Nitria was 62,[12] Pambo and Serapion were each 70,[13] Benjamin was 81,[14] Paphnutius was

---

[4]A 80 (Ward, pp. 18-19).
[5]A 58, A 70, A 72, A 74 (Ward, pp. 12, 15, 16, 17).
[6]HL 38, 1; 38, 10; 38, 13.
[7]HL 2, 1.
[8]HL 35, 4; 35, 11-12.
[9]A 486 (Ward, p. 134).
[10]HL 17, 2.
[11]HL 1, 1.
[12]HL 8.
[13]HL 10, 5; 37, 14.
[14]HL 12, 1.

more than 80,[15] Mark was close to 100 and, like Antony, still had all his teeth.[16] Moses and Pachon were both septuagenarians.[17] The *History of the Monks* mentions two elders who were 110 — Cronides in Nitria and Elias in the Thebaid[18] — as well as Copres who was still in great shape at 90.[19] Old Chaeremon was more than 100 but couldn't get around anymore except on all fours.[20] Finally, always wanting his hero to surpass all the others, Saint Jerome has his Paul dying at 113.[21]

Illnesses and Disabilities

The desert "reporters," Palladius and Cassian, were not concerned at all about inquiring into the sanitary conditions of the anchoritic areas of Egypt. What interested them was moral health and the manner in which the Desert Fathers treated spiritual illnesses. When they speak of physical illnesses in passing, it is in relation to asceticism and the soul's health. Illness often can be, all at the same time, a consequence of asceticism, when provoked by excessive austerity; an asceticism itself, by the sometimes heroic patience it requires; and also the touchstone of asceticism. Sickness is thus sometimes presented as a proof of virtue and holiness. If a certain anchorite was sick, it was because he took on, with courage and generosity, the ascetic labors, without sparing his pain. It is said of two elders in Scetis that they became ill because they submitted themselves to too severe a diet.[22] These excesses of asceticism most of the time dealt with food and the practice of remaining on one's feet rather than sitting, kneeling, or lying down. They often led to problems with the digestive system and wounds to the feet. For example, Dioscorus had internal bleeding and foot ulcers but accepted no

---

[15]HL 47, 3.
[16]HL 18, 26.
[17]HL 19, 11; 23, 1.
[18]HM 7, 1; 20, 13.
[19]HM 10, 1. Cf. P. DeVos, "Les Nombres dans l'Historia monachorum in Aegypto," in *Analecta Bollandiana* 92, 1974, pp. 97-108.
[20]Cassian, Conf. 11, 4.
[21]*Life of Paul*, 7.
[22]N 174, N 357.

remedy, not even the saffron suggested by his disciple. He just kept his feet wrapped in rags until the Lord healed him.[23] Similarly, John had "feet that gave out due to lengthy immobility and produced secretions and pus." He was cured by an angel.[24]

Again it is Palladius who gives us the most precise details of the illnesses of a few anchorites. He himself who had suffered from dropsy, as we said, tells about a Nitrian monk stricken with the same illness but in far worse condition. His body swelled so much that, after his death, it was necessary to enlarge the door to get the cadaver out of the cell.[25] Macarius' disciple John was stricken with elephantiasis as punishment for his avarice.[26] A priest was healed by Macarius of a cancer in his head with which he had been afflicted because of his sins of impurity.[27] The chastisement of illness can also be preventative: at the moment when the monk Heron entered a prostitute's place to commit evil, a carbuncle appeared on his genitals, which got so bad that after a few months "his parts became gangrenous and fell off."[28] Another, Stephen the Libyan, edifying in every respect, suffered a similar illness, a cancerous ulcer, and these same members had to be amputated.[29] To these cases, duly diagnosed by Palladius, there is little to add except the excision of the inflamed uvula of Machetes, reported by Cassian.[30]

In our day, there's little talk about the spleen except when an accident causes its rupture. The ancients often pinpoint it as a cause when they suffer digestive troubles. Palamon's disciples thought their master had developed an illness of the spleen. The doctor they sent for told them it was nothing, that the illness was caused only by an excess of fasting.[31] In his works, Evagrius took pleasure in listing the different thoughts that can come to the

---

[23]Ch 255.
[24]HM 13, 7.
[25]HL 12, 2.
[26]HL 17, 4.
[27]HL 18, 19.
[28]HL 26, 5.
[29]HL 24, 2.
[30]Cassian, Inst. 5, 30.
[31]Veilleux, p. 38.

mind of the anchorite in his cell.[32] Among thoughts inspired by greed, there are those that suggest to the monk the many ills he can develop by fasting too much: "pains of the stomach, of the liver, of the spleen and dropsy...." They urge him to drink wine on the pretext that "water harms the liver or spleen,..." they pinpoint "his stomach, his liver, his spleen, dropsy, a long illness, the lack of essentials and the absence of a doctor."

Often a demon may be involved, attacking the anchorite's very body, as happened to Antony and Moses,[33] and noted by Amma Syncletica: "In fact, he brings on very serious illnesses, by divine permission, so as to discourage souls. He destroys the body with very high fevers and torments it with an intolerable thirst...."[34] Another Amma, Theodora, also appears to speak from experience:

> He overwhelms the body with diseases and debility, weakness of the knees and all the members; he dissipates the vigor of the soul and of the body, to get us to say, "I'm sick; I don't have the strength to recite the office." But if we are vigilant, all these temptations fall away. There was a monk who, at the moment of starting the office, was stricken by chills and fever along with violent headaches. He said to himself, "I am ill and near to death; so I will get up before I die and recite the office." As soon as he finished praying, the fever left.[35]

In general, sick monks did everything they could to hold fast to their rigorous asceticism, declining the relief their companions wanted to provide for them. Isaac had a serious illness that wouldn't go away. His disciple made him a little porridge and added some prunes to it. But the elder refused it, saying, "Really, brother, I would prefer to spend thirty years with this illness."[36] Another elder, who was always sick, recovered for a year and complained about it. Crying, he said, "God abandoned

---

[32]Evagrius, *Praktikos* 7 and texts cited in note SC 171, pp. 509-511.
[33]VA 8; HL 19, 9.
[34]A 898 (Ward, p. 232).
[35]A 311 (Ward, p. 83).
[36]A 381 (Ward, p. 101); N 156.

me and no longer visited me."[37] In the Cells, a brother never stopped repeating this prayer, "Lord, send me a sickness because, when I'm well, I disobey you."[38] Copres, sick and bedridden, never stopped thanking God;[39] for Poemen, as well as for Joseph and Rufus, this is perfection achieved.[40] Understandably, the demons did everything possible to impede such acts of thanksgiving, going so far as to urge the invalid into keeping his customary fasts and an upright position, in order to tire him out and discourage him.[41]

Care and Visitation of the Sick

When the apothegms speak of a sick anchorite, it is almost always to underline either the virtue of the invalid or the charity of the brothers who visit and look after him. The elder who became disabled and bedridden usually had a disciple or brothers to care for him. Sisoes had his faithful Abraham and wanted no one else to serve him.[42] For twelve years, Ammoes always had John the Theban with him.[43] Another brother used to read to the sick Agathon;[44] some brothers looked after Antionus, infirm and blind, even putting food in his mouth.[45] An elder, who lived alone and isolated in the Cells, was helped by an angel,[46] but normally the sick anchorite was not abandoned. At the weekend gathering, if they noticed a brother missing, they would go to inquire about his health, comfort him and bring him everything he needed: food, clothing and medicine.[47] So long as an invalid remained bedridden, his neighbors called on him frequently.[48] This is why Theodore of Pherme received many visitors. They

---

[37]N 209.
[38]N 504.
[39]A 442 (Ward, p. 118).
[40]A 424, A 603, A 802 (Ward, pp. 110, 171, 210).
[41]Evagrius, *Praktikos*, 40.
[42]A 849, A 852, A 853 (Ward, pp. 220, 221).
[43]A 132, A 420 (Ward, pp. 30,109).
[44]A 104 (Ward, p. 23).
[45]A 153 (Ward, p. 37).
[46]N 212.
[47]N 4; Eth 14, 33.
[48]Sozomen, *Hist. Eccl.* VI 31 (PG 67, 1388B).

never stopped bringing him food but he would give it away bit by bit and when the hour for his meal arrived, he happily ate whatever was left.[49] Those who could not come themselves to see the invalid sent him something: figs, grapes,[50] a small fish,[51] some sweets or a fresh loaf of bread, which Macarius fetched from Alexandria.[52]

Visiting sick brothers was a duty of charity which took precedence over any other work. It was "the commandment of God" *par excellence*, even for Theodore who was never the most sociable.[53] This was better than spending the whole week in the cell.[54] Agathon would go so far as to spend four months in town to nurse an invalid stranger.[55] Lot even showed his constant concern for a sick monk who agreed with the errors of Origen.[56] Serving the sick required patience and courage, especially when it involved caring for an elder whose purulent wounds gave off an unbearable stench[57] or when the illness was prolonged for years and the invalid never expressed any gratitude to his infirmarian.[58]

Sometimes the invalid was transported to church, where the brothers prayed for him and sprinkled holy water on him to effect a cure.[59] Unctions of oil were also administered.[60] Each one waited most of all for a healing from the Lord, "the great doctor of souls and bodies."[61] However, sometimes earthly doctors were brought in, especially when a surgical operation was required.[62] A doctor was brought in for a sick Palamon.[63] There were,

---

[49]A 293 (Ward, pp. 77-78).
[50]N 494; Cassian, Inst. 5, 40.
[51]A 776 (Ward, p. 198).
[52]A 461 (Ward, p. 129); N 348.
[53]A 278 (Ward, p. 75).
[54]N 355.
[55]A 109 (Ward, p. 24).
[56]A 447 (Ward, p. 121).
[57]N 356.
[58]A 420 (Ward, p. 109).
[59]N 351.
[60]N 635.
[61]Am 180, 12.
[62]N 261, N 493; HL 24, 2.
[63]Veilleux, p. 38.

apparently, no practicing doctors in the Cells and Scetis but, according to Palladius, there was one in Nitria.[64] A certain Apollonius had become a traveling pharmacist. From morning until night he went everywhere, going to all the cells to see if anyone was sick and bringing grapes, pomegranates, eggs, bread made from fine wheat flour and all the useful medicine he picked up in Alexandria.[65]

Generally, monks who were ill remained in the desert and didn't return to the towns and villages to obtain better care. One Scetis elder, seriously ill, wanted to spare the brothers the trouble of looking after him and, despite a warning from Moses, went to Egypt to be cared for by a moniale. Once cured, he fell into temptation and slept with her, making her pregnant.[66]

The Thought of Death

Having come to the desert to await the Promised Land, the anchorites did not fear death any more than they did illness, which often resulted in it. All thought and spoke about it constantly. "Live each day as if you're dying," Antony repeated all through his long life.[67] Evagrius and Cassian each reported Macarius as stating, "The monk must always keep himself ready, as if he were to die the next morning, and vice-versa, use his body as if he were to live with it for many years."[68] It was an excellent way to avoid discouragement and backsliding.[69] The apothegms often show how the monks put this rule into practice. In working with a spindle, an elder would think of death each time he brought it back up.[70] Amma Sara did the same before climbing up a ladder, a measure of prudence always in season.[71] An elder said, "I expect death morning and night, each day."[72] A

---

[64]HL 7, 4.
[65]HL 13, 1.
[66]N 187.
[67]VA 19, VA 91.
[68]Evagrius, *Praktikos* 29; Cassian, Inst. 5, 41.
[69]N 121.
[70]N 58; Sy 3, 52.
[71]A 889 (Ward, p. 230).
[72]Bu I 334.

brother in Sinai had come across a small tablet bearing this inscription: "Moses to Theodore: I am present and I witness." Each day he would take the tablet and ask, "Where are you now, you who said, 'I am present and I witness'?" And remembering death, he couldn't stop crying.[73] An elder, when sending a disciple on an errand, would stay by the door and say, "Who will come first, this one or another, an angel coming to take and guide me to the Lord?"[74] The Rhaithou elder who constantly asked while moaning, "What will happen to me?" spent his days meditating continually about his departure from the body.[75] "When you lie down," advised another, "ask yourself: 'Will I wake up in the morning, or not?' "[76]

The Approach of Death

Death can, in fact, arrive anytime without warning. The brother for whom Patermuthius had obtained an extension of life for three years, so that he could do penance, died all of a sudden, as if falling asleep.[77] Several monks knew the moment of death in advance and often announced it: John of Lycopolis, Paphnutius and the monks named Isidore.[78] One elder knew three days in advance that he would die. Calling together his disciples, he announced it to them and, indeed, died three days later.[79] Alonius learned from Semyas that his elder would die. He arrived to assist him in his final moments and at death.[80] In the Cells, a brother thought death was approaching because he was crying copiously, but death didn't come and he cried even more.[81]

Normally, the approach of death cannot be imagined without a few tears, if not from the dying one, at least among those around him. When Macarius was nearing the end, the elders in

---

[73]N 519.
[74]N 522.
[75]N 531.
[76]N 592/45.
[77]HM 10, 19.
[78]HM 1, 65; 14, 23; 17, 3.
[79]N 418.
[80]Eth 13, 39.
[81]N 537.

Nitria sent a delegation to plead with him to come see them one last time. He did so, and the elders asked him to address the brothers gathered there. Said Macarius, "Let us weep, brothers, and may our eyes shed tears before we go where our tears will burn our bodies." All wept and fell at his feet, saying, "Father, pray for us."[82]

And yet, in general, the anchorites were not at all afraid to see the day of their death arriving. Egyptians have always looked kindly upon death. From Antiquity, their religious concepts led them to live half of the time on earth and half in the other world. Christianity only accentuated this orientation towards a future life, the real life. And this is the perspective that gives all its meaning to the existence of the Desert Fathers. In their attitude toward death, one must see a reflection of their ancestral beliefs and at the same time the expression of their Christian convictions. Among most of them, a certain fear is intermingled with joy and serenity, but it is a fear inspired by humility. One finds in the apothegms a little of all the nuances, sometimes with a note of humor that matches the naturally playful character of the Egyptians.

An elder of Scetis, whose name is unfortunately unknown, was ready to die, and the brothers around his bed were crying. Opening his eyes, he broke out three times in laughter. When the brothers asked him why, he replied, "I laughed first of all because all of you are afraid of dying; I laughed a second time because you're not ready; and I laughed a third time because I am quitting work to go rest." And straightaway he gave up the ghost.[83]

As Guillaumont noted, humor "can be a very discreet way of saying something serious,"[84] and also to veil an emotion. Regardless of what one might think at first glance, this elder was obviously not insensitive to the brothers' sorrow at the thought of an imminent separation, but his pleasant reaction was a way

---

[82]A 487 (Ward, p. 136).

[83]N 279.

[84]*Hommages à François Daumas*, Montpellier, 1986, p. 376.

of distracting them and inviting them not to make a drama out of an event which, for him, was very simple.

Death Without Witnesses

It is surely to spare their companions this kind of sorrow that made some Desert Fathers want to die without witnesses. Paul of Thebes asked Antony to fetch the coat given him by Athanasius so he could use it as his shroud, "wanting," says his biographer, "to soften the distress caused by his death."[85]

John of Lycopolis asked to be left alone for three days. Then with his knees bent in prayer, he expired and returned to God.[86] Often anchorites who knew each other well, went to see each other one last time before dying.[87] However, sometimes one of them, advised of the imminent death of a brother, preferred to remain in his cell and put off the meeting until the great reunion in the hereafter.[88]

There are also cases of a few hermits who died in their isolated cells some days or years before, and whose cadavers or skeletons were found later by visitors.[89] But the dying anchorite is usually surrounded by elders and brothers who comfort him by their presence and their prayers, but who also carefully take note of his last words.

Last Words of the Elders

The apothegms have left us a good number of words spoken by the Fathers just before dying. Their variety reflects the main ideas of those who expressed them. Bessarion, for example, simply said, "The monk must be all eyes, like the cherubim and seraphim."[90] Benjamin, as a final recommendation to his disciples, quoted verses of Paul to the Thessalonians: "Rejoice always.

---

[85]*Life of Paul*, 12.
[86]HM 1, 65.
[87]A 353 (Ward, p. 93); Bu II 420.
[88]A 286 (Ward, p. 76); N21.
[89]N 132A; HM 20, 7.
[90]A 166 (Ward, p. 42).

Pray without ceasing. No matter what happens, never cease giving thanks."[91]

Sometimes a disciple would ask his elder for words summing up everything he should do to be saved. When asked for this, James of the Cells replied, "Go. Don't act to please people, because those who want to please people kill them. Stay away from them and you'll be saved."[92] Another Cells elder, John, told his disciple, "Go. Love your neighbor as yourself and all your enemies will fall down at your feet."[93] The words aren't always explicitly requested but are then all the more memorable. Paphnutius' disciples said to him, "Happy are you, our Father, because you are going to the Kingdom." To which he replied, "Me, for sure, I've made a laughing stock of my life."[94]

The replies of some elders deliver a barely-hidden note of warning or reprimand. Nadbay the Persian declared, "What to tell you? Generations will come after you. They'll eat their fill, they'll tittle-tattle and won't work, but will try to enlighten their predecessors."[95] And Isaac of Cells, the priest, said, "See how I walked before you. If you wish, you too can follow and keep God's commandments. He'll send his grace and guard this place. Otherwise, you won't stay here...."[96] Sometimes the elder shied away because of humility, at other times he offered himself modestly as an example: "I don't recollect ever having asked any of you to do anything without first making up my mind not to get angry if he didn't do what I asked; this is how, throughout our lives, we lived in peace."[97] An Abba John, on the verge of drawing his last breath, was full of joy, thinking he was returning to his own country. He left his disconsolate disciples these words, "Never have I carried out my own will nor taught anyone to do something I hadn't first practiced myself."[98] Before dying,

[91]A 171 (Ward, p. 44).
[92]Eth 13, 34.
[93]Eth 13, 85.
[94]Eth 13, 82.
[95]Eth 13, 23.
[96]A 382 (Ward, p. 101).
[97]A 803 (Ward, pp. 210-211).
[98]A 431 (Ward, p. 114).

Pambo had declared, "Since the day I came here and built the cell where I live, I don't recall having eaten any bread I didn't earn through my own work, and I never regretted a word I said. And yet I go to God as if I had not yet begun serving God."[99] This is also how Matoes felt when he declared, "When I was young, I told myself: 'Perhaps I'll do something good?' Now that I'm old, I see there's not a single good act in me."[100]

Likewise, Sisoes "was not aware of having begun," and asked the angels coming to get him for a bit more time "to do a little penance." And yet he could see the prophets and apostles, and his face shone like the sun.[101] Arsenius admitted of always having with him the same fear that had accompanied him since he became a monk.[102] On the point of death, Agathon's eyes remained open and immobile for three days. The brothers shook him and asked, "Agathon, where are you?" "I'm keeping myself before the judgment seat of God." They asked him, "How come you too, Father?" "Of course," he declared, "I did everything possible to keep the commandments of God, but I'm a man. How do I know if my work pleased God?" Then the old man put an end to the dialogue: "For charity's sake, don't speak to me anymore because I'm busy." And he died full of joy. They saw him depart like a man saying farewell to his friends.[103] Another monk also had a beautiful death, in silence. This was Zacharias. Next to him was Moses, his elder, who, seeing him as if in ecstasy, asked him what he could see. The dying one replied, "Is it right for me to speak?" "No," said Moses. And Zacharias died.[104]

A brother of Pharan, Aretas, also went to God full of joy. And yet he had not always been the most fervent of monks. When his elder reminded him of this, he replied, "Yes, Father, that's true. But since becoming a monk, I never judged anyone and always forgave anyone who did me wrong. I also intend to

---

[99] A 769 (Ward, p. 197).
[100] A 515 (Ward, p. 143).
[101] A 817 (Ward, pp. 214-215).
[102] A 78 (Ward, p. 18).
[103] A11 (Ward, p. 3).
[104] A 247 (Ward, p. 68); Eth 14, 35.

tell God, 'You said, oh Master, Judge not that ye be not judged; forgive and ye shall be forgiven.' "[105]

Another brother, however, had reason to worry about imminent death. Ares related how, each day, one of his neighbors would steal the money he earned by selling the mats he made. When Ares left to refill his water jug, the thief would enter his cell with a skeleton key and take the money. After six months of this, Ares divided the money in two and left a note asking the thief to leave him one-half for his subsistence. The other did nothing and continued his daily thievery for three more years, after which he took sick and, feeling death approaching, sent for his victim and asked to be forgiven. Ares simply kissed the hands and feet of the dying one, saying, "May the Lord bless these hands and feet, because they taught me to become a monk!" Then the brother died and Ares buried him.[106]

One last account of an edifying death should really be mentioned. It deals with two brothers, so attached to each other that the Lord allowed them to die together. One became ill and could not attend the Saturday liturgy. The other announced this to the brothers at church and, on Saturday, all of them gathered at the invalid's bedside. On Sunday, they found him dying. His brother then told him, "My brother, are you going to die and abandon me? Excuse me, but I'm not going to let you die and leave me." He asked for a mat and as soon as he lay on it, he caught a fever and died. After that, his brother died, too, and both were buried together.[107]

Death and Burial

If the last moments of the Desert Fathers are often mentioned, details about the death itself and burial are sparse. The soul's withdrawal and ascension to heaven are sometimes mentioned, but the descriptions carry the pious clichés of classical hagiography. Thus elders saw angels greeting Anouph's soul

---

[105]N 530.
[106]Eth 13, 80; Cf. N 7 and N 339.
[107]Eth 14, 33; Cr. N 4 and N 622.

with choirs of martyrs and taking him to heaven,[108] or Paphnutius' soul rising to heaven "among choirs of the just and of angels
praising God."[109] Pachomian accounts are more detailed. The
burial of an anchorite was undoubtedly done in the simplest way
possible. They dug a grave in the sand, with or without the help
of obliging lions, the corpse was lowered and covered with sand.
But there were specialists. Patermuthius took very good care of
the dead. His disciple asked to be given the same treatment. He
died, in fact, before his elder and the latter, after carrying out his
funeral duties, asked him at the top of his voice before everyone,
"Did I take care of you, my son, or is there still a little something
to be done?" And they heard the deceased reply from underground, "It's enough, Father. You kept your promise."[110]

Before burial, the corpse was usually washed and prepared.
This is how the identity of a woman, who had lived in the desert
and passed herself off as a monk, was eventually discovered.[111]
In Nitria, as noted earlier, Melania took charge herself of performing these last duties for Pambo: "Having cleaned him for
the funeral and wrapped the body in linen, she placed him in the
ground."[112] Most of the anchorites didn't worry too much about
what became of their bodies. Arsenius told his disciples, who
were asking themselves what to do, because they didn't know
how to bury someone, "Wouldn't you know how to tie a cord to
my feet and drag me to the mountain?"[113] (Arsenius was, at that
time, in the valley, in Troë, not far from the Nile. The Egyptians,
however, always had their tombs in the mountains, that is, above
the inhabited and cultivated lands which were largely covered,
now and then, by the flooding river.)

A monk in the Sinai asked his neighbor to take his cadaver
to the desert after death, so that it could be eaten by wild beasts
and birds of prey because, he said, "I've sinned greatly against
God and don't deserve a tomb." Despite a few scruples, the

[108]HM 11, 8.
[109]HM 14, 24.
[110]HM 10, 9; N 8.
[111]A 159 (Ward, p. 41); N 132C.
[112]HL 10, 5.
[113]A 78 (Ward, p. 18).

neighbor carried out the wish of the deceased.[114] As for Antony, he feared they would embalm him and turn his body into a mummy. This is why, shortly before his death, he withdrew to the mountain with two disciples who had lived near him for fifteen years. He advised them to let no one take his body away but to bury it in a spot known only to them. They carried out their master's instructions so well, says the biographer, that "no one, apart from these two, knew where he was buried."[115]

The story is told of an elder who obtained from God the favor of seeing the Fathers in glory, saw them all but, to his utter astonishment, Antony was not among them. When he asked why, he got the reply, "Where God is, there is Abba Antony."[116] The great patriarch of the monks being now hidden in God, it was also right for his body to remain invisible to the eyes of humanity until the last day.

---

[114]N 520.
[115]VA 90-92.
[116]A 28 (Ward, p. 7).

Epilogue

In the desert of Scetis, in the Wadi Natrun, about two miles from the Amba Pshoi monastery, people could still see even a few years ago the "tree of obedience," which grew there in the fourth century from a piece of dry wood planted and watered by John the Dwarf on orders from his elder.[1] The tree is undoubtedly not as old as they claim, but is, in any case, a symbol of the vitality and fecundity of the original stock planted in this desert by the faith of the first hermits who established themselves there. The film-maker Andrei Tarkovski repeated the anecdote in his film, *The Sacrifice*. The film's hero, Alexander, tells his "young boy," who is mute, the story of John the Dwarf and has him water a dried-out tree each morning. At the end of the film, after his father's heroic sacrifice, the child still waters the dry tree and, cured of his muteness, tries to pronounce the phrase he often heard from the mouth of his father: "In the beginning was the Word.... Why, daddy?"

It is truly the Word, the Word of God incarnated in Jesus, the beloved Son of the Father, who led the hermits into solitude, who nourished them in the silence and who made them become the abbas of the desert. It is said of Tarkovski that he never "stopped being haunted in his life and works by the mystery of human and divine paternity."[2] It is therefore not surprising that he, too, should be drawn to the Desert Fathers — and especially St Antony — who was to be the subject of a film that death unfortunately prevented the film-maker from creating. The sacrifice of Alexander, who burned down his house, condemns himself voluntarily to silence and cuts himself off from everything he loves by pretending to be insane, recalls the total renunciation of the first Egyptian anchorites. Jacques Lacarrière asks himself if they "were fools or saints."[3] But aren't all saints fools in the eyes

---

[1] A 316 (Ward, p. 85). Cf. Evelyn White, pp. 108-109 and plate V.

[2] Edwin Carels and Charles H. de Brantes, in *La France catholique*, no. 2088, 9 January 1987, p. 8.

[3] J. LaCarrière, *Les Hommes ivres de Dieu*, p. 11.

239

of a completely human wisdom? Wasn't it folly to go live in the heart of the desert and spend one's whole existence doing apparently useless and weird things, such as watering a piece of dry wood or putting together baskets that were burned at the end of the year? In John Colobos' apothegm, the wood comes alive again after three years; in another version of the episode, reported by Cassian,[4] it stays dry. Never mind the visible result. Christian holiness doesn't depend on spectacular exploits but on humble gestures carried out each day with love by the sons who seek only to please their Father, by doing everything he asks them to do with a ready heart. This was the main point of the desert hermits' daily life, seen as an intricate design through their words and the recollections of their disciples.

One can rightly be astonished that such a simple and humble lifestyle had this extraordinary influence, which we have observed, upon the entire Christian world for fifteen centuries. By human standards, Egyptian monasticism in the desert did not have much of a future. The hermitages closest to populated areas —those of Nitria and the Cells especially—were doomed to disappear, by the very reason of this proximity which did not suit the solitude and silence of the anchorites. From the end of the fourth century, doctrinal controversies caused troubles and dissension among them. As for the centers founded deeper in the desert, they were constantly threatened by incursions and raids from nomads. Scetis was devastated several times in the course of the fourth century. But surrounded later by fortified enclosures, the monasteries became the high places and heart of the Coptic church. With the patriarch and bishops chosen from among the monks, there was always a symbiosis between Egyptian Christianity and desert monasticism, a symbiosis which certainly played a large part in maintaining the Christian faith under Moslem domination. And so it is that the Desert Fathers continue to maintain the vitality of the Coptic church in the very same locales where they had lived and where their descendants faithfully remember them.

---

[4]Cassian, Inst. 4, 24 (SC 109, p. 156).

The influence of the Fathers which had, from the fourth century, spread just about everywhere, then reached churches of all denominations including those which didn't share the Coptic Monophysite belief. Their influence was felt mainly in Palestine, Syria, Asia Minor, Greece and Russia, thanks to the distribution of the *Lives* and apothegms, translated into various languages. Through the work especially of Cassian, who adapted the teachings of the Egyptian hermits for the use of western cenobites, St Benedict collected this heritage and transmitted it to his innumerable posterity. But Benedictine and Cistercian monks are not the only sons of the Desert Fathers. One can say that all Christians who try to follow Christ on the road of Gospel teachings, walk in the footsteps of the first anchorites. All the founders or reformers of religious orders in the Middle Ages and modern times were inspired by them, by their lives, their words and their teachings. From the Carthusians, Dominicans, Franciscans and Jesuits to the Little Brothers of Jesus and Sisters of Bethlehem — despite the diversity of ideas and observances — all admire and imitate, to a degree, the Fathers of the Desert. Dom Mabillon and the Maurists along with Abbot de Rancé and his Trappists claim to be inspired by them. Jansenists and Jesuits quoted them and published their works. After Father Rosweyde had published the *Vitae Patrum* in Latin, Arnauld d'Andilly translated them into French. In general, Protestants didn't have much esteem for the ancient anchorites, but a number of them have now come to appreciate them more. Seminars and symposia have drawn reformed adherents of every denomination, along with Catholics and Orthodox, to study what the Desert Fathers can contribute to Christians of the twentieth century.[5]

What is particularly remarkable in today's renewal of interest in the Desert Fathers is that it shows up in scientific circles as well as in the practice of Christian life. Historians, philosophers and sociologists now take seriously these personalities who were long considered fanatics or mad men. An eminent contemporary

---

[5]We should at least mention the study weeks held at the monastery of Chevetogne in 1974 and 1977, as well as the seminars at the Yale Divinity School (cf. Henri Nouwen, *The Way of the Heart*, New York, 1981).

English historian, Peter Brown, a specialist in Late Antiquity, sees in their apothegms "an unrivaled collection of proverbial wisdom,"[6] "the last and one of the greatest products of the Wisdom Literature of the ancient Near East."[7]

In recent years, one of his students, who wrote a thesis on "Scripture and the Quest for Holiness in the *Apophthegmata Patrum*" for a doctorate in philosophy at the University of Berkeley, also gave spiritual conferences on the "Words of the Fathers" in his parish church. In Paris, Professor Antoine Guillaumont brilliantly introduced the Desert Fathers at the Ecole des Hautes Etudes and the Collège de France, while a Christian radio station in the south of France offers listeners an apothegm and a brief spiritual commentary every morning.

Today's fascination with the hermits of the past is all the more surprising when we observe how our times are so far removed from the mores and spirit of the first anchorites. Yet perhaps the new generations are more inclined than preceding ones to appreciate the Desert Fathers, envy them, indeed even to seek from them the human and Christian values which are not much honored these days: solitude and silence, asceticism and contemplation, interiority and self-giving, spiritual paternity and obedience, renunciation and humility. To all those who painfully feel the emptiness of an existence devoted entirely to the quest for material well-being and ephemeral pleasures, the elders of the desert are blunt reminders of the conditions for true happiness. As John Paul II has said, "The message of these enthusiasts for God rings out again today, more up-to-date than ever, [for] these formidable athletes of the faith were witnesses of an admirable radicality in the search for the Kingdom, of a unique mastery for penetrating the secrets hidden in the heart of man." They encourage and help us "rediscover in the hubbub of modern civilization creative solitudes where we can walk in the search for truth without masks, alibis or lies."[8]

---

[6]P. Brown, *Society and the Holy in Late Antiquity*, Berkeley, CA, 1982, p. 111.

[7]P. Brown, *The Making of Late Antiquity*, Cambridge, MA, 1978, p. 82.

[8]Pope John Paul II, Homily at the Coptic liturgy, August 14, 1988 at the church of Saint Mary Major.

Chronological Landmarks

The Church and the World	Monastic Egypt
249-251 Persecution by Decius	251 Birth of Antony Paul of Thebes retires to the desert
	271 Antony embraces the
284 Emperor Diocletian	ascetic life
	285 Antony to Pispir
	292 Birth of Pachomius
	293 Birth of Macarius of Alexandria Birth of Hilarion near Gaza
	300 Birth of Macarius the
303-311 Persecutions	Egyptian
	304 Birth of Pambo Birth of John of Lycopolis
	306 Birth of Apollo in the Thebaid
	311 Antony to Alexandria to assist the martyrs
313 Edict of Milan	313 Antony to Mount Colzim
End of persecutions	Baptism of Pachomius
315-325 Arius preaches in Alexandria	
325 Council of Nicea condemns Arius	
328 Athanasius, Patriarch of Alexandria	
	330 Amoun to Nitria Macarius the Egyptian to Scetis
	333 Baptism of Macarius of Alexandria
335-337 Athansius' first exile	

The Church and the World	Monastic Egypt
339-346 Exile of Athanasius to the West	338 Antony to Alexandria and to Nitria Foundation of the Cells 340 Macarius the Egyptian ordained priest 341 Antony meets Paul Death of Paul 346 Death of Pachomius John becomes a hermit at Lycopolis 352 Death of Amoun 356 Death of Antony 357 Hilarion visits Mt. Colzim
361 Emperor Julian the Apostate	Sisoes leaves Scetis and goes to Mount Colzim Athanasius writes the *Life of Antony*
373 Death of Athanasius	373-375 Rufinus and Melania in Egypt Death of Pambo 383 Evagrius to Nitria
385 Theophilus, Patriarch of Alexandria	385 Evagrius to the Cells Jerome and Paula to Alexandria and to Nitria 388 Palladius to Alexandria Cassian in Egypt 390 Death of Macarius the Egyptian Palladius to Nitria 391 Palladius to the Cells 393 Death of Macarius of Alexandria 394 Arsenius to Scetis The Authors of the *History of the Monks* in Egypt 395 Death of Apollo Death of John of Lycopolis
398 John Chrysostom, Bishop of Constantinople	399 Death of Evagrius Palladius and Cassian leave Egypt

The Church and the World	Monastic Egypt
400 Synod of Alexandria condemns Origenism	400 Postumianus in Egypt
	406 *History of the Monks in Egypt*
407 Death of John Chrysostom	407-408 First devastation of Scetis
	Death of Moses
412 Cyril, Patriarch of Alexandria	Poemen and his brothers to Terenuthis
	419 *Lausiac History* by Palladius
	421 *Institutes* of Cassian
	426 *Conferences* of Cassian
428 Nestorius, Bishop of Constantinople	
431 Council of Ephesus Deposition of Nestorius	
	434 Second devastation of Scetis
	Arsenius to Troë
444 Death of Cyril of Alexandria	449 Death of Arsenius
451 Council of Chalcedon Condemnation of Monophysitism	

Bibliography

I. SOURCES

[In this section, the author listed only those works available in French translations. Where available, we have given the English translations. Readers wishing to refer to the original texts will find in these books any references needed.]

Apophtegmes des Pères, trans. by Lucien Regnault and the monks of Solesmes in *Les Sentences des Pères du désert*, 5 volumes, Solesmes, 1966-1985.
The "Alphabetical Collection" is available in English as *The Sayings of the Desert Fathers*, trans. by Benedicta Ward, SLG, Kalamazoo, MI: Cistercian Publications, 1975.

     Since the sixth century, the memorable words and actions of the Desert Fathers have been termed "apothegms." First passed down orally in Coptic, they were collected and translated into Greek, then into all languages. The main collections were created in Palestine at the end of the fifth century. The one called the "Alphabetical-Anonymous Collection" gives, in alphabetical order of the names, the apothegms of known personalities plus the anonymous items. In the "Systematic Collection," items are set out in chapters according to the main observances and monastic virtues. The latter collection was translated into Latin by two Roman deacons, Pelagius and John, at the beginning of the sixth century. Each was later elected Pope in turn.

     In the different written traditions, the collections are infinitely varied, exaggerated, abridged or revised to suit the copyists, so that in order to reassemble all the preserved apothegms, one must go back to different collections, small and large, passed down in Greek, Latin, Syriac, Armenian, Georgian, Arabic and Ethiopian. The results of such research has been edited and published in five volumes by Solesmes.

Athanasius (Saint), *Life of Antony*, trans. by H. Ellershaw, *Nicene and Post-Nicene Fathers*, Second Series, Grand Rapids, MI: Wm. B. Eerdmans Publishing Co., 1980.

     Composed soon after the death of the saint, the *Life of Antony* became the best-seller of its day in the West as well as in the East, due to the notoriety of its author. Translated into Latin before 375 A.D., the

246

Life led to many conversions and monastic vocations in Gaul and Italy, including that of St Augustine.

Cassian, *Conferences* and *Institutes*, trans. by E. C. S. Gibson, *Nicene and Post-Nicene Fathers*, Second Series, Grand Rapids, MI: Wm. B. Eerdmans Publ. Co., 1982.
John Cassian (360-435 A.D.), probably born in the Balkans, was a Bethlehem monk and lived a dozen years in Egypt (388-399). After 466, he founded the Monastery of St Victor in Marseilles along with a monastery of nuns. His writings made known the customs and teachings of the Desert Fathers to western monasticism.

Evagrius, *Outline Teaching on Asceticism and Stillness in the Solitary Life*, trans. by G.E.H. Palmer et al, in *The Philokalia*, London, 1979, pp. 31-37.
The Praktikos and Chapters on Prayer, trans. by John Eudes Bamberger, OCSO, Kalamazoo, MI: Cistercian Publications, 1981.
The Mind's Long Journey to the Holy Trinity: The Ad Monachos *of Evagrius Ponticus*, trans. by Jeremy Driscoll, Collegeville, MN, 1993.
Evagrius Ponticus (346-399 A.D.) had been ordained deacon by Gregory Nazianzen. Having left Constantinople after a sentimental misadventure, he reached Jerusalem, then Egypt, where he lived among the anchorites of Nitria and the Cells. An original thinker in the tradition of Origen, he was one of the few monks in the desert to write. These give the teachings of the elders, though systematized and associated with sometimes doubtful theories. References are only to writings quoted in this book.

The Lives of the Desert Fathers: The Historia Monachorum in Aegypto, trans. by Normal Russell, London: Mowbray and Kalamazoo, MI: Cistercian Publications, 1980.
This work gives an account of a trip around Egypt in 394-395 by a group of Palestinian monks who went first to the Thebaid, then down the Nile Valley as far as the Delta. The tour ended with a brief visit to Scetis, the Cells and Diolcos. Written in Greek by one of the travelers, the work was then translated, with a few changes, into Latin by Rufinus.

Isaiah, *Recueil ascétique*, trans. by H. de Broc, 3rd Edition, Bellefontaine, 1985 (Spiritualité orientale n° 7 bis). (A small selection of Isaiah's teachings can be found in *The Philokalia*, London, 1979, listed above.)
Isaiah was a monk in Scetis, then in Gaza, where he died in 491. By his teachings and writings, he made the tradition of the Egyp-

tian anchorites known in Palestine. He had a strong influence on Barsanuphius, John and Dorotheus of Gaza.

Jerome (Saint), *Life of Paul the First Hermit* and *Life of Hilarion*, trans. by W. H. Fremantle et al, *Nicene and Post-Nicene Fathers*, Second Series, Grand Rapids, MI: Wm. B. Eerdmans Publ. Co., 1983.

Even during the author's lifetime, the historical quality of these biographies was already being questioned. However, it is generally accepted that Paul and Hilarion really did exist. The accounts by Jerome were best-sellers and made the two subjects popular heroes.

Palladius, *The Lausiac History*, trans. by R. T. Meyer, *Ancient Christian Writers Series*, New York: Newman Press, 1964.

Born in Galatia, Palladius spent a few years with the Egyptian monks (388-399) before becoming deacon in Constantinople, then bishop of Helenopolis. This work, dedicated to Lausus, chamberlain to the Emperor, summarizes biographical notes on the main ascetics, monks and moniales he knew in Egypt and Palestine.

Sulpicius Severus, *Dialogue*, trans. by A. Roberts, *Nicene and Post-Nicene Fathers*, 2nd Series, Grand Rapids, MI: Eerdmans Publ. Co., 1982.

Becoming a monk in Aquitaine following the death of his wife, Sulpicius Severus wrote a biography of St Martin, to which he added two books of *Dialogues*, with the intention of proving that Martin had greater saintliness and miraculous powers than the Egyptian anchorites. The acts reported about the latter come from his friend Postumianus, who had gone on a pilgrimage to Egypt around 400 A.D.

Life of Saint Pachomius, trans. by Armand Veilleux, *Pachomian Koinonia*, vol. 1, Kalamazoo, MI: Cistercian Publications, 1980.

Before founding his communities, Pachomius lived as an ascetic near his village, under the direction of Palamon. Many comparisons can be made between Pachomian customs and those of the other Desert Fathers. This excellent work by Armand Veilleux provides all the appropriate cross-references.

II. GENERAL BIBLIOGRAPHY

Besse, J.M., *Les Moines d'Orient antérieurs au concile de Chalcédoine (451)*, Paris-Poitiers, 1900.

Bouyer, L., *La Vie de saint Antoine*, Bellefontaine, 1978 (Spiritualité orientale n° 22).

Brémond, J. & H., *Les Pères du désert*, Paris, 1927.

Budge, E.A.W. (trans.), *The Wit and Wisdom of the Christian Fathers of Egypt*, London, 1934.

Chitty, D.J., *The Desert a City*, Crestwood, New York, 1966.

"Chrétiens du désert au IVe siècle, Saint Antoine et les moines du désert," *Dossiers Histoire et Archéologie*, n° 133, December, 1988.

Draguet, R., *Les Pères du désert*, Paris, 1949.

Evelyn White, H.G., "The Monasteries of the Wadi 'n Natrun," Part II, *The History of the Monasteries of Nitria and Scetis*, New York, 1932.

Festugière, A.J., *Les moines d'Orient I, culture ou sainteté, Introduction au monachisme oriental*, Paris, 1961

Guillaumont, A., *Aux origines du monachisme chrétien*, Bellefontaine, 1979 (Spiritualité orientale n° 30).

Heussi, K., *Der Ursprung des Monchtums*, Tubingen, 1935.

Judge, E.A., "Fourth-century Monasticism in the Papyri," in *Proceedings of the 16th International Congress of Papyrologists*, Chico, CA: Scholar's Press, 1981.

Lacarrière, J., *The God-Possessed*, trans. by Roy Monkcom, London, 1963.

Leloir, L., *Désert et Communion*, Bellefontaine, 1978 (Spiritualité orientale n° 26).

Meinrardus, O., *Christian Egypt ancient and modern*, 2nd Edition, Cairo, 1977; *Monks and Monasteries of the Egyptian Deserts*, Cairo, 1961.

Montet, P., *Everyday Life in Egypt in the Days of Ramesses the Great*, trans. by A.R. Maxwell-Hyslop and M.S. Drower, Philadelphia, 1981.

Regnault, L., *Les Pères du désert à travers leurs Apophtegmes*, Solesmes, 1987.

Vie spirituelle (La), 669-670, 1986, t. 140, pp. 148-379.

III. SPECIAL STUDIES

Chapter 1: In the Heart of the Desert

Amélineau, E., *La Géographie de l'Egypte à l'époque copte*, Paris, 1893.
Guillaumont, A., "La Conception du désert chez les moines d'Egypte," in *Aux origines...*, pp. 69-87.

Chapter 2: The Men

Ayrout, H., *The Egyptian Peasant*, trans. by J.A. Williams, Boston, 1963.
Blackman, *The Fellahin of Upper Egypt*, London, 1927.
Martin, A., "L'Eglise et la khôra égyptienne au IVe siècle," in *Revue des études augustiniennes*, vol. XXV, 1979, pp. 3-26.

Chapter 3: Women and Children

Desroches-Noblecourt, C., *La Femme au temps des Pharaons*, Paris, 1986.
Guillaumont, A., "Ascèse et sexualité dans le christianisme des premiers siècles," in *Annuaire du Collège de France*, 82nd Year (1981-82), pp. 425-431; "Le célibat monastique et l'idéal chrétien de la virginité ont-ils des motivations ontologiques et protologiques?" in *La Tradizione dell'enkrateia*, Milan, 1982, pp. 83-107.
Leloir, L., "La Femme," in *Désert et Communion*, pp. 136-158.
Rousselle, A., *Porneia, On Desire and the Body in Antiquity*, trans. by F. Pheasant, London, 1988.
Ward, B., *Harlots of the Desert*, London, 1987.

Chapter 4: Habitat

Husson, G., "L'Habitat monastique en Egypte à la lumière des papyrus grecs, des textes chrétiens et de l'archéologie," in *Hommages à la mémoire de S. Sauneron*, vol. II, IFAO, Cairo, 1979, pp. 191-207.
Sauneron, S., *Les Hermitages chrétiens du désert d'Esna*, IFAO, Cairo, 1972, vols. I & IV.

Chapter 5: Clothing

Guillaumont, A. & C., Notes on the Prologue of Evagrius' treatise "Praktikos" in *Sources chrétiennes* 171, pp. 484-491.
Oppenheim, P., *Das Monchskleid im Christlichen Altertum*, Fribourgen-B, 1931; *Symbolik und religiose Wertung des Monchskleides im Christlichen Altertum*, Munster, 1932.

Chapter 6: Diet

Devos, P., "Règles et pratiques alimentaires selon les textes," in *Le Site monastique copte des Kellia. Actes du colloque de Genève*, Aug. 13-15, 1984, Geneva, 1986, pp. 73-84.
Festugière, A.J., *Les moines d'Orient*, I, pp. 59-74.

Chapter 7: Life in the Cell

Guillaumont, A., "Les fondements de la vie monastique selon Evagre le Pontique," *Annuaire du Collège de France*, 78th Year (1977-78), pp. 469-475.
Hausherr, I., "L'Hésychasme," in *Orientalia Periodica*, XXII, 1956, pp. 5-40.

Chapter 8: A Day in the Life of the Anchorite

Guillaumont, A., "Le Travail manuel dans le monachisme ancien," in *Aux origines...*, pp. 117-128; "Le problème de la prière continuelle dans le monachisme ancien," in *L'Expérience de la prière dans les grandes religions*, Homo religiosus 5, Louvain-la-Neuve, 1980, pp. 285-294.
Heussi, K., *Der Ursprung des Monchtums*, pp. 210-218.
Regnault, L., "La prière continuelle monologistos dans les Apophtegmes des Pères," in *Les Pères du désert...*, pp. 113-139.
Evelyn White, H.G., *The Monasteries...*, pp. 197-205.

Chapter 9: The Hidden Activity

Hausherr, I., "L'Hesychasme," pp. 262-285.
The Name of Jesus, Kalamazoo, MI, 1978, pp. 157-180.
Penthos: The Doctrine of Compunction in the Christian East, Kalamazoo, MI, 1982.

251

Chapter 10: Elders and Disciples

Hausherr I., *Spiritual Direction in the Early Christian East*, Kalamazoo, MI, 1990.
Louf, A., "La paternité spirituelle dans la littérature du désert," in *La Vie spirituelle*, 66, 1986, pp. 335-360.
Regnault, L., *Les Pères du désert...*, pp. 28-36; 96-109.

Chapter 12: Outings and Trips

Guillaumont, A., "Le dépaysement comme forme d'ascèse dans le monachisme ancien," in *Aux origines...*, pp. 89-116.

Chapter 13: The Community Weekend

Donahue, C., "The Agapè of the Hermits of Scété," in *Studia Monastica*, vol. I, 1959, pp. 97-114.
Evelyn White, H.G., *The Monasteries...*, pp. 207-213.

Chapter 14: Angels and Demons

Festugière, A.J., *Les Moines d'Orient*, I, pp. 23-29.
Guillaumont, A. & C., "Le démon dans la plus ancienne littérature monastique," in *Dictionnaire de spiritualité*, vol. 3, 1957, col. 189-212.

Chapter 15: The Desert Bestiary

Brémond, J. & H., *Les Pères du désert*, Introduction, pp. XXXI-XXXV.
Cazin, P., *Le Bestiaire des deux Testaments*, Paris, 1928, pp. 102-141.
Festugière, A.J., *Les Moines d'Orient*, I, pp. 53-57.

Chapter 16: The Marvels of God

Guillaumont, A., "Les visions mystiques dans le monachisme oriental chrétien," in *Aux origines...*, pp. 136-147.
Heussi, K., *Der Ursprung des Mönchtums*, pp. 172-181.
Ward, B., "Signs and Wonders, Miracles in the Desert Tradition," in *Studia Patristica*, vol. XVII, Oxford, 1982, pp. 539-542.

Index of Names

(This index includes only the Desert Fathers and Mothers and their contemporaries who had contact with them. Monks with the same names are distinguished wherever possible. When monks quoted by Cassian are noted, his name is added in brackets.)

Athanasius, ix, 8, 9, 34, 41, 53,
59, 80, 92, 127, 146, 147, 168,
181, 233

Bane, 80, 99, 109
Benjamin, 17, 74-75, 217, 224,
233
Bes, 136, 198
Bessarion, 26, 39, 93, 108, 109,
173, 192, 208, 219, 233

Carion, 35, 38, 133
Cassian, ix, 10, 11, 19, 20, 28-29
42, 44, 45, 47, 49, 52, 55, 57,
58, 64, 65, 66, 68, 70, 71, 72,
73, 75, 78, 79, 83, 85, 87-88,
89, 94, 98, 103, 104-105, 107,
109, 117, 119, 120, 134, 137,
140, 143, 146, 148, 151, 160,
163, 165, 167, 170, 172, 179,
181, 185, 187, 190, 204, 211,
214, 217, 218, 222, 225, 226,
230, 240, 241
Chaeremon [Cassian], 63, 74,
109, 134, 225
Chaeremon of Nitria, 41, 43, 78
Copres of Scetis, 173, 228
Copres of the Thebaid, 55, 193,
215-216, 219, 225
Cronides, 225
Cronius, 131, 136, 183, 214

Daniel, disciple of Arsenius,
56, 80, 102, 135, 136, 145,
161, 166
Daniel of Scetis, 26
Didymus of Alexandria, 141
Didymus of Nitria, 206
Dioscorus, former scribe, 19,
47, 57, 83. 89, 91, 225
Dioscorus of the Thebaid, 189
Domecius, 22

Dorotheus (=Apollinaris), 25
Dorotheus the Theban, x, 44,
69, 79, 100, 109, 129, 224
Doulas, 26

Elias of Antinoe, 40, 63, 69, 215,
219, 225
Elias of Athribe, 179
Elpidius, 41, 108
Epiphanius, 105
Eucarpius, 172
Eucharistus, 157
Eudemon, 38
Eulogius, 62
Eulogius (priest), 166, 208
Evagrius, ix, 21, 22, 30, 33, 40,
55, 56, 58, 66, 71, 72, 78, 87-
88, 102, 104, 105, 106, 119,
124, 137, 142, 143, 173, 176,
177, 178, 181, 183, 185-186,
215, 224, 226, 230

Gerasimus, 205
Germanus [Cassian], 70, 73, 143

Helladius, 80, 81, 166
Helle, 21, 40, 54, 62, 72, 129,
130, 178, 200, 208, 220
Hephestion, 89
Heron, 62, 159, 168, 226
Hierax, 84, 190
Hilary, 25
Hilarion, ix, 53, 128, 185, 190

Isaac, disciple of Bes, 136
Isaac [Cassian], 45, 70, 103
Isaac, priest at Cells, 36, 57, 92,
131, 136, 158, 163, 164, 170,
227, 234
Isaac of Scetis, 59, 213
Isaac the Theban, 76, 180
Isaiah of Scetis, ix, 57, 67, 69,

174, 178, 183, 185, 208, 209,
210, 225, 227, 230-231, 235

Nadbay, 234
Nathaniel, 37
Nesteros [Cassian], 105, 222
Nisterus, 135, 136, 197

Olympius, 32, 146, 212
Or, 5, 44, 56, 59, 62, 63, 69, 131,
144, 178, 180, 188, 193

Pachomius, viii, 55, 67, 83, 99,
107, 108, 109, 127, 129, 133,
153, 154, 165, 198, 213
Pachon, 27, 187, 225
Paësia, 153, 176
Paësius, 171
Paësius [Cassian], 107
Paësius, brother of Isaias, 18
Paësius, brother of Poemen, 35
Palamon, 55, 74, 81, 99, 108,
129, 153, 226, 229
Palladius, ix, 10, 18, 20, 24, 39-
40, 41, 42, 49, 55, 62, 64, 65,
66, 78, 80, 82, 107, 108-109,
124, 129, 137, 141, 144, 163,
168, 178, 179, 195, 200, 217,
218, 224, 225, 226, 230
Pambo, 17, 29, 42, 43, 54, 57,
107, 146, 163, 168, 190, 208,
223, 224, 235, 237
Paphnutius Bubalis [Cassian],
11, 38, 42, 58, 77, 84, 158,
166, 180
Paphnutius Kephalas, 67, 224
Paphnutius, copyist, 102
Paphnutius, disciple of
Macarius, 200
Paphnutius the Sindonite, 234
Paphnutius of the Thebaid,
176, 231, 237

Patermuthius, 5, 20, 55, 59, 62,
69, 211, 216, 219, 221, 231,
237
Paul, 198, 204
Paul [Cassian], 28, 98, 136, 218
Paul the Great, 69, 78, 90, 103
Paul of Pherme, 97, 106
Paul the Simple, 18, 54, 64, 65,
100, 108, 129-130, 192, 210
Paul of Thebes, ix, x, 4, 41, 53,
59, 128, 194, 201, 225, 233
Paula, 146
Peter, 133
Phocas, 58
Piammonas, 179, 212
Piamoun, 77, 144, 165, 218
Pinufius [Cassian],55, 160
Pior, 77, 80, 154, 173, 217
Pityrion, 40, 64, 193
Poemen, 11, 19, 21, 29, 31, 35-
36, 37, 40, 60, 61, 64, 65, 68,
75, 76, 77, 79, 97, 111, 113,
115, 116, 117, 118, 119, 120,
121, 122, 123, 128, 131, 132,
133, 136, 137, 139, 140, 145,
146, 148, 149, 150, 152, 160,
167, 204, 210, 213, 220, 228
Postumianus, 70, 72, 203
Ptolemy, 168

Rufinus of Aquilea, ix, 146
Rufus, 84, 228

Sarmatas, 61, 84, 109
Sara, 25, 221, 230
Semyas, 231
Serapion, 84, 92, 153
Serapion [Cassian], 66, 141
Serapion the Sindonite, 39, 54,
105, 224
Serenus [Cassian], 73, 85, 179,
181, 183, 185

Silvanus, 48, 111, 136, 160, 210, 211
Simon, 75, 145
Sisoes, 10, 24, 41, 47, 64, 68, 70, 71, 76, 84, 92, 102, 104, 131, 136, 146, 147, 148, 170, 176, 177, 178, 184, 209, 211, 221, 228, 235
Stephen the Lybian, 226
Sulpicius Severus, 52, 200, 203
Syncletica, 25, 227

Theodora, 25, 227
Theodore, 45
Theodore of Pherme, 57, 67, 92, 103, 124-125, 128, 131, 136, 140, 145, 147, 149, 170, 191, 209, 228

Theodore, disciple of Pachomius, 83
Theon, 48, 69, 141, 203, 215
Theon [Cassian], 66
Theophilus, 30, 73, 122, 145, 146, 154-155, 160
Timothy, 153

Valens, 101, 168, 187, 214

Xanthias, 77, 193, 197
Xoius, 66, 219

Zacharias, 35, 38, 66, 133, 208, 210, 235
Zeno, 37, 45, 103, 178, 192
Zoïlus, 135, 136